The New Additi...
Breaker

Everything you should know about additives in your food

Maurice Hanssen with Jill Marsden
Revised for Australia by
Betty Norris
Complete number guide for Australia and New Zealand

LOTHIAN PUBLISHING COMPANY PTY LTD
Melbourne Sydney Auckland

This book is based on the UK edition, *E for Additives* (Thorsons, 1984), revised as the *New E for Additives* (Thorsons, 1987). Winner of the 1988 Glenfiddich Special Award for excellence in food and wine writing.

Of this UK edition, judge and broadcaster Derek Cooper wrote in the *Listener*, 'This book has done more than any other publication to persuade the food industry their unnecessary over-processing is not in their interest or the interest of the public.'

A Lothian book
Lothian Publishing Company Pty Ltd
11 Munro Street Port Melbourne Victoria 3207

This edition first published 1989
Copyright © Maurice Hanssen 1989

National Library of Australia
Cataloguing-in-Publication data

Hanssen, Maurice.
The new additive code breaker.

ISBN 0 85091 325 6.

1. Food additives. 2. Food additives — Toxicology.
3. Food — Labelling. I. Marsden, Jill. II. Norris, Betty.
III. Hanssen, Maurice. Additive code breaker. IV. Title.
V. Title: The additive code breaker.

664'.06

Designed by Marius Foley
Typeset by Bookset
Printed by The Book Printer, Maryborough

Foreword

Many foods of our modern society are seasonal in nature and must be preserved from times of plenty if we are to enjoy them throughout the year. Others are grown in areas far from our cities, and must be processed to ensure their safe arrival at major centres of consumption. Some foods need to be modified by high technology processes to make them quick and convenient to use in the home. In short, there are very few foods in our diets that have not been subject to some form of controlled processing to meet our requirements.

Some of these processes, but not all, require the use of food additives which, in Australia, are as closely controlled as in any country of the world. Food additives are permitted only when their use is essential and when their safety-in-use has been established.

Yet there are some people who suffer adverse reactions to some food ingredients, and also to some food additives, that are of no consequence to the large majority of consumers. There are also some consumers who simply wish to know the nature of the particular additive in foods offered for sale, so that they can exercise their own personal judgement.

This welcome book has been produced in an easy-to-follow form to help the Australian people make a more informed decision about the foods they buy. The information in this book, the information on food labels and the increasing awareness of the role of food selection in maintaining our health and well being, are all matters of related importance. Let us remember that there is no bad food, but only a bad use of food that this book will help to correct.

Professor R. A. EDWARDS
Head, Department of Food Science & Technology
University of New South Wales

About the authors

Maurice Hanssen is chairman of the academic and parliamentary consumer group in England, the National Association for Health, which monitors all food and medicines legislation. He is in close contact with the development of European law relating to food, medicines and consumer affairs, and is a member of the European Food Law Association.

All opinions expressed in this book are the author's and not necessarily those of the other contributors.

Jill Marsden, B.Sc., Dip.Ecol., Dip.Ed., Research Assistant to Maurice Hanssen

Betty Norris, B.Sc., C.Chem., M.R.S.C., Dip.Ed., Secretary to the NHMRC Food Standards Committee (1979–87)

Tom Heyhoe, Dip.Tech., AAIFST, ARACI, C.Chem., Food industry consultant

Contents

Introduction

Since 1 January 1987 Australia has had an approved system of labelling for additives in packaged foods. All ingredients and additives in foods are controlled by food laws and food additives are permitted only where necessary. No new additive is approved for use in food before its safety has been established by the National Health and Medical Research Council (NHMRC). Under this system each additive has to be named or numbered using numbers the same as those used on food labels in Europe, but without the prefix 'E' used there.

This book is mainly concerned with the specific identification of food additives in packaged food and includes information on all additives approved for use in food in Australia for which code numbers have been allocated at this time.

The Labelling of Packaged Foods

In recent years there has been much interest in food labelling. This has been brought about, in part, by the increase in the market-place of pre-packaged processed food and the consumer's need for more information about the ingredients of such foods.

Food regulations throughout Australia require that the labels on all packaged foods include the following information:

- the prescribed name or appropriate designation of the food;
- the name and business address, in Australia, of the manufacturer, the packer or vendor and, in the case of imported food, the name and address of the importer;
- a mark identifying the premises where the food was prepared, and the production lot involved;
- a statement of the country of origin of the food;
- a statement of ingredients in descending order of proportion;
- in the case of foods with a minimum durable life of less than two years a date-mark as required by the standard for the date-marking of packed food.

In addition, those foods whose labels include nutrition claims must also include a set nutrition information panel. There are also specific labelling requirements for some foods.

This book is designed to assist people to make informed choices when buying packaged foods, particularly about the additives they contain. It should make shopping a lot easier and less worrying for people with allergies to a particular additive or additives, and also provide a lot more information for the ever-growing number of people who take a serious interest in what they and their families eat.

Ingredients

Throughout Australia the labels of all packaged foods must carry a statement of ingredients in descending order of proportion by weight except that:

- dehydrated or concentrated ingredients in a food shall be declared in the list of ingredients in the position determined by their reconstituted weights in the food;
- dehydrated or concentrated foods intended to be reconstituted in accordance with directions in the label may declare their ingre-

dients in descending order of proportion by weight in the reconstituted product, provided that the ingredient statement is headed by the words 'INGREDIENTS WHEN RECONSTITUTED';

- alcoholic beverages and food in small packages (total surface area less than 100 square centimetres) are exempt from the total-ingredient labelling requirement but if they contain any added preservative, colour, flavouring or antioxidant the presence of these must be declared;
- the presence of added water may be declared at the end of an ingredient statement provided it is declared as 'water added'.

Food additives must be declared in the ingredient statement by approved class names that reflect the functions they perform in the packaged food. Approved class names and the functions they perform are:

- *anti-caking agents* ensure that products such as salt flow freely and that the particles do not stick together;
- *antioxidants* prevent foods that contain fats and oils from becoming rancid and other foods such as cut fruits from discolouring on exposure to the air;
- *artificial sweetening substances* are used to sweeten low-joule foods and brewed soft drinks;
- *bleaching agents* whiten foods, for example, flour;
- *colours* restore colour lost during processing and storage and ensure a uniform colour in the finished product;
- *emulsifiers* ensure that oil and water mixtures do not separate into layers;
- *enzymes* break down foods, for example, milk into curds and whey;
- *flavour enhancers* bring out the flavour of the food without imparting a flavour of their own;
- *flavours* restore flavours lost during processing and maintain uniformity;
- *flour treatment agents* improve flour performance in bread making;
- *food acids* maintain a constant acid level in food despite variations in the acid level of the ingredients;
- *humectants* prevent foods from drying out and becoming hard and unpalatable;
- *minerals* are added to certain foods to supplement dietary intake;

- *mineral salts* enhance the texture of foods such as processed meats which might lose fats and meat juices;
- *preservatives* prolong the shelf-life of foods;
- *propellants* are used in aerosol containers;
- *thickeners* ensure constant consistency;
- *vegetable gums* also ensure constant consistency;
- *vitamins* are added to foods to make up for losses in processing and storage.

Except in the case of flavours, since 1 January 1987 these class names must be immediately followed, in brackets, by either the prescribed name, appropriate designation or code number of each food additive present belonging to that class. For example, food containing the preservative sodium metabisulphite has to show in the statement of ingredients in the label: PRESERVATIVE (SODIUM METABISULPHITE) or PRESERVATIVE (223). A person who is allergic or sensitive to sodium metabisulphite would therefore be alerted to its presence and avoid this food.

Any approved food additive not belonging to one of the above classes that is present in a packaged food must be declared in the ingredient statement by its prescribed name or appropriate designation.

What are Food Additive Code Numbers?

Food Additive Code Numbers recommended by NHMRC are the same as those used on food labels in Europe. The number system was developed by the European Economic Community (EEC) as part of its effort to harmonise laws so that foods can be moved from country to country more easily. The European numbers are 'E' numbers, for example, E223. The Australian numbers do not utilise the 'E' prefix, i.e. 223 is used instead.

Some food additives used in Europe are not used in Australia, hence the Australian number list is shorter than the 'E' number list. This book gives information about many of the additives on the 'E' number list. Those additives with code numbers which are not prefixed are permitted to be used both in Australia and Europe. Those numbers in this book that are prefixed by an 'E' are not currently permitted to be used in Australia. This does not necessarily imply that they are not generally recognised as safe. It may mean that no Australian food manufacturer has applied to the NHMRC asking to use them.

Some food additives approved for use in Australia do not have 'E' numbers and do not appear in this book. For these food additives the name must appear in the statement of ingredients in the label.

If an additive which is not permitted to be used in food in Australia is included in the label of a food purchased in Australia, the relevant State/Territory Health Department should be contacted.

Additions are made to the list from time to time as new substances are found to be suitable for use in foods. Substances are removed from the list if they are found to present problems or if they can be replaced by a more effective substance with greater safety.

It is interesting to note that the Codex Committee on Food Additives of the Joint Food and Agriculture Organisation and the World Health Organisation Codex Alimentarius Commission currently has under consideration a Draft International Code Numbering System for Food Additives also based on the 'E' number list but without using the 'E' prefix, i.e. similar to the Australian system.

What is a Food Additive?

According to the Codex Alimentarius, a food additive is: 'Any substance not normally consumed as a food by itself and not normally used as a typical ingredient of food, whether or not it has nutritive value, the intentional addition of which to food for a technological (including organoleptic) purpose in the manufacture, processing, preparation, treatment, packing, packaging, transport or holding of such food results in, or may be reasonably expected to result (directly or indirectly) in it or its by-products becoming a component of or otherwise affecting the characteristics of such. The term does not include "contaminants" or substances added to food for maintaining or improving nutritional qualities.' ('Organoleptic' means sight, taste, smell and texture as perceived by the senses.)

Because manufacturers can use either the code number or the proper name of the additive as an alternative, they often choose to use the name on the premise that it is less 'frightening' than a code number. On the other hand, some ingredients which have valuable nutritional properties can cause confusion because they have names that look very much like additives, whereas in fact they are not in that class.

A good example is soya protein isolate, which is the valuable protein part of the soya bean in a very pure state and is an extraordinarily good source of very nutritious protein. It can make meat products in particular, such as sausages and pies, as well as a number of other dishes and drinks, more nutritious than they would be without it, and also has useful technical properties in giving the product a better appearance and texture.

Again, if you use an egg yolk because of the emulsifying properties of its natural lecithin then it is declared as the ingredient 'egg-yolk' and not as '322', lecithin.

Are Additives Necessary?

Sugar and salt are perhaps the most common food ingredients which are important in the preservation of foods. But excessive sugar and salt is not healthy. There is a likely relationship between too much salt and high blood pressure and between excessive sugar and dental decay as well as overweight. So their use is valuable but their consumption needs to be moderated. The same is true of most additives — they are tested for safety — but if you read your labels carefully you can control your intake.

Quite a few of the additives are substances that occur in nature, such as vitamin C and lecithin.

This book is to help you to decide whether the additives in your food are the sort that are essential to keep it in good condition (such as when the preservation of meat products is far more important than the risks of possibly fatal food poisoning from eating tainted meat), whether it is just to assist the manufacturing processes which produce the food, or whether it is to colour, to enhance the flavour or even to allow the manufacturer to add extra water or to hide excess fat without the awareness of the consumer.

We now have enough information appearing on labels to enable us to choose whether the additives are the sort that we are happy to use or would prefer to do without. Remember too, that although perhaps one in ten will find the yellow colour tartrazine does not suit them, nine out of ten will find that it does! Question whether the additives are just for the convenience of the manufacturer, enabling him to use lower quality raw materials or processing methods without the knowledge of the consumer, or whether they enable the food to be brought to you tasting better and in better condition than would be possible without the use of additives. So learn to read the label wisely.

There is, at present, no requirement for added food flavours to have an additive number. This is because of the extremely complex nature of food flavour — for example natural coffee aroma consists of several thousand odorous materials, each composed of a different chemical type. This is the case for all characteristic food flavours.

Typical labels

Frankfurters

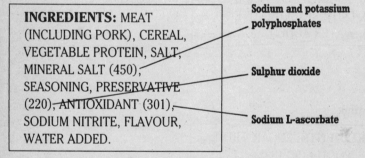

INGREDIENTS: MEAT (INCLUDING PORK), CEREAL, VEGETABLE PROTEIN, SALT, MINERAL SALT (450), SEASONING, PRESERVATIVE (220), ANTIOXIDANT (301), SODIUM NITRITE, FLAVOUR, WATER ADDED.

Sodium and potassium polyphosphates

Sulphur dioxide

Sodium L-ascorbate

Devon

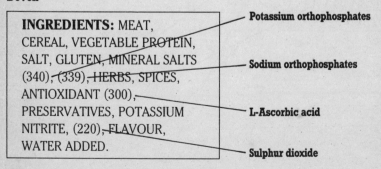

INGREDIENTS: MEAT, CEREAL, VEGETABLE PROTEIN, SALT, GLUTEN, MINERAL SALTS (340), (339), HERBS, SPICES, ANTIOXIDANT (300), PRESERVATIVES, POTASSIUM NITRITE, (220), FLAVOUR, WATER ADDED.

Potassium orthophosphates

Sodium orthophosphates

L-Ascorbic acid

Sulphur dioxide

Drink base

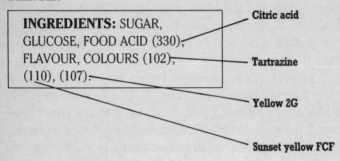

INGREDIENTS: SUGAR, GLUCOSE, FOOD ACID (330), FLAVOUR, COLOURS (102), (110), (107).

Citric acid

Tartrazine

Yellow 2G

Sunset yellow FCF

Orange fruit juice drink

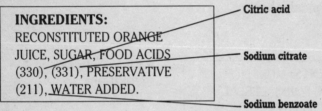

INGREDIENTS: RECONSTITUTED ORANGE JUICE, SUGAR, FOOD ACIDS (330), (331), PRESERVATIVE (211), WATER ADDED.

Citric acid

Sodium citrate

Sodium benzoate

Orange drink

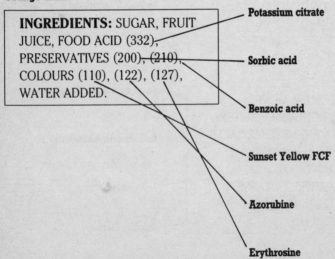

INGREDIENTS: SUGAR, FRUIT JUICE, FOOD ACID (332), PRESERVATIVES (200), (210), COLOURS (110), (122), (127), WATER ADDED.

Potassium citrate

Sorbic acid

Benzoic acid

Sunset Yellow FCF

Azorubine

Erythrosine

Apricot pie

INGREDIENTS: FLOUR, APRICOTS, MARGARINE, SUGAR, THICKENERS (1412), (1420), BAKING POWDER, FOOD ACID (296), EMULSIFIER (471), FLAVOUR, WATER ADDED.

— Distarch phosphate

— Starch acetate

— Malic acid

— Mono- and di-glycerides of fat-forming fatty acids

Ice confection

INGREDIENTS: SKIM MILK, VEGETABLE FAT, GLUCOSE SYRUP, THICKENER (GELATINE), EMULSIFIER (436), VEGETABLE GUMS (407), (410), SALT, FLAVOURS, COLOURS (102), (110), WATER ADDED.

— Polysorbate 65

— Carrageenan

— Locust bean gum

— Tartrazine

— Sunset yellow FCF

Chocolate cake mix

INGREDIENTS: SUGAR, WHEAT FLOUR, ANIMAL AND VEGETABLE FATS, COCOA, SKIM MILK POWDER, THICKENER (1400), BAKING POWDER, SALT, COLOUR (155), EMULSIFIER (442), ANTIOXIDANT (320), FLAVOUR, VEGETABLE GUM (413).

— Dextrins

— Brown HT

— Ammonium phosphatides

— Butylated hydroxyanisole

— Tragacanth

Flavoured yoghurt

INGREDIENTS: MILK, SUGAR, SKIM MILK POWDER, CULTURE, FLAVOUR, VEGETABLE GUM (407), COLOUR (160b), (162).

Carrageenan

Annatto extracts

Betanin

Table margarine

INGREDIENTS: ANIMAL FATS, VEGETABLE OILS, SALT, SKIM MILK, EMULSIFIER (471), ANTIOXIDANTS (310), (320), VITAMINS, FLAVOURS.

Mono- and di-glycerides of fat-forming fatty acids

Propyl gallate

Butylated hydroxyanisole

Sweet orange marmalade

INGREDIENTS: SUGAR, GLUCOSE SYRUP, ORANGES, VEGETABLE GUM (440(a)), FOOD ACIDS (331), (333).

Pectin

Sodium citrate

Calcium citrate

Smoky ham cheese spread

INGREDIENTS: CHEDDAR CHEESE, BUTTER OIL, SKIM MILK POWDER, HAM, EMULSIFIER (433), FLAVOURS, WATER ADDED.

Polysorbate 80

Peanut butter

INGREDIENTS: PEANUTS, PEANUT OIL, SALT, EMULSIFIER (471).

Mono- and di-glycerides of fat-forming fatty acids.

Fish fingers

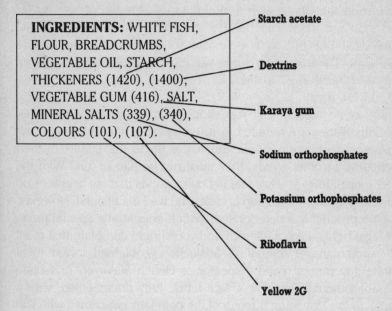

INGREDIENTS: WHITE FISH,
FLOUR, BREADCRUMBS,
VEGETABLE OIL, STARCH,
THICKENERS (1420), (1400),
VEGETABLE GUM (416), SALT,
MINERAL SALTS (339), (340),
COLOURS (101), (107).

Starch acetate

Dextrins

Karaya gum

Sodium orthophosphates

Potassium orthophosphates

Riboflavin

Yellow 2G

Date marking

Date marking is now required on most pre-packed foods (with a few exceptions, such as small ice creams, filled bread rolls and wine) unless they have a shelf-life of at least two years. Even products with a very long shelf-life may be marked, but this is not mandatory. This shall be expressed as either:
- Date of packing and minimum durable life

or:
- Use-by date

Date of packing means the date the food was packaged. It will be written as 'PACKING DATE', 'PACKED ON' or 'PKD' followed by the date in brackets.

Minimum durable life means the period, starting from the date of packing, during which the food can be expected to retain its normal quality, if it is stored in the manner stated on the label. It will be followed by the number of days, weeks, months or years in brackets.

A 'Use-by date' in Australia means the date on which the minimum durable life of a food will be over. It will be written as 'USE BY' or

'BEST BEFORE' followed by the date in brackets. However foods with a very short life (those with a minimum durable life of less than 7 days) must use the words 'USE BY' and are not permitted to use the words 'BEST BEFORE'. A 'Use-by date' will be shown in the form of 06 JUN 89. There may be some variation to these rules (between States and Territories) in the case of bread, milk, cream and pre-packed fresh meat.

There is no reason why you should not buy overdue products, especially if they are reduced in price, because the onus is on the shopkeeper to provide goods which live up to the quality of their description. In other words, they must not be bad or 'off'. With the longer time datings you are safe in buying goods that are near the end of their expiry date if the shop is clean and well maintained. However, if such a product has deteriorated, even if bought at a special price, your legal rights are not affected and you should complain first of all to the shop manager, then, if no satisfaction is obtained, to your local or State government Food Inspector or Health Surveyor. It is often preferable, though, to write a nice letter, fully documented, with a sample, to the Managing Director of the company concerned who will often, for the sake of goodwill (and most of the good companies are very jealous of their reputation), refund your cost and may even give you something extra besides. However, if you are on the make, beware, because most manufacturers keep very accurate records of complainants and get wise to the person who frequently finds a dead mouse in the meat pie.

Nutrition information

Packaged foods with labels which contain a nutrition claim must also provide nutrition information. In effect, this means that if a claim is made in the label that states, suggests or implies that a food has a nutritional property then the label must contain a nutrition information panel detailing the energy value of the food and its protein, fat, total carbohydrate, sugars, sodium and potassium contents per serving and per 100 grams (or 100 millilitres in the case of a liquid food). For example, the nutrition information panel of a wholemeal bread might appear as follows:

Slices per package — 33
Slice size — 27 g

	Per slice 27 g	Per 100 g
Energy	270 kJ (65 Cal)	1000 kJ (240 Cal)
Protein	2.7 g	10.0 g
Fat	0.8 g	3.1 g
Carbohydrate		
— total	12.1 g	45.0 g
— sugars	0.7 g	2.6 g
Sodium	33 mg	120 mg
Potassium	106 mg	390 mg

A product with a label that carries a claim for salt, sodium or potassium only, is not required to include a full nutrition-information panel, only nutrition information relating to the sodium and potassium contents.

Nutrition labelling was introduced into Australia to enable consumers to select foods for a healthy and nutritious diet.

Dietary guidelines for Australians

In 1979 the Commonwealth Department of Health adopted a food and nutrition policy which aims to ensure that all Australians consume a nutritionally adequate diet. To assist Australians to reach this goal the Department drew up a set of eight dietary guidelines:
- promote breast feeding;
- choose a nutritious diet from a variety of foods;
- eat more breads and cereals (preferably wholegrain) and vegetables and fruit;
- control your weight;

- avoid eating too much fat;
- avoid eating too much sugar;
- use less salt;
- limit alcohol consumption.

A nutritious diet is one that contains a variety of foods consumed in such quantities that a desirable body weight can be maintained. To this end Australians have been advised for many years to choose a good diet by selecting a variety of foods from the following five food groups:

- breads and cereals;
- vegetables and fruit;
- meat, poultry and fish, eggs, legumes and nuts;
- milk, cheese and yoghurt;
- butter or table margarine.

The nutrition-labelling requirements for packaged foods, for which nutrition claims are made, which were introduced in 1987 will help consumers compare the nutritional value of similar foods and those who are watching their weight will be very interested in the kilojoule content of packaged foods.

Hyperactivity in Children

Hyperactive children bring much strain and exhaustion to parents who have to manage offspring who sleep only a few hours out of twenty-four, may suffer from eczema and asthma and cannot be calmed down.

As they grow older they become even more active and can easily be hurt. Difficulties are experienced with speech, balance and learning, even if the IQ is high. They suffer from excessive thirst and often are prone to respiratory difficulties.

It was to help such parents and children that the Hyperactive Children's Support Group was formed in the UK in 1977 (HACSG). It is now a registered charity.

The group recommends that parents try a diet based on the work of the American doctor, Ben Feingold. First, this means cutting out all food and drink containing synthetic colours or flavours, avoiding glutamates, nitrites, nitrates, BHA, BHT and benzoic acid. Second, for the first four to six weeks, food containing natural salicylates (which are chemically similar to aspirin) should be avoided and then re-introduced **one at a time** to see if they cause problems. Such foods include almonds, apples, apricots, peaches, plums, prunes, oranges, tomatoes, tangerines, cucumbers, most soft fruits, cherries, grapes and raisins.

The numbers of additives that the HACSG recommend should be avoided are:

102	Tartrazine	151	Black PN
E104	Quinoline yellow	E154	Brown FK
107	Yellow 2G	155	Brown HT
110	Sunset yellow FCF	160(b)	Annatto
120	Cochineal	210	Benzoic acid
122	Carmoisine	211	Sodium benzoate
123	Amaranth	220	Sulphur dioxide
124	Ponceau 4R	250	Sodium nitrite
127	Erythrosine	251	Sodium nitrate
E128	Red 2G	319	*tert*-Butylhydroquinone
132	Indigo carmine	320	Butylated hydroxyanisole
133	Brilliant blue FCF	321	Butylated hydroxytoluene
150	Caramel		

Additives which are either dangerous to asthmatics or aspirin-sensitive people, and could reasonably be added to the HACSG listing or not allowed in food intended for babies or young children are:

212	Potassium benzoate	310	Propyl gallate
213	Calcium benzoate	311	Octyl gallate
E214	Ethyl 4-hydroxybenzoate	312	Dodecyl gallate
E215	Ethyl 4-hydroxybenzoate, sodium salt	621	Monosodium L-glutamate
216	Propyl 4-hydroxybenzoate	622	Monopotassium L-glutamate
E217	Propyl 4-hydroxybenzoate, sodium salt	623	Calcium di-L-glutamate
218	Methyl 4-hydroxybenzoate	627	Disodium guanylate
E219	Methyl 4-hydroxybenzoate, sodium salt	631	Disodium inosinate
221	Sodium sulphite	E635	Sodium 5'-ribonucleotide
222	Sodium bisulphite		
223	Sodium metabisulphite		
224	Potassium metabisulphite		

In the *Lancet* (Editorial, 20 March 1982, p. 662) the view was taken that most clinicians will say that the evidence 'does not yet justify prescribing the treatment, but does justify supporting families who have decided to try it themselves'.

A resource list of organisations for asthma, allergies and hyperactivity in Australia and New Zealand is at the end of this book.

How to Use This Book

Many additives have several different uses but, in general, code numbers follow a numerical system according to their main function. The first part of this book is laid out numerically, according to the code number, so that you can quickly look up the information on the label.

Each entry lists the number, the name of the substance, its origin, functions, effects and acceptable daily intake (A.D.I.) (see glossary), whether or not it occurs naturally and, from time to time, notes for the consumer. At the end is an alphabetical list of food additives so that any ingredient given by name instead of number can be checked out.

The labelling regulations state that ingredients, except water, must be given in descending order by weight so it is a useful indicator of the amount of the additive present to see, for example, whether it comes above or below salt.

In this book an attempt has been made to gather as much information as possible and there will inevitably be some sins of omission. Indeed the EEC will certainly make continual changes in their proposals and the NHMRC will be making additions to the Australian list. Any changes will be rectified, where appropriate, in subsequent editions. The products listed are generally those in which the additive is permitted, though the list is not always exhaustive. The best way to check out permitted food additives is to consult the food regulations of the State or Territory in which you live. However a good guide is the NHMRC publication *Food Standards Code* which is available from the Australian Government Publishing Service.

Food Additives

100 ✓✓ **Curcumin (C.I. 75300)**

Origin   Extract of dried rhizome of
Curcuma longa (turmeric), a member
of the ginger family, grown in India,
West Pakistan, China and Malaya. The
side shoots of lateral rhizomes contain
the most colouring materials, known
as curcuminoids. Curcumin, the pure
colouring principle of the spice
turmeric, is obtained by solvent
extraction of turmeric using methanol,
hexane and acetone.

Function   Oil soluble orange-yellow
colour depending on pH (yellow
between pH 1–7; orange above pH
7.5). Used in many new products as a
replacement for tartrazine (102). Its
usefulness is limited by its poor light
stability. It is heat stable but is
bleached by sulphur dioxide.

Effects   Curcumin has been
demonstrated to have anti-
inflammatory properties, to lower
cholesterol levels, to increase the
liver's secretion of bile and stimulate
its passage on to the duodenum and to
protect the liver from toxic substances.
It has a beneficial effect on blood sugar
in diabetics. In laboratory tests

curcumin prevented harmful
substances such as tobacco extract
and cigarette smoke from causing the
genes in bacteria to mutate. There were
no adverse effects seen in rats and
mice fed 0.1 per cent curcumin over 90
days, but the thyroid weight of pigs
increased when fed 60–1550mg/kg
body weight curcumin for over 100
days, and the thyroid cells multiplied
abnormally. Long-term studies in rats
are in progress to try to help
understand these results.

A.D.I.   0–0.1mg/kg body weight
(temporary to 1989).

Typical products
Savoury rice
Curry powders
Margarine
Processed cheese
Flour confectionery
Fishcakes, fingers and breaded fish

100   **Turmeric**
see curcumin (100)

101 ✓ Riboflavin (lactoflavin; vitamin B₂)

Origin   Occurs naturally in liver, kidneys, green vegetables, malted barley, eggs and milk, and a small amount is synthesised by bacteria in the large intestine. Manufactured from yeast or other fermenting organisms, such as *Ashbya gossypii* or *Eremothecium ashbyii*, or more often by synthesis starting with o-xylene, D-ribose or alloxan.

Function   Yellow or orange-yellow colour; vitamin B_2. Has poor solubility, so is difficult to incorporate into many liquid foods, and is also sensitive to light.

Effects   Little riboflavin is stored in the body; excess of requirements is excreted in the urine. No toxicological problems even with intakes far exceeding the nutritionally required levels. There is a suggestion that riboflavin in the diet may prevent the reduction of azo dyes (see glossary) by intestinal bacteria.

A.D.I.   0–0.5mg/kg body weight.

Typical products
Processed cheeses
Margarine
Note: Riboflavin may be used in the production of foods intended for infants and young children only in amounts necessary to restore that lost in processing and during normal shelf-life.

101 Riboflavin-5′-phosphate-sodium

Origin   Prepared by chemical action on riboflavin. Riboflavin-5′-phosphate sodium consists mainly of the monosodium salt of the 5′-monophosphate ester of riboflavin dihydrate.

Function   Yellow or orange-yellow colour; vitamin B_2 — a more soluble form of riboflavin, but also more expensive.

Effects   The phosphate is rapidly hydrolysed after ingestion to yield riboflavin. Riboflavin and riboflavin-5′-phosphate sodium are in metabolic equilibrium after absorption. There are no toxicological problems with riboflavin even when taken in amounts far exceeding the nutritionally required levels or any likely food use.

A.D.I.   0–0.5mg/kg body weight (temporary).

Typical products
Cheeses
Margarine

102 ✗ Tartrazine (C.I. 19140; FD and C yellow 5)

Origin   Synthetic, an azo dye (see glossary).

Function   Yellow colour.

Effects   Tartrazine appears to be the most reactive of all the azo dyes. In a double-blind crossover placebo-controlled trial with 76 selected overactive children, tartrazine and benzoic acid (210) provoked a response in 79 per cent of those tested but no child reacted to either substance individually.
   In a study of 88 children with severe frequent migraine headaches tartrazine caused symptoms in 12 of them.
   Tartrazine provokes a response in some adult asthmatics, particularly

those sensitive to aspirin, although aspirin-intolerant people are not necessarily intolerant to tartrazine. It also makes the condition worse in between 10 and 40 per cent of patients with chronic urticaria (nettle rash), and possibly intensifies the reactions of a higher proportion still of aspirin-sensitive individuals. However, the 1987 UK Food Advisory Committee's report on the Colouring Matter in Food Regulations states that placebo-controlled provocation studies are shedding doubt on the aspirin/tartrazine association and the matter is as yet unresolved.

Other adverse reactions in susceptible people include itching, rhinitis (runny nose), blurred vision, and purple patches on the skin, and it has been suggested that tartrazine in fruit flavour cordials may be responsible for wakefulness in small children at night.

There appears to be no clear scientific explanation of how tartrazine causes a response in sensitive individuals. Some reactions, because they happen quickly on low doses, suggest an allergy. Tartrazine has been shown to raise the plasma histamine levels of normal healthy adults when large doses of more than 50 mg are given. Skin tests with tartrazine, however, often fail to produce a reaction, so it may mean that a breakdown product of tartrazine is responsible.

An assessment of tartrazine sensitivity in the general population can be only a guess. One source (BIBRA) supposes that 0.06–0.24 per cent of the population as a whole might be sensitive to tartrazine. This would represent between 34 000 and 134 000 people in the UK. Survey work undertaken on behalf of the Ministry of Agriculture, Fisheries and Food (UK) suggests that intolerance to *all* food additives is something approaching 0.4 per cent (or 222 000) of the population.

A.D.I. 0–7.5mg/kg body weight.

Typical products
Confectionery
Soft drinks
Mint sauce and jelly
Packet dessert topping
Fruit juice cordial
Canned fruit
    flavoured pie filling
Canned peas
Marzipan
Pickles
Brown sauce

A very commonly used colour.

E104 Quinoline yellow (C.I. 47005)

Origin   Synthetic 'coal tar' dye (see glossary), the disodium salt of disulphonic acid. There are two quinoline yellows, the so-called 'earlier' and 'later' quinoline yellows; the latter is about 30 per cent methylated, the former is non-metholated.

Function   Dull yellow to greenish-yellow colour.

Effects   Short-term studies of quinoline yellow in dogs and rats showed that the dye was poorly absorbed from the food canal. There were no dose-related effects following a three generation study in the rat and a long-term/carcinogenicity study in the mouse was satisfactory. On this basis the Food Advisory Committee (UK) recommended that the use of quinoline yellow in food was acceptable.

A.D.I. 0–10mg/kg body weight.

Typical products Not permitted in Australia.

✗ 107 Yellow 2G (C.I. 18965)

Origin Synthetic 'coal tar' dye, and azo dye (see glossary).

Function Food colour.

Effects Yellow 2G belongs to a group of chemical dyes known as azo dyes. People who suffer from asthma and those sensitive to aspirin may also show an allergic reaction to this colour.

A.D.I. No A.D.I. allocated.

Typical products
Soft drinks

✗ 110 Sunset yellow FCF (C.I. 15985; FD and C yellow 6)

Origin Synthetic 'coal tar' dye, and azo dye (see glossary).

Function Yellow colour, especially useful for fermented foods which must be heat-treated.

Effects An azo dye to which some people have an allergic reaction. Hypersensitvity may occur especially in people showing aspirin sensitivity, producing urticaria (nettle rash), angioedema (swelling on the skin), gastric upset and vomiting.

The dye is minimally absorbed in rats, mice, guinea pigs, rabbits and man, and is able to cross the placenta.

In 1984 animal studies in the United States showed this dye to be weakly carcinogenic. These results are not, however, consistent with other work with rats and mice.

In view of all the results, the Food Advisory Committee (UK) did not consider the findings in the recent experiments attributable to Sunset Yellow FCF and are happy with its continued use as a food colour.

A.D.I. 0–2.5 mg/kg body weight.

Typical products
Fruit juice cordial
Marzipan
Fruit butters
Packet trifle mix
Hot chocolate mix
Packet soup
Confectionery

120 ✓ Cochineal; (carmines; carminic acid; C.I. 75470)

Origin Cochineal is the natural red colour which accumulates in the bodies of pregnant scale insects (*Dactilopius coccus* (Dactilopiidae)). The insects breed and feed on particular cacti (species of *Nopalea*) and both are indigenous to Central America. Commercial supplies are obtained from Peru, the Canaries, Algiers and Honduras. An aqueous extract is obtained from the dried female insects. This is reacted with alumina to produce the aluminium lake of carminic acid which is known as carmine.

Function Expensive but effective red colouring for liquids and (ammonium carmine) solids. The water-soluble form is used exclusively for colouring alcoholic drinks; the insoluble form (calcium carmine) has wider colouring applications.

Effects A long term carcinogenicity study on the liquid form of cochineal in rats showed no carcinogenic or other adverse effects.

A.D.I. 0–5 mg/kg body weight.

Typical products Now used fairly rarely because of high cost, but available as cochineal food colour for home cooking. Largely replaced by Ponceau 4R (124) in manufacturing.

✗122 Azorubine (carmoisine; C.I. 14720)

Origin Synthetic azo dye (see glossary).

Function Red colour, especially for foods which are heat-treated after fermentation.

Effects Azorubine produces no serious toxicological responses in rats, mice or pigs and does not cross the placenta in rats, but the dye is decolorised by lactic acid bacteria. The dye is broken down in the gut and eliminated in the faeces. It did not cause the genes of bacteria or a yeast to mutate. It is an azo dye, producing adverse reactions in sensitive people, or people with aspirin allergy, or asthmatics. These reactions may include urticaria (nettle rash) or oedema (water retention).

A.D.I. 0–4 mg/kg body weight.

Typical products
Blancmange powder
Jelly crystals
Confectionery
Brown sauce
Pre-packed Swiss roll
Pre-packed sponge pudding
Marzipan

✗123 Amaranth (C.I. 16185; FD and C red 2)

Origin Synthetic 'coal tar' dye and azo dye (see glossary).

Function Purplish-red colour, especially useful for blackcurrant products.

Effects New studies in 1982 on metabolism and mutagenicity revealed no evidence of potential toxicity of amaranth, but because the results of long-term feeding studies it had requested in 1978 were not available the Joint FAO/WHO Export Committee on Food Additives (JECFA) extended the previously established temporary A.D.I. of 0–0.75 mg/kg body weight pending these results. In 1984 JECFA considered the requested results which enabled the evaluation of amaranth to be completed and an A.D.I. of 0–0.5 mg/kg body weight was allocated. The dye was banned in 1976 in the United States by the Food and Drug Administration after experiments demonstrated that amaranth increased the number of malignant tumours in female rats. Some amaranth is absorbed from the food canal.

It is an azo dye, therefore to be avoided by people with aspirin sensitivity as it may cause urticaria (skin rash).

A.D.I. 0–0.5 mg/kg body weight.

Typical products
Packet cake mix
Packet trifle mix
Fruit-flavoured fillings
Jelly crystals

124   Ponceau 4R (brilliant scarlet 4R C.I. 16255)

Origin   Synthetic 'coal tar' dye and azo dye (see glossary).

Function   Red colour.

Effects   An azo dye, so should be avoided by people with aspirin sensitivity, and by asthmatics. The colour is absorbed from the gut and excreted in the urine and faeces without tissue accumulation. Long-term studies in rats showed an absence of carcinogenic potential.

A.D.I.   0–4 mg/kg body weight.

Typical products
Packet trifle mix
Packet cheescake mix
Packet cake mix
Dessert topping
Jelly crystals
Canned strawberries
Canned cherry, redcurrant and
   raspberry flavoured pie fillings

127   Erythrosine (C.I. 45430; FD and C Red 3)

Origin   The disodium salt of 2', 4', 5', 7'-tetraiodofluorescein, a derivative of fluorescein. Synthetic 'coal tar' dye (see glossary).

Function   Cherry pink to red colour. Erythrosine is insoluble in acid solutions and is particularly used to colour cherries in tinned fruit cocktail as it doesn't stain the other fruit. It is also used in disclosing tablets for revealing plaque on teeth. Erythrosine is partly degraded during food processing at high temperatures over 200°C, to release iodide.

Effects   Fears have been expressed that erythrosine might increase the thyroid hormone levels because of its high (577 mg/gram) iodine content and lead to hyperthyroidism (overactive thyroid). Experiments were carried out with rats to see if this was so, and male rats' thyroid gland weights increased abnormally, and they developed benign tumours when they were fed diets containing 4 per cent erythrosine.

Japanese experiments show that man and rats absorb little iodine from erythrosine. The possibility still remains that large dietary intakes of erythrosine could affect the thyroid although normal intakes would not. Children consuming food with high levels of erythrosine can have intakes approaching the levels which could cause problems.

Erythrosine has been shown to have a toxic effect on the genes of some strains of yeast cells, so the Food and Drug Administration in the United States has recommended that this dye be banned as a carcinogen. The UK Food Advisory Committee on Mutagenicity has studied the available data and advised that there is now sufficient evidence from well-conducted studies to conclude that erythrosine is probably not mutagenic.

Erythrosine has been implicated in minimal brain dysfunction in children.

Erythrosine can cause phototoxicity (sensitivity to light) and when common houseflies were fed erythrosine in 0.25 and 1 per cent concentrations and were then exposed to sunlight, 100 per cent of them died within 3 hours.

A.D.I. 0–0.6 mg/kg body weight (temporary).

Typical products
Glacé cherries
Scotch eggs
Quick custard mix
Biscuits
Pre-packed Swiss roll
Canned red cherries,
    strawberries and rhubarb
Packet trifle mix

E 128   Red 2G (C.I. 18050)

Origin Synthetic 'coal tar' dye, and azo dye (see glossary).

Function Red colour, particularly useful in meat products because it is not affected by sulphur dioxide (220) and metabisulphite (223 and 224), which bleach many colours. Not for use in foodstuffs subject to high temperature during processing, nor in products of high acidity, when Red 2G hydrolyses to the amine Red 10B, a rather suspect colour.

Effects Further toxicological studied required. The main debate on Red 2G has concerned its ability to be converted to aniline in the gut. Aniline can interfere with the haemoglobin of the red blood corpuscles, and rats fed on Red 2G have become anaemic.

A.D.I. 0–0.1 mg/kg body weight.

Typical products
Not permitted in Australia.

129   Allura red AC (C.I. 16035; food red 17; FD and C red 40)

Origin An artificial dye introduced in 1971 in the USA to replace Amaranth (123).

Function Red colour.

Effects Allura red has been shown to be non-genotoxic. It does not cause cancer in rats or mice, but para-cresidine, a compound used in the production of the dye, causes bladder tumours in rodents. No free para-cresidine has been found in food-grade Allura Red.

There were no birth defects in rats or rabbits, nor skin sensitivity in rabbits and man.

Of 52 people who were prone to nettle rash or puffy skin reactions given 1 or 10 mg by mouth, 8 of them responded hypersensitively.

Allura red is broken down and mostly eliminated in the faeces in the first 24 hours.

A.D.I. 0–7 mg/kg body weight.

Typical products
Many of those permitted to contain Amaranth (123)
Chocolate biscuits.

E 131   Patent blue V (C.I. 42051)

Origin Synthetic 'coal tar' dye (see glossary).

Function Dark bluish-violet colour and diagnostic agent, used to colour the lymph vessels.

Effects   To be avoided by those with a history of allergy. Allergic reactions may occur immediately or after a few minutes. They consist of skin sensitivity, itching and urticaria (nettle rash). More severe reactions, including shock and breathing problems, occur rarely. Nausea, low blood-pressure and tremor have been reported. Detailed toxicological work has shown that Patent Blue V does not harm the genes.

A.D.I.   No A.D.I. allocated.

Typical products   Not permitted in Australia.

132   Indigotine (indigo carmine; C.I. 73015; FD and C Blue 2)

Origin   Synthetic 'coal tar' dye (see glossary).

Function   Blue colour and diagnostic agent (used to test whether the kidneys are functioning normally by producing blue urine after Indigo Carmine is injected into veins or muscles).

Effects   People with a history of allergy should avoid this colour. May cause nausea, vomiting, high blood-pressure and occasionally allergic reactions such as skin rash, pruritus (itching) and breathing problems.

   Short-term feeding studies on dogs in the US showed they were more sensitive to fatal viral disease when fed with this dye. Studies in Britain on the genotoxicity of this colour have proved inconclusive and further research is required.

A.D.I.   0–5mg/kg body weight.

Typical products
Blancmange mix
Biscuits
Confectionery

133   Brilliant blue FCF (C.I. 42090; FD and C Blue 1)

Origin   Synthetic 'coal tar' dye (see glossary).

Function   Blue colour which can produce green hues in combination with tartrazine.

Effects   This dye does not cause genes to mutate, nor is it metabolised in the food canal.

A.D.I.   0–12.5mg/kg body weight.

Typical products
Canned processed peas

140   Chlorophyll (C.I. 75810)

Origin   Chlorophyll is the green pigment in the cells of leaves responsible for absorbing light energy for photosynthesis. Pure chlorophyll is not easy to isolate and the chlorophyll which is commercially available contains other plant pigments, fatty acids and phosphatides, and is known as 'technical chlorophyll'. The usual souces are nettles, spinach, grass and lucerne. The chlorophyll is obtained by solvent extraction using acetone, ethanol, light petroleum, methyl ethyl ketone and dichloromethane. Chlorophylls may also contain other substances such as oils, fats and waxes derived from the plant material. The pigment lutein (161(b)) may also be extracted at the same time and from the same source as chlorophyll.

Function   Oil soluble. Olive to dark green colour. Chlorophyll extracts exhibit limited stability towards heat and light. Whilst stability is enhanced under alkaline conditions, special acid-resistant forms are available.

Effects   No adverse effects are known. Chlorophyll has always been part of man's diet.

A.D.I.   Not limited.

Typical products
Naturally green fruits preserved in a
   liquid.
Soups
Sauces

E141 ✓ Copper complexes of chlorophyll and chlorophyllins (C.I. 75810; copper phaeophytins)

Origin   Copper complexes of chlorophyll are derived from chlorophyll (140) by substitution of the magnesium ion with copper, to increase stability. Copper complexes of chlorophyllins are obtained by processing of chlorophyll extracts obtained by solvent extraction from dried ground grass or lucerne, and replacing the magnesium present in natural cholorphyll with copper. Saponification yields the water soluble copper chlorophyllins. Chlorophyllins also contain other pigments which may be presented as the copper derivative, and other substances such as the sodium or potassium salts of fatty acids, derived directly or indirectly from the source material.

Function   The copper complexes are olive-green oil-soluble colours; the chlorophyllins are green water-soluble colours.

Effects   No adverse effects are known.

A.D.I.   0–15mg/kg body weight as sum of both complexes.

Typical products   Not permitted in Australia.

142 ✕ Green S (acid brilliant green BS; food green S; lissamine green; C.I. 44090)

Origin   Synthetic 'coal tar' dye (see glossary).

Function   Green colour.

Effects   Green S is poorly absorbed from the food canal except in high doses and not metabolised in rats and guinea pigs. In rats given massive doses of 1500mg/kg body weight, there was slightly increased food intake and body weight gains in males, and mild anaemia, increased protein in the urine and mild thyroid degeneration in females. None of these changes was seen at a dose of 500 mg/kg.

A.D.I.   No A.D.I. allocated.

Typical products
Packet cheesecake mix
Canned peas
Packet breadcrumbs
Gravy granules
Mint jelly and sauce

150 Caramel

Origin   The term 'caramel colour' relates to products of a more or less intense brown colour. It is not the sugary aromatic product obtained from heating sugar, which is used for flavouring purposes, but has poor colour intensity.
   Caramel colours are dark brown to black liquids or solids having an odour of burnt sugar and a pleasant, somewhat bitter taste. They are prepared by the controlled heat treatment of carbohydrates (commercially available glucose syrup,

sucrose, dextrose invertase, etc.) in the presence of food-grade ammonia, ammonium sulphate, sulphur dioxide and/or sodium hydroxide in amounts consistent with good manufacturing practice (GMP) to promote caramelisation. The number of types of caramel available has been reduced to the six proposed by the British Caramel Manufacturers' Association to meet all the needs of the British food industry.

Subsequently new specifications have been submitted by the International Technical Caramel Association, encompassing worldwide caramel products, and enabling a potential greater variability within caramels. The European Commission has proposed that the various forms of caramel be designated in the following way:

E150 (a) Plain (spirit) caramel. Caramel prepared by the controlled heat treatment of carbohydrates with or without the presence of alkali or acids.

E150 (b) Caustic sulphite caramel. Caramel prepared by the controlled heat treatment of carbohydrates with sulphur dioxide or sulphur containing compounds.

E150 (c) Ammonia caramel. Caramel prepared by the controlled heat treatment of carbohydrates with ammonia.

E150 Sulphite ammonia caramel. Caramel prepared by the controlled heat treatment of carbohydrates with ammonia and sulphite-containing caramels.

Function Caramel colour constitutes about 98 per cent of all colouring matter added to food (approximately 8800 tonnes/year in 1984). Depending on their method of production, the caramel colours are suitable for different products: for example, cola drinks and vinegar employ sulphite-ammonia caramel; whisky, brandy and ice cream (in the US) caustic caramel colour; and beer, stouts and gravy brownings ammonia caramel colour.

Effects For plain (spirit) caramel colour there appear to be no toxicological problems.

Industry is considering conducting short-term toxicity studies on caustic sulphite caramel colour.

Because the sulphite ammonia caramel colour is used so extensively in soft drinks, a lot of toxicity studies have been done on this kind of caramel colour. Rats fed high concentrations understandably find it unpalatable, drink less, eat less and lose weight. Their stools become darker coloured and soft. The caecum (first part of the large intestine) enlarges, which is thought to be associated with higher concentrations of indigestible components and is not serious, so this caramel colour is not considered to be toxic, nor does it cause reproductive abnormalities. When sulphite ammonia caramel was tested on human subjects they reported gastro-intestinal symptoms including soft to liquid faeces and increased frequency of bowel movements.

Ammonia caramel colour fed to rats decreased white cells counts, although in another experiment when rats had sufficient vitamin B_6 their white cells were not reduced. The effect of ammonia caramel colour on white cell count was dose-related, the lowest effect-producing dose being 200–500 mg/kg body weight caramel/day.

The effect was transient and reversible. The immediate health implications of this are uncertain and no experiments have taken place to discover whether other animals' white cells behave in the same way, and especially under conditions of low vitamin B_6.

Toxicological Committees seem to be seriously concerned at the difficulty in knowing which caramel colour is which, and call for greater clarity within and between the caramel colour categories which have not been chemically defined.

A.D.I. Plain (Spirit) Caramel colour — Not specified.
Caustic Sulphite Caramel colour — No A.D.I allocated.
Ammonia Caramel colour 1–200 mg/kg body weight (1–150 mg/kg body weight on solids basis).
Sulphite Ammonia Caramel colour 0–200 mg/kg body weight (1–150 mg/kg body weight on solids basis).

Typical products
Chocolate dessert whip
Oyster sauce
Biscuits
Packet soup
Canned sauce
Scotch eggs
Beer
Whisky
Brandy
Sweet pickle
Pickled onions
Mint jelly
Pre-packed cakes
Soya sauce
Fruit sauce

151 Brilliant black BN (brilliant black PN; C.I. 28440)

Origin Synthetic 'coal tar' dye, and azo dye (see glossary).

Function Black colour.

Effects Apart from the finding of intestinal cysts in pigs given Brilliant Black BN in a 90-day feeding study, no toxicological significant effects have been observed in teratogenicity (fetal abnormality), reproduction, multigeneration, carcinogenicity or metabolic studies.

The colour is broken down by bacteria in the gut and the metabolites are readily excreted in the urine.

A.D.I. 0–1mg/kg body weight.

Typical products
Blackcurrant cheesecake mix
Brown sauce

153 Vegetable carbon (carbon black)

Origin Carbon black can be prepared from animal charcoal, furnace black, lampblack or activated charcoal. Only carbon black prepared from vegetable sources is permitted for use in foods in Australia. The main commercial source is plant material.

Function Black colour.

Effects In 1976 Carbon black was banned by the Food and Drugs Administration in the United States in the belief that the impurities released during dye manufacture could cause cancer.

Despite no decision having been made on an A.D.I., Carbon black continues to be permitted in the EEC as specific purity criteria are said to ensure a minimum of impurities. More tests need to be done.

A.D.I. Decision postponed.

Typical products
Jams
Jelly crystals
Liquorice

E 154 ╳ Brown FK (kipper brown; food brown)

Origin Synthetic mixture of six azo dyes (see glossary) and subsidiary colouring matters together with sodium chloride and/or sodium sulphate as the principal uncoloured components.

Function Brown colour, especially for kippers. In the smoking process, fish first have to be gutted and preserved by soaking in a saturated salt solution to kill bacteria, and at the same time dye (Brown FK) is added. Brown FK is considered to be the most suitable dye because it is the only colour of the correct hue stable to and soluble in brine. It produces an even colour throughout the herring flesh which does not leach or fade during storage or cooking.

A minor use is to give a 'barbequed' look to precooked poultry. Brown FK is currently permitted in all foods in the UK. The 1987 Food Advisory Committee report recommends that in future Brown FK be restricted to use in smoked and cured fish only, to a maximum level of 20mg/kg. As many people are now happy to purchase smoked fish which has not been coloured, the need for 154 must be questionable.

Effects Experiments with bacteria have shown that two of the colour's constituents (components I and II) cause genetic mutation. When Brown FK was fed to rats and mice at huge daily oral doses (100mg/kg body weight) there was a degeneration of skeletal and heart muscle. Muscle damage also occurred after repeated oral dosing of rabbits, guinea pigs and miniature pigs. Enzyme activity was increased and disturbed and a dark pigment associated with the breakdown of enzyme bodies in the cells was apparent. The same pigment was deposited in conventional feeding studies in the rat and pig.

It is supposed that the azo dye components I and II were broken down by the gut bacteria into two amines, triamino-benzene and triamino-toluene. Both substances are mutagenic to *Salmonella* bacteria and triaminotoluene is a presumed animal carcinogen.

It is fair to assume that Brown FK is similarly metabolized in the human food canal and that potentially toxic amines will be formed, since human faeces contain gut bacteria capable of reducing these azo dyes.

The minimum concentration for Brown FK to cause gene mutation in bacteria is 1mg/1ml culture. As much as 29mg/kg dye has been found in kippers. A rough calculation is that 2 small kippers weighing 200g each would yield enough dye for activity to be detected.

A.D.I. No A.D.I. allocated.

Typical products Not permitted in Australia.

155 ✕ Brown HT (chocolate brown HT; C.I. 20285)

Origin Synthetic 'coal tar' dye and azo dye (see glossary).

Function Brown colour, especially when manufacturers wish to use neither cocoa nor caramel in cakes.

Effects An azo dye, therefore to be avoided by people with asthma, aspirin sensitivity and skin sensitivity.

High oral doses of Brown HT in rats and mice led to the accumulation of a soluble pigment in the lymph nodes, but this was not found in pigs, nor long-term in rats. Brown HT undergoes azo-reduction in the food canal and is largely excreted in the urine or eliminated in the faeces in rats and guinea pigs. A small amount (0.05–0.25 per cent) has been shown to accumulate in the tissues, and some crosses the placenta. Despite this, experiments with developing animals in utero showed there were no adverse effects on survival, growth, intrauterine development, post-natal development, or on the pathology of any tissues, including the lymph nodes and kidneys. Rats given huge doses (500 mg/kg) of Brown HT showed increased kidney weight and in some females caecum weight increased. (The caecum is at the junction of the large and small intestines.)

A.D.I. 0–1.5 mg/kg body weight.

Typical products
Chocolate flavour cake mixes

160(a) ✓ α-Carotene, β-Carotene, γ-Carotene (C.I. 75130)

Origin Carotenes are orange or yellow plant pigments which occur in all higher plants but are found especially in carrots, green leafy vegetables, tomatoes, apricots, rosehips and oranges. Carotenes of commerce are manufactured in the laboratory (nature-identical substances) but some commercial carotene is extracted from carrots and some algae with hexane. It consists mainly of beta-carotene, with some alpha- and gamma-carotene present. Mixed carotenes also contain other pigments and other substances such as oils, fats and waxes derived from the source material. An edible oil (e.g. peanut oil) has to be added immediately after extraction to stabilise the product.

Function Orange-yellow colour; becomes vitamin A in the body. Carotenes are insoluble in water and soluble in oils, fats and hexane. Normally stable to heat, pH change and sulphur dioxide but the colour fades on exposure to light.

Effects People with cancer have been found to have below-normal blood levels of beta-carotene and vitamin A. However, it is not yet known whether the low levels cause or result from the cancers.

A.D.I. No A.D.I. allocated.

Typical products
Margarine
Dairy blend
Yogurt dessert whip
Pre-packed coffee sponge cake
Sandwich cake

160(b) Annatto extracts (annatto; bixin; norbixin; C.I. 75120)

Origin A vegetable dye from the pericarp (seed coat) of the tropical Annatto tree (*Bixa orellana*). The shrub is 2 to 5 metres high. The fruit is rather like a sweet chestnut, with burrs and contains between 10 and 50 seeds covered with a thin layer of soft, slightly sticky orange pulp.

Annatto may be extracted by water-soluble or oil-soluble methods. Water-soluble annatto is extracted by agitation in aqueous alkali (sodium or potassium hydroxide) of the outer coating of the seeds. It contains norbixin (the hydrolysis product of bixin) as sodium or potassium salts as the major colouring principle.

Oil-soluble annatto (as a solution or suspension) is extracted by mechanical abrasion of the outer seed coats with warm food-grade vegetable oil to separate the pericarp from the waste seeds. The major colour component is bixin, a carotenoid.

Bixin is extracted with organic solvents such as acetone, hexane or methanol followed by removal of the solvent. The extracted bixin may be further processed by aqueous alkali to produce norbixin. Annatto is therefore regarded as a 'natural' colour, whereas bixin is not.

Function Yellow to peach or red colour, traditionally used in the dairy industry, more recently as an alternative to tartrazine. Because annatto, bixin and norbixin are either oil- or water-soluble they are versatile and allow manufacturers flexibility of use. They are stable in processing and baking, and in brine which makes them useful for smoked fish.

Effects There is only sparse scientific data available on bixin.

A.D.I. 0–0.065 mg/kg body weight (expressed as bixin).

Typical products
Margarine
Cheshire cheese
Pre-packed sponge pudding
Smoked fish

E 160(c) Capsanthin (capsorubin)

Origin Paprika extract is prepared by solvent extraction of the fruit pods and seeds of *Capsicum annuum* (red pepper). Although originally a native of tropical America and cultivated by the American Indians in prehistoric times, it is the Hungarian variety (which is rather hotter than the sweet pepper used in salads) from which the paprika spice comes, but Spain is the major producer of the Capsanthin colour. The major colouring principles of paprika extracts are Capsanthin and Capsorubin, although a wide variety of other coloured compounds are present.

Function A spice extract used primarily for its red to orange colour. Used particularly in poultry feed to deepen the colour of egg yolks. With the more widespread use of natural colours it is finding a new use in meat products.

Effects Not known.

A.D.I. Not specified.

Typical products Not permitted in Australia

E160(d) Lycopene (C.I. 75125)

Origin Natural plant extract from tomatoes.

Function Red colour.

Effects Appeciable amounts of lycopene are consumed daily from sources such as tomatoes, so Lycopene was considered by the Food Advisory Committee in 1987 to be provisionally acceptable for potential use in food, with metabolism studies required in the future.

A.D.I. Not specified.

Typical products Not permitted in Australia.

160(e) β-Apo-8′-carotenal (β-8′-apocarotenal)

Origin Only synthesised pigments are available.

Function Orange to yellowish-red colour.

Effects No adverse effects are known.

A.D.I. 0–5 mg/kg body weight.

Typical products
Cheese slices

160(f) β-Apo-8′-carotenoic acid ethyl ester

Origin Only synthesised pigments are available.

Function Natural orange to yellow colour.

Effects No adverse effects are known.

A.D.I. 0–5 mg/kg body weight.

Typical products —

161 Xanthophylls — flavoxanthin

Origin Xanthophylls are prepared by physical means and are hydroxy derivatives of alpha-, beta- and gamma-carotenes (160a) and their naturally occurring epoxides and the fatty acid esters of those compounds present in natural food. Xanthophylls are obtained by hexane extraction of the food and subsequent removal of the solvent. The extract may then be mixed with edible vegetable oils. Xanthophylls may contain other substances, such as oils, fats and waxes derived from the source material.

Function Yellow colour. Flavoxanthin is not commerically available.

Effects Flavoxanthin is consumed as part of the normal daily diet and so is unlikely to pose a health hazard when used as a food colour, provided the level of use is not high.

A.D.I. No A.D.I. allocated.

Typical products —

161 Xanthophylls — lutein

Origin Related to carotene, one of the plant pigments present in abundance in green leaves and marigolds. Also present in egg yolks.

Lutein is commercially available as a natural plant extract and may be obtained from the same sources and at the same time as Chlorophyll (140).

Function Yellow to reddish colour. Used especially in poultry feed to deepen the colour of egg yolks.

Effects   Lutein is consumed as part of the normal daily diet and so is unlikely to pose a hazard to health when used as a food colour, provided the level of use is not high.

A.D.I.   No A.D.I. allocated.

Typical products —

161   Xanthophylls — cryptoxanthin

Origin   Related to carotene, especially well presented in the petals and berries of the *Physalis* (Bladder Cherry, Cape Gooseberry) genus (*Solanaceae*, the potato and tomato family) and also present in orange rind, egg yolk and butter.

Cryptoxanthin is not commerically available either as a plant extract or as a synthesised pigment.

Function   Yellow colour.

Effects   Cryptoxanthin is consumed as part of the normal daily diet and so is unlikely to pose a hazard to health when used as a food colour, provided the level of use is not high.

A.D.I.   No A.D.I. allocated.

Typical products —

161   Xanthophylls — rubixanthin

Origin   Related to carotene, especially present in rosehips, but is not available commercially.

Function   Yellow colour.

Effects   Rubixanthin is consumed as part of the normal daily diet and so is unlikely to pose a health hazard when used as a food colour, provided the level of use is not high.

A.D.I.   No A.D.I. allocated.

Typical products —

161   Xanthophylls — violaxanthin

Origin   Natural extract from the plant pigment carotene, especially isolated from yellow pansies (*Viola tricolor*), but is not available commercially as a food colour.

Function   Yellow colour.

Effects   No adverse effects are known.

A.D.I.   No A.D.I. allocated.

Typical products —

161   Xanthophylls — rhodoxanthin

Origin   A naturally occurring carotenoid pigment found only in small amounts in, for example, the seeds of the yew tree (*Taxus baccata*). (All parts of the yew tree are poisonous, including the berries.)

Function   Yellow colour.

Effects   No adverse effects are known.

A.D.I.   No AD.I. allocated.

Typical products   Not commerically available.

161(g)   Xanthophylls — canthaxanthin (C.I. 40850)

Origin   A fairly rare carotenoid pigment which can be isolated from some mushrooms, for example the chanterelle, various crustacea and fish and flamingo feathers. It can be produced commercially as part of the synthesis of beta-carotene, or from retinal.

Function   Natural orange colour. Used on fish farms to increase the flesh pigmentation of trout and salmon, to levels at harvest of around 2–4 mg/kg in trout and 8–10 mg/kg in salmon, and given to flamingos in zoos to enhance the colour of their feathers.

Effects   No adverse effects are known, when canthaxanthin is taken in the amounts in which it would occur as a colour for fish, which could be 1–5 mg/day, but would not be on a regular basis. Concern has been expressed because it is known from the use of canthaxanthin tablets as tanning promoters that the retina of the eye can become spotted. Users of these tablets may take 30–120 mg/day for several weeks or years and have complained of deterioration of twilight vision, sensitivity to glare and delay in dark adaptation time. As canthaxanthin is being used as a food colour increasingly because it is 'natural', in confectionery, pickles and sauces, it is thought that regular users of canthaxanthin-containing foods could be taking 1–3 mg/day and this amount is considered undesirable.

A.D.I.   0–25 mg/kg body weight (1974) but because of the ocular problems associated with non-food use it is expected to be reduced to 0.05 mg/kg body weight awaiting ophthalmological data.

Typical products   Mallow biscuits

162   Beet red (betanin)

Origin   Natural extract of beetroot. The principle colouring compound is beta-d-glucopyranoside of betanidine.

Function   Deep purplish-red colour. Not a particularly useful colour because of its instability in many food-processing conditions. Also has a rather 'earthy' taste.

Effects   No adverse effects known. Beet red may contain sodium nitrate (251) up to 25 mg/kg of the produce (in liquid or solid forms) so at high levels there may be reasons for elimination from the diets of babies and young children.

A.D.I.   No A.D.I. allocated.

Typical products   Oxtail soup

163   Anthocyanins

Origin   Anthocyanins are natural plant pigments (red, blue or violet) which are present in the cell sap of many flowers, fruits and vegetables. The most common commercially-available anthocyanin is grape-skin extract and red cabbage is another alternative. They are extracted with water, methanol or ethanol. Anthocyanins contain the common components of the source material (anthocyanin, tartaric acid, tannins, sugars, minerals, etc.).

Function   Red, blue or violet food colouring. The colour obtained is pH-dependent, being reddest and most intense in very acid conditions. The shade becomes bluer as the pH rises. Anthocyanins are not suitable for the meat industry since at the pH of meat they exhibit a purple/blue colour.

Effects It seems unlikely that the consumption of anthocyanins as added food colours would significantly increase the daily intake. Information on the metabolism and toxicity of anthocyanins is limited and interpretation is complicated as there are several different, though chemically related, anthocyanins, and studies have been done with certain specific anthocyanins as well as with mixtures extracted from fruits. No adverse effects were recorded on rats or dogs fed colour from purple corn in huge amounts of 2.5 g/kg and 10 per cent of the diet respectively.

In the UK anthocyanin extracts are permitted to contain not more than 1000 mg/kg of sulphur dioxide (220) in liquid extracts and not more than 5000 mg/kg in dried extracts and, as sulphur dioxide is dangerous to asthmatics, anthocyanins should be avoided by this group of people.

Anthocyanins found in red wine can inactivate the enzymes which inactivate other harmful substances and may explain why red but not white wine causes migraine in some people.

A.D.I. No A.D.I. allocated.

Typical products
Soft drinks
Jams and preserves

170 Calcium carbonate (chalk; C.I. 77220)

Origin Naturally occurring white mineral.

Function Alkali sometimes used for deacidification of wine; firming agent for canned fruit and vegetables;

releasing agent (in vitamin tablets); in calcium supplements and as a surface food colorant.

Effects No adverse effects are known.

A.D.I. Not limited.

Typical products
Bread
Biscuits
Buns and cakes
Confectionery
Canned fruit and vegetables

171 Titanium dioxide (C.I. 77891)

Origin Prepared from the naturally occurring mineral ilmenite.

Function White colour to provide a barrier to colour in sweets with contrasting centres.

Effects No adverse effects are known.

A.D.I. Not limited.

Typical products
Pan sugar-coated confectionery   5 g/kg (only permitted use in Australia)

172 Iron oxides (yellow: C.I. 77492; red: 77491; black: 77499)

Origin Naturally occurring pigments of iron.

Function Yellow, red, orange, brown and black colour.

Effects The iron present in these oxides is in the ferric form and is not therefore very actively available to the body tissues. The results of feeding experiments in dogs and cats with high levels of iron did not result in any adverse effects.

A.D.I.   0–0.5 mg/kg body weight.

Typical products
Salmon and shrimp paste or
spread   500 mg/kg

E173   Aluminium (C.I. 77000)

Origin   Naturally occurring, from the
ore bauxite. The normal dietary intake
from cereal and vegetables is 5–6 mg/
day.

Function   Metallic colour for surface
only.

Effects   Insoluble forms of aluminium
taken orally are poorly absorbed and of
very low toxicity. Toxic effects are not
seen when aluminium is present in
drinking water. There is an increasing
body of evidence, however, to suggest
that an accumulation of aluminium in
the cells of the nervous system could
be potentially toxic and is found in the
brain cells of people with Parkinson-
type diseases and senile dementia.
(Aluminium is permitted to contain not
more than 10 mg/kg of lead as
impurities.) Several reports also
suggest that a high aluminium intake
may have adverse effects on the
metabolism of phosphorus, calcium or
fluoride in the human body and may
induce or intensify skeletal
abnormalities.

A.D.I.   No A.D.I. allocated.

Typical products   Not permitted in
Australia.

E174   Silver (C.I. 77820)

Origin   Naturally occurring metal.

Function   Metallic surface colour.

Effects   Silver salts are toxic to bacteria
and lower life-forms. Long, regular
consumption can lead to argyria, a
blue-grey skin, which is not dangerous.
The small amounts consumed on
special occasions would not
accumulate in the tissues to any extent
or constitute a health hazard.

A.D.I.   Decision postponed.

Typical products   Not permitted in
Australia.

E175   Gold (C.I. 77480)

Origin   Naturally occurring metal.

Function   Metallic surface colour.

Effects   Chemically very inactive —
therefore harmless — but expensive.

A.D.I.   No A.D.I. allocated.

Typical products   Not permitted in
Australia.

E180   Pigment rubine (Lithol rubine BK: C.I. 15850)

Origin   Synthetic, an azo dye (see
glossary).

Function   Reddish colour.

Effects   No adverse effects known.
Toxicity studies in rats and rabbits did
not show any treatment-related effects.

A.D.I.   No A.D.I. allocated.

Typical products   Not permitted in
Australia.

181   Tannic acid (tannins)

Origin   Tannin is obtained from nut-galls of young twigs of oaks such as *Quercus infectoria*, from nut galls of Sumacs (*Rhus* sp.) or from the seed pods of Tara (*Caesalpinia spinosa*). The ground nut galls are treated with a mixture of water and alcohol. The resulting solution contains tannic acid and other related compounds. Food-grade tannin is purer than tannin from tea leaves.

Function   Clarifying agent in alcoholic drinks, to remove cloudiness caused by protein.

Effects   In the same way as tannin in tea stains teapots, it turns the skin brown when used internally. Large doses can cause vomiting or irritate the stomach, and liver and kidney damage can occur through the formation of tannic acid. Tannins inhibit the absorption of nutrients such as iron. A cup of tea or coffee contains 100–500 mg of tannins, so the problems associated with excessive intake have more meaningful consequences for heavy imbibers than for consumers of food items in which tannins are used in small safe amounts as additives.

A.D.I.   0–0.6 mg/kg body weight (temporary).

Typical products
Beer
Wine

200   Sorbic acid

Origin   Occurs naturally in some fruits. May be obtained from the berries of mountain ash (*Sorbus aucuparia*), and manufactured synthetically for commercial use from ketene.

Function   Preservative, inhibiting the growth of yeasts and moulds between a pH range of 4.0–6.0, but only marginally effective against bacteria. This makes sorbic acid particularly advantageous as a cheese preservative, permitting the fermenting action of lactic acid bacteria. It cannot be used in pasteurised food as it breaks down at high temperatures. Permitted in oenicological (wine-making) practices and processes.

Effects   Possible skin irritant, when directly applied. Sorbic acid is metabolised in a manner comparable with that of similar fatty acids, which is a good indication that it is unlikely to be hazardous at the current exposure level.

A.D.I.   0–25 mg/kg body weight (sum of sorbic acid, its calcium, potassium and sodium salts expressed as sorbic acid).

Typical products & maximum permitted levels

Bread	1.2 g/kg dry weight
Brewed soft drinks	400 mg/kg
Cheese (other than processed cheese) in flexible packaging material	3 g/kg
Cheese spread	3 g/kg
Cherries, preserved	1 g/kg
Cider	400 mg/L
Cottage cheese	500 mg/kg
Dips with more than 85% dairy products	500 mg/kg
Dried tree fruits other than figs (water content greater than 200 g/kg)	1 g/kg
Essences (liquid only)	800 mg/L
Figs (water content greater than 240 g/kg)	500 mg/kg
Fish marinades, fish semi-preserves	1 g/kg
Flavoured cordial, flavoured syrup, flavoured topping	800 mg/kg
Flour products other than bread	1 g/kg
Fruit drink	400 mg/kg
Fruit flavoured drink	400 mg/kg
Fruit juice	400 mg/kg
Fruit juice drink	400 mg/kg
Fruit juice cordial, fruit juice syrup, fruit juice topping	800 mg/kg
Fruit juice for manufacturing purposes	2.1 g/kg
Fruit salad, fresh	375 mg/kg

Fruit yoghurt, vegetable yoghurt,
   nut yoghurt   50 mg/kg
Imitation fruit   400 mg/kg
Liquorice   1 g/kg
Low joule jam   1 g/kg
Olives in salt   500 mg/kg
Perry   400 mg/kg
Processed cheese, sliced   2 g/kg
Reduced fat cheese spread   3 g/kg
Reduced fat processed cheese,
   sliced   3 g/kg
Soft drinks   400 mg/kg
Tomato juice, non-canned
   (pH less than 4.5)   400 mg/kg
Tomato juice, concentrated non-
   canned (pH less than 4.5)   400 g/kg
Wine   200 mg/L

201 Sodium sorbate

Origin Manufactured by neutralisation of sorbic acid (200).

Function Preservative.

Effects None known.

A.D.I. 0–25 mg/kg body weight (see sorbic acid (200)).

Typical products Many of those permitted to contain sorbic acid (200).

202 Potassium sorbate

Origin Manufactured by neutralisation of sorbic acid (200) with potassium hydroxide.

Function Antifungal and antibacterial preservative, more soluble than sorbic acid (200). Permitted in oenicological (wine-making) practices and processes.

Effects None known.

A.D.I. 0–2.5 mg/kg body weight (see sorbic acid (200)).

Typical products Many of those permitted to contain sorbic acid (200).

203 Calcium sorbate

Origin Manufactured by neutralisation of sorbic acid (200).

Function Antifungal and antibacterial preservative.

Effects None known.

A.D.I. 0–2.5 mg/kg body weight (see sorbic acid (200)).

Typical products Many of those permitted to contain sorbic acid (200).

210 Benzoic acid

Origin Occurs naturally in many edible berries, fruits and vegetables. Commercially available benzoic acid is made by chemical synthesis.

Function Preservative — antibacterial and antifungal — but effective only in an acid medium.

Effects People who suffer from asthma or who have recurrent urticaria (nettle-rash) are likely to be sensitive to benzoic acid. It may also cause gastric irritation if consumed in large quantities. It has been reported to be responsible for neurological disorders and to react with the preservative sodium bisulphite (222).

When hyperactive children were given a diet containing few varieties of food, and provoking foods were identified by their weekly reintroduction, benzoic acid along with tartrazine provoked a hyperactive response in 27 out of 34 children (79 per cent).

The body excretes benzoic acids as hippuric acid within 9–15 hours of eating food containing it.

A.D.I. 0–5 mg/kg body weight (sum of benzoic acid, its calcium, potassium and sodium salts expressed as benzoic acid (210)).

Typical products & maximum permitted levels

Brewed soft drinks	400 mg/kg
Cherries, preserved	1 g/L
Cider	400 mg/L
Essences, liquid only	800 mg/L
Fish marinades, fish semi-preserves	1 g/kg
Flavoured cordial, flavoured syrup, flavoured topping	800 mg/kg
Fruit drink	400 mg/kg
Fruit flavoured drink	400 mg/kg
Fruit juice	400 mg/kg
Fruit juice drink	400 mg/kg
Fruit juice cordial, fruit juice syrup, fruit juice topping	800 mg/kg
Imitation fruit	400 mg/kg
Perry	400 mg/kg
Low joule jam	1 g/g
Soft drink	400 mg/kg
Tomato juice, non-canned (pH less than 4.5)	400 mg/kg
Tomato juice, concentrated non-canned (pH less than 4.5)	1.4 g/kg

211 Sodium benzoate

Origin The sodium salt of benzoic acid.

Function Preservative — antibacterial and antifungal — effective only in slightly acid environment.

Effects People who suffer from asthma, or who have recurrent urticaria, may be sensitive to sodium benzoate and have allergic reactions. Sodium benzoate and tartrazine (102) exacerbate the condition in between 10 and 40 per cent of patients with chronic urticaria, and possibly a higher proportion still of aspirin-sensitive individuals.

A.D.I. 0–5 mg/kg body weight (see benzoic acid (210)).

Typical products Many of those permitted to contain benzoic acid (210).

212 Potassium benzoate

Origin The potassium salt of benzoic acid.

Function Preservative — antibacterial and antifungal.

Effects People who suffer from asthma or are allergic to aspirin or have recurrent urticaria (nettle-rash) may be sensitive to potassium benzoate and show allergic reactions.

A.D.I. 0–5 mg/kg body weight (see benzoic acid (210)).

Typical products Many of those permitted to contain benzoic acid (210).

213 Calcium benzoate

Origin The calcium salt of benzoic acid.

Function Preservative — antibacterial and antifungal.

Effects JECFA claims there are reports of a relatively high incidence of adverse reactions to calcium benzoate in susceptible individuals. They say, 'It is not clear to what extent these reactions are manifestations of immunological hypersensitivity or of idiosyncratic hyper-reactivity . . . but both can be regarded as forms of intolerance'.

People who suffer from asthma, recurrent urticaria or are allergic to aspirin are likely to be sensitive to calcium benzoate.

A.D.I. 0–5 mg/kg body weight (see benzoic acid (210)).

Typical products Many of those permitted to contain benzoic acid (210).

E214 Ethyl 4-hydroxybenzoate (ethyl *para*-hydroxybenzoate)

Origin Produced from benzoic acid.

Function Preservative — antibacterial and antifungal.

Effects Some people are hypersensitive to benzoates, especially those sensitive to aspirin, asthmatics and those with recurrent urticaria. This substance may cause allergic contact dermatitis, although relatively few cases have been described. There is no evidence that esters of benzoic acid accumulate in the body; they are readily absorbed, broken down and excreted. There may also be a numbing effect on the mouth, as it has anaesthetic properties.

A.D.I. 0–10 mg/kg body weight (sum of ethyl, methyl and propyl esters).

Typical products Not permitted in Australia.

E215 Ethyl 4-hydroxybenzoate, sodium salt (sodium ethyl *para*-hydroxybenzoate)

Origin Produced from benzoic acid.

Function Preservative — antibacterial and antifungal.

Effects This substance may cause allergic contact dermatitis, although relatively few cases have been described. There is no evidence that esters of benzoic acid accumulate in the body; they are readily absorbed and de-esterfied. There may be a numbing effect on the mouth.

A.D.I. Not specified.

Typical products Not permitted in Australia.

216 Propylparaben (propyl 4-hydroxybenzoate; n-propyl p-hydroxybenzoate; propyl *para*-hydroxybenzoate)

Origin Produced from benzoic acid.

Function Preservative — antimicrobial.

Effects This substance may cause allergic contact dermatitis, although relatively few cases have been described. There is no evidence that esters of benzoic acid accumulate in the body; they are readily absorbed and de-esterfied. There may be a numbing effect on the mouth.

A.D.I.   0–10 mg/kg body weight (see ethyl ester (E214)).

Typical products & maximum permitted level
Food colours in aqueous solution   2.5 g/L in total with methylparaben (218) (The only permitted use in Australia.)

E217   Propyl 4-hydroxybenzoate, sodium salt (sodium n-propyl p-hydroxybenzoate; sodium propyl *para*-hydroxybenzoate)

Origin   Produced from benzoic acid.

Function   Preservative — antimicrobial.

Effects   Allergic reactions to this substance may develop in asthmatics, those with recurrent urticaria (nettle-rash), or people sensitive to aspirin. There may be skin sensitivity and/or a numbing effect on the mouth.
    Propylhydroxybenzoate forms complexes in solution with methylcellulose (461).

A.D.I.   Not specified.

Typical products   Not permitted in Australia.

218   Methylparaben (methyl 4-hydroxybenzoate, methyl *para*-hydroxybenzoate)

Origin   Synthetic.

Function   Preservative — antimicrobial agent.

Effects   Some people may exhibit allergic reactions to this substance, mainly affecting the skin or mouth. This substance is the main volatile compound in the vaginal secretions of female beagle dogs. A letter in the *Archives of Dermatology* (1985; 121:1107) suggests that when a male dog's sexual behaviour is socially embarrassing the presence of methyl paraben may be suspected as the unwilling target of his attentions.

A.D.I.   0–10 mg/kg body weight (see ethyl ester (E214)).

Typical products & maximum permitted level
Food colours in aqueous solution.   2.5 g/L in total with propylparaben (216) (The only permitted use in Australia.)

E219   Methyl 4-hydroxybenzoate, sodium salt (sodium methyl *para*-hydroxybenzoate; sodium methyl hydroxybenzoate)

Origin   Produced from benzoic acid.

Function   Preservative — active against fungi and yeasts, but less active against bacteria.

Effects   Allergic reactions have occurred when preparations containing hydroxybenzoates have been applied to the skin. Similar reactions have also occurred following intravenous or oral administration. Hydroxybenzoates have a numbing effect on the mouth.

A.D.I.   0–10 mg/kg body weight.

Typical products   Not permitted in Australia

220   Sulphur dioxide

Origin   Occurs naturally but produced chemically by the combustion of sulphur or gypsum.

Function   One of the oldest food additives known to man, sulphur dioxide was employed by the Romans, Ancient Greeks and Egyptians as a preservative for wine. Sulphur was burnt before sealing the wine into barrels. Today it is the most reactive food additive in use and one of the most versatile, preventing food spoilage (whether it be introduced by micro-organisms, browning (enzymic or non-enzymic) or oxidation); and used as a bleaching agent for flour; as an improving agent; and for physical modification of dough in biscuit manufacture; for stabilisation of vitamin C and to inhibit nitrosamine formation in the kilning of barley. It is also used in the malting process in beer-making to reduce excess loss of carbohydrate from the germinated barley rootlets, and also to prevent further growth of the barley during the dehydrating period after germination.

Seasonally available soft fruit is stored as sulphited fruit pulp to permit jam manufacture to proceed all the year round. Much of the sulphur dioxide is lost during the jam boiling process.

It is used as a bleaching agent in the manufacture of maraschino cherries and to improve the translucency of candied citrus peels. Table grapes may be fumigated with sulphur dioxide to inhibit *Botrytis cinerea* — a fungus which causes deterioration. Salad bars in the USA used to spray sulphur dioxide on to salads to keep them looking fresh, excessive use causing

an estimated 8 deaths from asthma.

In the wine industry sulphur dioxide is still employed today to prevent enzymic browning in the grape must (especially important for white wines), and to inhibit the growth of lactic acid or acetic acid bacteria, ensuring the required yeast will dominate the fermentation. It stabilises the wine colour, behaves as an antimicrobial agent and antioxidant, and traps undesirable acetaldehyde. The term 'sulphur dioxide' as a food additive is a collective one and includes the sulphites (221-228).

Effects   Sulphur dioxide destroys the vitamin B_1 or thiamine in foods. Foods that contain a significant source of thiamine — meat, cereals, dairy products — should not be treated. Bleaching of flour reduces its vitamin E content.

Sulphurous acid, produced when sulphur dioxide is dissolved, may cause gastric irritation. Healthy people have no problem metabolizing sulphur dioxide: the kidneys and liver both produce enzymes which oxidise sulphites, but those with impaired kidneys or liver may need to avoid sulphites.

Foods containing sulphites may precipitate an asthmatic attack in asthma sufferers, who are very sensitive to the irritant effects of sulphur dioxide gas which may be liberated from the foods containing it and inhaled as the food is swallowed.

A.D.I.   0–0.7 mg/kg body weight (included in the sulphur dioxide and sulphites group).

Typical products & maximum permitted levels

Avocado spread, frozen	300 mg/kg
Beer	25 mg/L
Brewed soft drink	115 mg/kg

Cabbage, dehydrated	1.5 g/kg
Carrots, dehydrated	1 g/kg
Cider	200 mg/L
Cooked manufactured meat	260 mg/kg
Crystallised pineapple	280 mg/kg
Desiccated coconut	50 mg/kg
Dried fruit	3 g/kg
Essences (liquid only)	230 mg/L
Flavoured cordial, flavoured syrup, flavoured topping	230 mg/kg
French beans, dehydrated	750 mg/kg
Fruit drink	115 mg/kg
Fruit flavoured drink	115 mg/kg
Fruit juice	115 mg/kg
Fruit juice drink	115 mg/kg
Fruit juice cordial, fruit juice syrup, fruit juice topping	230 mg/kg
Gelatine	1 g/kg
Glucose syrup	300 mg/kg
Glucose syrup, dried	40 mg/kg
Imitation fruit	3 g/kg
Low joule jam	285 mg/kg
Maraschino cherries, cocktail cherries	300 mg/kg
Mixed dried fruit	3 g/kg
Peas, dehydrated	1 g/kg
Perry	200 mg/L
Pickles	750 mg/kg
Potatoes, dehydrated	500 mg/kg
Potatoes, raw peeled	50 mg/kg
Silver beet, dehydrated	1.5 g/kg
Soft drink	115 mg/kg
Sausage meat, uncooked	500 mg/kg
Tomato juice, non-canned (pH less than 4.5)	115 mg/kg
Tomato juice, concentrated non-canned (pH less than 4.5)	400 mg/kg
Vinegar (except vinegar prepared from wine)	25 mg/kg
Vinegar prepared from wine	100 mg/kg
Wine	300 mg/L

221 Sodium sulphite

Origin A sodium salt of sulphurous acid.

Function In food processing sulphites are used to sterilise fermentation equipment and food containers, to selectively inhibit undesirable micro-organisms in fermentation industries, prevent oxidative discoloration and control enzymic browning of pre-peeled and sliced/chipped apples or potatoes, especially for catering or baking use. Sulphiting agents also control non-enzymic browning. In the US sulphites were used in restaurant foods to keep salad bar vegetables and fruits looking fresh and prevent browning. Used in processing sugar beet, corn sweeteners, food starches and gelatine.

Treatment of foods with sulphites reduces their thiamine (vitamin B_1) content, so foods which contain a significant amount of thiamine — meat, cereals, dairy products — should not be treated.

In some countries sulphiting agents may be applied to specific products, e.g. fresh sausage in the UK, in which their function is to act as antimicrobial agents especially in controlling *Enterobacteriaceae* (gut bacteria) including *Salmonellae*. They also preserve the bright-red colour of meat by inhibiting the oxidation of myoglobin to metamyoglobin, and prevent the discoloration of shrimps and lobsters due to the action of the enzyme tyrosinase.

Sulphites modify the properties of dough by the sulphitolysis of disulphite bonds in the gluten. This has several technological advantages, reducing the time it takes to mix a batch of dough and reducing the elasticity of the dough. It eliminates the need for standing time for stress relaxation to occur, and allows continuous biscuit plants to make satisfactory dough sheets. They help to produce a consistent baked product even though various varieties of wheat may be used.

Effects Asthmatics are very sensitive to the irritant effects of sulphur dioxide gas which is liberated from sulphites in acid food and inhaled when the food is swallowed. This may trigger an asthmatic attack.

In other people, ingestion of sulphites may cause gastric irritation, nausea or diarrhoea due to liberation of sulphurous acid, or allergic reactions of nettle rash or swelling (angioedema). The exact mechanism of sulphite-induced reactions is unknown.

Sulphites are oxidised by enzymes produced in the kidneys and liver; those with impaired kidneys and liver should avoid all sulphites.

A.D.I. 0–0.7 mg/kg body weight (see sulphur dioxide (220)).

Typical products & maximum permitted levels
Many of those permitted to contain sulphur dioxide (220).
Uncooked prawns, uncooked shrimps 30 mg/kg

222 Sodium bisulphite (sodium hydrogen sulphite; acid sodium sulphite)

Origin A sodium salt of sulphurous acid.

Function Preservative for alcoholic beverages.

Effects Since 1982 some eight deaths have been linked to the use of sulphites in the USA, a result of eating salads at salad bars which had been sprayed with sulphites in uncontrolled amounts. This practice has now been banned. All the victims had asthma. Asthmatics are very sensitive to the irritant effects of sulphur dioxide gas which is liberated from sulphites in acid foods and inhaled as the food is swallowed. Ingestion of sulphites may cause gastric irritation in other people due to the liberation of sulphurous acid. They are a known cause of food aversion and allergic skin reactions.

Sulphites are oxidised by enzymes produced in the kidneys and liver; those with impaired organs should avoid all sulphites.

Treatment of foods with sulphites reduces their thiamine (vitamin B_1) content, so foods which contain a significant amount of thiamine, such as meat, cereals and dairy products should not be treated.

A.D.I. 0–0.7 mg/kg body weight (see sulphur dioxide (220)).

Typical products & maximum permitted levels
Many of those permitted to contain sulphur dioxide (220).
Uncooked prawns, uncooked shrimps 30 mg/kg

223 Sodium metabisulphite (disodium pyrosulphite)

Origin Commercially manufactured sodium salt of sulphurous acid.

Function Antimicrobial preservative; anti-oxidant; bleaching agent.

Effects Asthmatics are very sensitive to the irritant effects of sulphur dioxide gas which is liberated from sodium metabisulphite in acid foods and inhaled as the food is swallowed. Ingestion of sulphites may cause gastric irritation in other people due to liberation of sulphurous acid.

Sulphites are known to cause food aversion and allergic skin reactions. They are oxidised by enzymes produced in the kidneys and liver; those with impaired organs should avoid all sulphites. Treatment of foods with sulphite reduces their thiamine (vitamin B_1) content, so foods which contain a significant amount of thiamine — meat, cereals, dairy products — should not be treated.

A.D.I.   0–0.7 mg/kg body weight (see sulphur dioxide (220)).

Typical products & maximum permitted levels
Many of those permitted to contain sulphur dioxide (220)
Uncooked prawns,
   uncooked shrimps   30 mg/kg
Flour for bread
   making   60 mg/kg
Flour products other
   than bread   300 mg/kg

224   Potassium metabisulphite (potassium pyrosulphite)

Origin   Commercially manufactured potassium salt of sulphurous acid.

Function   Antimicrobial preservative, especially in the Campden process for preserving fruit and home-made wine. Used to halt fermentations in breweries. Antibrowning agent.

Effects   Asthmatics are very sensitive to the irritant effects of sulphur dioxide gas which is liberated from sulphites in acid foods and inhaled as the food is

swallowed. Ingestion of sulphites may cause gastric irritation due to liberation of sulphurous acid.

Sulphites are a known cause of food aversion and allergic skin reactions. They are oxidised by enzymes produced in the liver and kidneys; those with impaired organs should avoid all sulphites. Treatment of foods with sulphites reduces their thiamine (vitamin B_1) content, so foods which contain a significant amount of thiamine — meat, cereals, dairy products — should not be treated.

A.D.I.   0–0.7 mg/kg body weight (see sulphur dioxide (220)).

Typical products   Many of those permitted to contain sulphur dioxide (220).

225   Potassium sulphite

Origin   A white crystalline powder, a commercially available salt of sulphurous acid.

Function   Preservative.

Effects   Potassium sulphite has a diuretic effect (promotes excretion of urine). Asthmatics are very sensitive to the irritant effects of sulphur dioxide gas which is liberated from sulphites in acid foods and inhaled as the food is swallowed. Consuming sulphites may cause gastric irritation due to the liberation of sulphurous acid.

Sulphites are a well recognised cause of food aversion and allergic skin reactions. They are oxidised by enzymes produced in the liver and kidneys so if these organs are impaired, all sulphites should be avoided. Treatment of foods with sulphites reduces their vitamin B1 or thiamine content, so foods which contain a significant amount of thiamine such as meat, cereals and dairy products should not be treated.

A.D.I. 0–0.7 mg/kg body weight (see sulphur dioxide (220)).

Typical products Many of those permitted to contain sulphur dioxide (220).

E226 Calcium sulphite

Origin A calcium salt of sulphurous acid.

Function Preservative; firming agent in canned fruits and vegetables; disinfectant in brewing vats.

Effects Established asthmatics are very sensitive to the irritant effects of sulphur dioxide gas which is liberated from sulphites in acid foods and inhaled in low concentrations as the food is swallowed. Ingestion of sulphite may cause gastric irritation due to the liberation of sulphurous acid.

Sulphites are a known cause of food aversion and allergic skin reactions. They are oxidised by enzymes produced in the kidney and liver; those with impaired organs should avoid all sulphites. Treatment of foods with sulphite reduces their thiamine (vitamin B_1) content, so foods containing a significant source of thiamine (meat, cereals, dairy products) should not be treated.

A.D.I. 0–0.7 mg/kg body weight (see sulphur dioxide (220)).

Typical products Not permitted in Australia.

E227 Calcium hydrogen sulphite (calcium bisulphite)

Origin A calcium salt of sulphurous acid.

Function Preservative; prevents secondary fermentation in brewing, and is used in washing beer casks to prevent the beer becoming cloudy or sour; firming agent in canned fruits and vegetables.

Effects Established asthmatics are very sensitive to the irritant effects of sulphur dioxide gas which is liberated from sulphites in acid food and inhaled in low concentrations as the food is swallowed. Ingestion of sulphites may cause gastric irritation due to liberation of sulphurous acid. Sulphites are a known cause of food aversion and allergic skin reactions. They are oxidised by enzymes produced in the kidneys and liver; those with impaired organs should avoid all sulphites. Treatment of foods with sulphite reduces their thiamine (vitamin B_1) content, and may contribute to a vitamin deficiency.

A.D.I. 0–0.07 mg/kg body weight (see sulphur dioxide (220)).

Typical products Not permitted in Australia

228 Potassium bisulphite (potassium hydrogen sulphite)

Origin A potassium salt of sulphurous acid.

Function Preservative, especially for wine.

Effects Asthmatics are very sensitive to the irritant effects of sulphur dioxide gas which is liberated from potassium bisulphite in wine and inhaled as the wine is swallowed. Ingestion of sulphites may cause gastric irritation in other groups of people due to liberation of sulphurous acid.

Sulphites are known to cause food aversion and allergic skin reactions. They are oxidised by enzymes produced in the liver and kidneys: so if these organs are impaired, all sulphites should be avoided.

A.D.I. 0–0.7mg/kg body weight (see sulphur dioxide (220)).

Typical products Many of those permitted to contain sulphur dioxide (220).

E**230** Biphenyl (diphenyl)

Origin Synthetic, produced by action of heat on benzene.

Function Fungistatic agent; food preservative which inhibits the growth of species of *Penicillium*, especially *P. digitatum*, which cause citrus fruits to go mouldy. Can penetrate the skin of fruit and might be included in food or drink prepared from fruit. Sometimes fruit is wrapped in paper impregnated with diphenyl.

Effects More soluble in alcohol than in water, although it is considered that those consuming sufficient gin and tonic with lemon to be at risk have a substantially greater chance of cirrhosis than of harm from biphenyl. Workers exposed to diphenyl reported nausea, vomiting and irritation to eyes and nose.

A.D.I. 0–0.05mg/kg body weight.

Typical products & maximum residue limits
Not considered as a food additive in Australia, however it is permitted to be used as an agricultural chemical on certain specified crops provided that the maximum residue limit (MRL) in the food is not exceeded. The presence of agricultural chemical residues in food is not required to be declared.

Citrus fruit	110mg/kg

231 2-Hydroxybiphenyl (o-phenyl phenol; orthophenylphenol)

Origin Prepared from phenyl ether or from dibenzofuran.

Function Preservative — antibacterial and antifungal.

Effects None known.

A.D.I. 0–0.2mg/kg body weight.

Typical products & maximum residue limits
Not considered as a food additive in Australia, however it is permitted to be used as an agricultural chemical on certain specified crops provided that the maximum residue limit (MRL) in the food is not exceeded. The presence of agricultural chemical residues in food is not required to be declared.

Pears	25mg/kg
Carrots and peaches	20mg/kg
Plums, prunes and sweet potatoes	15mg/kg
Cantaloupes, citrus fruit, cucumbers, pineapples, tomatoes and peppers	10mg/kg
Cherries and nectarines	3mg/kg

E232 Sodium biphenyl-2-yl oxide (sodium o-phenylphenol; sodium orthophenylphenate)

Origin Synthetic (with a strong smell of soap).

Function Preservative — antifungal. Alternative form of 231.

Effects None known.

A.D.I. 0–0.2 mg/kg body weight.

Typical products & maximum residue limits
Not considered as a food additive in Australia, however, it is permitted to be used as an agricultural chemical on certain specified crops provided that the maximum residue limit (MRL) in the food is not exceeded. The presence of agricultural chemical residues in food is not required to be declared.

Pears	25mg/kg
Carrots and peaches	20 mg/kg
Plums, prunes and sweet potatoes	15 mg/kg
Cantaloupes, citrus fruit, cucumbers, pineapples, tomatoes and peppers	10 mg/kg
Cherries and nectarines	3 mg/kg

E233 2-(Thiazol-4-yl) benzimidazole (thiabendazole)

Origin Prepared by the reaction of 4-thiazolecarboxamide with O-phenylenediamine in polyphosphoric acid.

Function Preservative — fungicide, especially for spoilage control of citrus fruits. It is also used for the treatment of nematode worms in man.

Effects Thiabendazole given to pregnant rats on the ninth day of gestation led to foetal malformations of the skeleton and limbs. When radioactive thiabendazole was fed to pregnant mice it became bound to large molecules in various parts of the body, but especially to the foetus and skeletal cells.

Typical products & maximum residue limits
Not considered as a food additive in Australia, however it is permitted to be used as an agricultural chemical on certain specified crops provided that the maximum residue limit (MRL) in the food is not exceeded. The presence of agricultural chemical residues in food is not required to be declared.

Apples, pears and citrus fruits	10mg/kg
Potatoes	5 mg/kg
Bananas (whole)	3 mg/kg
Mushrooms	0.5 mg/kg
Bananas (pulp)	0.4 mg/kg
Meat	0.2 mg/kg
Milk	0.05 mg/kg

234 Nisin

Origin A polypeptide antibiotic substance produced by the growth of a bacterium called *Steptococcus lactis*. Several strains of cheese starter organisms produce nisin.

Function Preservative.

Effects None known.

A.D.I. 33 000 units/kg body weight.

Typical products
Canned soup
Canned tomatoes (pH less than 4.5)
Cheese spread

Processed cheese
Reduced fat cheese spread
Reduced fat processed cheese
Tomato paste
  (pH less than 4.5)
Tomato puree
  (pH Less than 4.5)

235 Natamycin (Pimaricin)

Origin Natamycin is an antibiotic produced by the growth of *Streptomyces natalensis*. It can behave either as an acid or as a base.

Function Anti-fungal preservative, which is either sprayed onto the surface of foods, incorporated into the plastic coating or food-wrapping material, or the foods may be dipped into a natamycin solution.

Effects Natamycin is used medically to treat *Candida albicans* (the yeast fungus responsible for 'thrush'). Nausea and vomiting, anorexia and diarrhoea have been caused when natamycin was given by mouth and it has caused mild irritation when applied to the skin. It is poorly absorbed from the gut and has been used to treat pregnant women without harm to the developing foetus.

A.D.I. 0–0.3 mg/kg body weight.

Typical products & maximum permitted levels

Uncooked fermented manufactured meat (Surface application)	$1.2 \, mg/dm^2$ when determined in a surface sample taken from a depth of not less than 3 mm and not more than 5 mm and including the casing
Cheese (applied to rind)	$2 \, mg/dm^2$ when determined in a surface sample taken from a depth of not less than 3 mm and not more than 5 mm.

(Only permitted uses in Australia.)

E236 Formic acid

Origin Occurs naturally in the bodies of ants; produced commercially by heating carbon monoxide and sodium hydroxide under pressure and decomposing the resulting sodium formate with sulphuric acid.

Function Preservative — antibacterial action; flavour adjunct.

Effects In amounts in which it would be present in food there is no danger, although Formic acid is very caustic to the skin and if absorbed has been known to cause urine disorders. It was formerly used as a diuretic.

A.D.I. 0–3 mg/kg body weight.

Typical products Not permitted in Australia.

E237 Sodium formate

Origin The sodium salt manufactured from formic acid.

Function Preservative.

Effects Has diuretic properties and was formerly used for this purpose.

A.D.I. Not specified.

Typical products Not permitted in Australia.

E238   Calcium formate

Origin   The calcium salt of formic acid.

Function   Preservative.

Effects   Has diuretic properties and was formerly used for this purpose.

A.D.I.   Not specified.

Typical products   Not permitted in Australia.

E239   Hexamine (hexamethylenetetramine)

Origin   Manufactured from formaldehyde and ammonia.

Function   Antimicrobial perservative.

Effects   Gastro-intestinal upsets may result from the prolonged use of hexamine by the production of formaldehyde. In addition, the urinary system may be affected and, less frequently, skin rashes may occur. In experiments with animals hexamine caused gene mutation and is suspected of being carcinogenic.

A.D.I.   0–0.15 mg/kg body weight.

Typical products   Not permitted in Australia.

249   Potassium nitrite

Origin   Potassium salt of nitrous acid.

Function   Curing agent for meat, converting the iron-containing pigments in the flesh to stable bright-pink compounds; preservative in meat, particularly inhibiting the development of spores of *Clostridium botulinum*, the dangerous bacterium responsible for botulism.

Effects   Nitrites are capable of entering the bloodstream and changing the nature of the haemoglobin of the red corpuscles responsible for oxygen transport. When the blood's ability to carry oxygen is impaired there may be difficulty in breathing and pallor, dizziness or headaches, a condition known as methemoglobinemia. Infants are far more susceptible to this condition than adults, and nitrites are not permitted in foods intended for infants and young children. Nitrites are also capable of reacting with substances called amines in the stomach to form nitrosamines which are potentially carcinogenic. There is also evidence that corresponding intakes of vitamins A, C and E in the form of fresh yellow-green vegetables is protective against stomach cancer which may be why no clear relationships have been established so far between the consumption of nitrites and cancer, with the possible exception of the Icelandics.

Without the nitrites and nitrates there would be many deaths from the growth of toxic micro-organisms in meats.

A.D.I.   0–0.2 mg/kg body weight (temporary; included in the group A.D.I. for sodium and potassium nitrite).

Typical products & maximum permitted levels

Canned cured meat, perishable	125 mg/kg
Canned cured meat, commercially sterile	50 mg/kg
Corned meat, cured meat, pickled meat, salted meat	125 mg/kg

Manufactured meat   125 mg/kg
Pressed corned meat,
    pressed cured
    meat, pressed
    pickled meat,
    pressed salt meat   125 mg/kg
Note — For the purpose of Australian food regulations, potassium nitrite and also sodium nitrite, potassium nitrate and sodium nitrate, are not classed as preservatives. Since they are not included in one of the Australian specified classes for food additives, they must, if present in a packaged food, be declared by their prescribed names, i.e. potassium nitrite, sodium nitrite, potassium nitrate or sodium nitrate and not by their code numbers.

250   Sodium nitrite

Origin   Not naturally occurring; derived from sodium nitrate by chemical or bacterial action.

Function   Curing agent for meat, converting the iron containing pigments in the flesh to stable bright-pink compounds; preservative in meat, particularly inhibiting the development of spores of *Clostridium botulinum*, the dangerous bacterium responsible for botulism.

Effects   Nitrites are capable of entering the bloodstream and changing the nature of the haemoglobin of the red blood corpuscles, responsible for oxygen transport. When the blood's ability to carry oxygen is impaired, there may be difficulty in breathing and pallor, dizziness or headaches, a condition known as methemoglobinemia. Infants are far more susceptible to this condition than adults, and nitrites are not permitted in foods intended for infants and young children.

Nitrites are also capable of reacting with substances called amines in the stomach to form nitrosamines which are potentially carcinogenic. There is also evidence that corresponding intakes of vitamins A, C and E in the form of fresh yellow-green vegetables is a considerable protection against stomach cancer which may be why no clear relationships have been established so far between the consumption of nitrites and cancer, with the possible exception of the Icelandics. A study commissioned by the US Department of Agriculture shows that 40ppm nitrite plus an inoculum of harmless bacteria (*Pediococcus acidilacti*) is as effective as the current 120 ppm in preserving bacon, but results in much lower levels of nitrosamines. See 249.

A.D.I.   0–0.2 mg/kg body weight (temporary; included in the group A.D.I. for sodium and potassium nitrite).

Typical products & maximum permitted levels
Canned cured meat,
    perishable   125 mg/kg
Canned cured meat,
    commercially sterile   50 mg/kg
Corned meat, cured
    meat, pickled
    meat, salted meat   125 mg/kg
Manufactured meat   125 mg/kg
Pressed corned meat,
    pressed cured
    meat, pressed
    pickled meat,
    pressed salted meat   125 mg/kg
See note at end of 249.

251 Sodium nitrate (Chile saltpetre)

Origin Naturally occurring mineral (especially in the Atacama desert, Chile).

Function Curing salt; colour fixative; preservative.

Effects Nitrates are capable of being converted to nitrites either when food spoils or by bacteria in the stomach (especially in infants). Nitrites can cause deoxygenation of the blood or form minute amounts of nitrosamines which are hazardous poisons and potentially carcinogenic. There is also evidence that corresponding intakes of vitamins A, C and E in the form of fresh yellow-green vegetables is a considerable protection against stomach cancer (see 250).

Without the nitrates and nitrites there would be many deaths from the growth of toxic micro-organisms in meats.

A.D.I. 0–5 mg/kg body weight (included in the group A.D.I. for potassium and sodium nitrate).

Typical products & maximum permitted levels
Slow dry-cured meat
of the prosciutto
ham type   500 mg/kg
Uncooked fermented
manufactured meat   500 mg/kg
See note at end of 249.

252 Potassium nitrate (saltpetre)

Origin Naturally occurring mineral, or artificially manufactured from waste animal and vegetable material.

Function Curing salt; colour fixative, preservative.

Effects Prolonged exposure to small amounts may cause anaemia, or inflammation of the kidneys. Ingestion of large quantities may cause gastroenteritis with severe abdominal pain, vomiting, vertigo, muscular weakness, and irregular pulse. Potassium nitrate may be reduced to potassium nitrite in the gut by bacterial action and this, once absorbed, can affect the haemoglobin in the red blood corpuscles preventing it carrying oxygen. Nitrites can produce minute amounts of nitrosamines which are potentially carcinogenic in man. There is also evidence that corresponding intakes of vitamins A, C and E in the form of fresh yellow-green vegetables is a considerable protection against stomach cancer (see 250). Without the nitrates and nitrites there would be many deaths from the growth of toxic micro-organisms in meats.

A.D.I. 0-5 mg/kg body weight (included in the group A.D.I. for potassium and sodium nitrate (251)).

Typical products & maximum permitted levels
Slow dry-cured meat of
prosciutto ham type   500 mg/kg
Uncooked fermented
manufactured meat   500 mg/kg
See note at end of 249.

260 Acetic acid

Origin The Monsanto process uses methanol from gas or oil and carbon monoxide to manufacture acetic acid. This method is also used by BP. An older route, still used by Hoechst, produces 100 per cent acetic acid from ethanol by oxidation. It is also manufactured by the destructive distillation of wood and from acetylene and water via acetaldehyde by oxidation with air. The acetic acid in vinegar is formed by the action of the bacterium *Acetobacter* on the alcohol in beer for malt vinegar, or cider or wine for those vinegars.

Function   Antibacterial, and at 5 per cent concentration may be bactericidal; substance permitted to stabilise the acidity of food; diluent for colouring matter; flavouring agent; used in the malting process in beer manufacture to reduce excess losses of carbohydrate from the germinated barley rootlets, and also at the brewery acetic acid may be added to the malt slurry to compensate for variations in the water supply to produce a beer of consistent quality. Used in the bread industry to inhibit mould growth.

Effects   No toxicological problems are known.

A.D.I.   Not limited.

Typical products   A wide range of foods including —
Pickles
Chutneys
Cheese
Salad cream
Fruit sauce
Brown sauce
Spicy brown sauce
Mint sauce and jelly
Horseradish cream

261   Potassium acetate

Origin   The potassium salt of acetic acid (260).

Function   To preserve natural colour of plant and animal tissues; buffer; neutralising agent.

Effects   Potassium salts, taken by mouth in healthy people, cause little toxicity since potassium is rapidly excreted in the urine, but should be avoided by people with impaired kidneys.

A.D.I.   Not limited.

Typical products   Many of those permitted to contain acetic acid (260).

262   Sodium hydrogen diacetate (sodium diacetate)

Origin   A 'bound' compound of sodium acetate (262) and acetic acid (260).

Function   Acidity regulator, sequestrant, preservative — anti-microbial inhibitor especially against the spores of *Bacillus mesentericus* and *B. subtilis*. These spores are heat-resistant and, if present in bread and permitted to germinate, convert the bread into sticky yellow patches, which are capable of being pulled into long threads, hence the term 'rope'.

Effects   None known.

A.D.I.   0–15 mg/kg body weight

Typical products & maximum permitted levels

Bread	3.6 g/kg dry weight
Flour products other than bread	3.3 g/kg

262   Sodium acetate (anhydrous) and sodium acetate

Origin   The sodium salt of acetic acid (260).

Function Buffer (acid or alkaline stabiliser).

Effects No adverse effects are known.

A.D.I. Not limited.

Typical products Many of those permitted to contain acetic acid (260).

263 Calcium acetate

Origin The calcium salt of acetic acid (260).

Function Antimould agent; anti-'rope' agent (prevents development of sticky yellow patches in bread); sequestrant; firming agent; stabiliser; buffering agent.

Effects No adverse effects are known.

A.D.I. Not limited.

Typical products Many of those permitted to contain acetic acid (260)
Packet cheesecake mix
Quick-setting jelly mix

264 Ammonium acetate

Origin The ammonium salt of acetic acid (260), it is prepared commercially from ammonia and acetic acid; it is a syrupy liquid.

Function Meat preservative; adjustment of pH (degree of acidity).

Effects It has a diuretic effect (promotes the excretion of urine) and a diaphoretic effect (promotes perspiration). It is completely metabolised, the metabolic products being urea and free acetate. Larger doses of ammonium salts than could

be ingested from foods irritate the stomach lining and may cause nausea and vomiting.

A.D.I. Not specified.

Typical products Many of those permitted to contain acetic acid (260).

270 Lactic acid

Origin Naturally occurring substance found in sour milk (as the result of the activity of lactic acid bacteria), molasses, apples and other fruit, tomato juice and in the seeds of many higher plants during germination. To produce lactic acid commercially, carbohydrates such as whey, cornstarch, potatoes or molasses are heated at high temperatures and fermented by bacteria such as *Bacillus acidilacti*, *Lactobacillus delbueckii* or *L. bulgaricus*.

Function Food preservative; capable of increasing the antioxidant effect of other substances; acid and flavouring; used in the malting process in brewing to reduce excess losses of carbohydrate from the germinated barley rootlets. Lactic acid may be added to the malt slurry to compensate for variations in the water supply to make a beer of consistent quality.

Effects Could cause problems in very young or premature babies who may have difficulty metabolising it. No toxicological problems with adults.

A.D.I. Not limited.

Typical products A wide range of foods including —
Infant formula
Confectionery

Soft drinks
Salad dressing
Carton salad in dressing
Pickled red cabbage
Sauce tartare

280   Propionic acid

Origin A naturally occurring fatty acid, one of the products of digestion of cellulose by the gut-inhabiting bacteria of herbivorous animals. It occurs in small amounts in many foods and dairy products, acting as a natural preservative in Swiss cheese. Commercially it is obtained by one of a number of different methods: from ethylene, carbon monoxide and steam; from ethanol and carbon monoxide or by oxidation of propionaldehyde; from natural gas; or it can be obtained from wood pulp waste liquor by the fermentation activity of *Propionibacteria* as a by-product in the pyrolysis of wood, or in small amounts by the activity of other micro-organisms.

Function Food preservative — antifungal agent against three families of fungi.

Effects No known toxicological problems.

A.D.I. Not limited.

Typical products & maximum permitted levels
Flour products other
than bread   2 g/kg

281   Sodium propionate

Origin The sodium salt of propionic acid (280). The propionates occur naturally in fermented foods, in human sweat and in the digestive products of ruminants.

Function Food preservative — an antimicrobial agent against three families of moulds one of which is the 'rope' micro-organism prevalent in bread. The spores of *Bacillus mesentericus* and *B. subtilis* are heat-resistant and if present in bread and allowed to germinate, convert the bread into sticky yellow patches which can be pulled into long threads. Sodium propionate is preferred to calcium propionate in cakes and pies.

Effects Some reports link propionates with migraine headaches. Rats fed 5% sodium propionate demonstrated reduced plasma cholesterol although liver cholesterol was increased.

A.D.I. Not limited.

Typical products & maximum permitted levels
Bread   2.4 g/kg
Flour products other
than bread   2 g/kg

282   Calcium propionate

Origin Occurs naturally in Swiss cheese, prepared commercially from propionic acid (280). The propionates occur naturally in fermented foods, in human sweat and in the digestive products of ruminants.

Function Preservative — antimicrobial mould inhibitor, especially of 'rope' micro-organisms, which occur in bread. The spores of *Bacillus mesentericus* and *B. subtilis* are heat resistant and, if present in bread and permitted to germinate, convert the bread into sticky yellow patches, which are capable of being pulled into long threads.

Effects   Some reports link propionates with migraine headaches.

A.D.I.   Not limited.

Typical products & maximum permitted levels
Bread	2.4 g/kg
Flour products other than bread	2 g/kg

283   Potassium propionate

Origin   The potassium salt of propionic acid (280). The propionates occur naturally in fermented foods, in human sweat and in the digestive products of ruminants.

Function   Preservative — mould inhibitor, especially of 'rope' micro-organisms which occur in bread. The spores of *Bacillus mesentericus* and *B. subtilis* are heat resistant and, if present in bread and permitted to germinate, convert the bread into sticky yellow patches, capable of being pulled into long threads.

Effects   Some reports link propionates with migraine headaches.

A.D.I.   Not limited.

Typical products & maximum permitted levels
Bread	2.4 g/kg
Flour products other than bread	2 g/kg

290   Carbon dioxide

Origin   Natural gas, present in atmospheric air but produced by fermentation, or the action of acid on a carbonate, or as a by-product in the manufacture of lime.

Function   Preservative; coolant; freezant (liquid form); packaging gas; aerator.

Effects   Some carbonates in the stomach increase the secretion of gastric acid and promote absorption of liquid by the mucous membranes, increasing the effect of alcohol.

A.D.I.   Not specified.

Typical products
Carbonated wine
Cider
Confectionery
Food packed in pressurised containers
Sparkling wine
Fruit drink
Fruit flavoured drink
Mineral waters, carbonated waters
Perry
Soft drinks

296   DL-Malic acid

Origin   Malic acid occurs in two mirror-image chemical forms, known as the D-form and the L-form. L-malic acid occurs in nature, especially in green apples, but also in pears, redcurrants, potatoes, etc., and is an important metabolite in all living cells. Commercial malic acid is usually a mixture of the D-form and the L-form and is made by chemical synthesis by heating malic acid with dilute sulphuric acid, under pressure.

Function   Acid, flavouring.

Effects   Because it is not known whether infants can metabolise the D-form of malic acid, it is important that foods containing it are not given to infants or young children.

A.D.I. Not specified.

Typical products A wide range of products including —
Tinned oxtail soup
Low calorie orange soft drink
Packet spaghetti sauce mix

297 Fumaric acid

Origin A naturally occurring organic acid especially important in cell respiration. Occurs in many plants, for example Common Fumitory (*Fumaria officinalis*), a herb used to treat eczema and dermatitis and for its laxative and diuretic properties, in the edible toadstool, *Boletus scaber* (Rough-stemmed Boletus) and in *Fomes igniarius* (a polypore fungus which grows on wood and yields a brown dye). It is prepared industrially by the fermentation of glucose by fungi such as *Rhizopus nigricans*.

Function Acidifier and flavouring agent; raising agent and antioxidant in baked goods. Its use is limited by its low solubility in water, but its low rate of moisture attraction means it helps to extend the shelf life of dry powdered foods.

Effects No adverse effects are known.

A.D.I. 0–6 mg/kg body weight.

Typical products A wide range of products including —
Packet cheesecake mix
Brewed soft drinks

300 - 381 Antioxidants, some Food Acids and Mineral Salts

300 Ascorbic acid (vitamin C; L ascorbic acid)

Origin Naturally occurring substance in many fresh fruits and vegetables; also manufactured by biological synthesis by one of several methods. One process uses glucose which is hydrogenated to sorbitol. The bacterium, *Acetobacter suboxydans* is then employed to oxidise the sorbitol to sorbate. Further chemical additions and then heating with hydrochloric acid produces ascorbic acid. A recent single fermentation process has been achieved by transferring the genetic material of two enzymes from different bacteria to a single bacterium.

Function Vitamin C; browning inhibitor in unprocessed cut fruits, fruit pulp and juices; improving agent for flour; meat colour preservative; used increasingly as an antioxidant in the brewing industry as more lager is produced, since the effects of oxidation are more apparent in delicately flavoured beers. Also improves shelf-life of beers, preventing haze development and 'off' flavours.

Effects Necessary for healthy teeth, gums, bones, skin and blood vessels. Essential for growth and promotes the absorption of iron. Usually well tolerated. Large doses may cause diarrhoea and/or dental erosion. More than 10g per day could result in kidney stones in susceptible people, but this level could not be obtained from normal foods.

A.D.I. Not specified.

Typical products & maximum permitted levels

Beer	40 mg/L*
Breakfast cereals	—
Cider	250 mg/L*
Confectionery hard tablet, hard pellet or hard roll type	1 g/kg*
Corned meat, cured meat, pickled meat, salted meat, cooked manufactured meat	—*
Flour for bread making	—
Flour products other than bread	100 mg/kg
Frozen cooked prawns, frozen cooked shrimps	400 mg/kg*
Frozen fish	400 mg/kg*
Perry	250 mg/L*
Pressed corned meat, pressed cured meat, pressed pickled meat, pressed salted meat	—

Foods for infants and young children in quantities necessary to restore that lost in processing and during normal shelf-life.

*When used in these products ascorbic acid (300) may be used either singly or in combination with any or all of the following additives: sodium ascorbate (301), erythorbic acid (317), sodium erythorbate (318).

301 Sodium ascorbate (vitamin C; sodium L-ascorbate)

Origin Prepared synthetically, the sodium salt of ascorbic acid (300).

Function Vitamin C; antioxidant; colour preservative.

Effects No toxicological problems in standard doses. Some trials have shown that in rats sodium ascorbate increases the adverse effects of known carcinogens. The relevance of this to man needs further research.

A.D.I. Not specified.

Typical products Many of those permitted to contain ascorbic acid (300).

302 Calcium ascorbate (calcium L-ascorbate)

Origin Prepared synthetically.

Function Vitamin C; antioxidant.

Effects There was some discussion in 1981 by JECFA of the theory that as oxalate is a major metabolite of ascorbate, the use of calcium ascorbate may increase the formation of calcium oxalate stones in the urine. However, they decided the intake of calcium from ascorbate in a normal diet would represent only a small fraction of the total dietary intake of calcium. It should, perhaps, be avoided by those with a predisposition to kidney stones.

A.D.I. Not specified.

Typical products
Infant formula (as a vitamin source).

303 Potassium ascorbate

Origin Potassium salt of ascorbic acid (vitamin C, 300).

Function Vitamin C; antioxidant.

Effects No adverse effects are known.

A.D.I. Not specified.

Typical products Many of those permitted to contain ascorbic acid (300).

304 Ascorbyl palmitate (palmitoyl-L-ascorbic acid)

Origin Ascorbic acid ester produced by synthesis. Comprises ascorbic acid and palmitic acid.

Function Performs the same function as vitamin C (300), but has the advantage at high temperatures of being fat-soluble. Antioxidant (prevents rancidity); colour preservative; prevents browning of cut fruit. An antioxidant synergistic effect exists between alpha-tocopherol (306/7) and ascorbyl palmitate, so manufacturers are likely to use them in combination.

Effects No adverse effect known.

A.D.I. 0–1.25 mg/kg body weight.

Typical products
Dairy blend
Dried instant mashed potato
Edible fats
Edible oils
Margarine
Essential oils
Salad oils
Lard
Dripping
Masticatory confectionery
Walnut and pecan nut kernels

306 Tocopherols concentrate, mixed (vitamin E)

Origin Extract of soya bean oil, wheat germ, rice germ, cottonseed, maize and green leaves, distilled in a vacuum.

Function Vitamin; antioxidant. For reasons which are not fully understood, alpha tocopherol has a greater antioxidant capacity than gamma tocopherol (308) in animal systems, but not in cells nor in non-biological systems.

Effects Helps the supply of oxygen to the heart and muscles. It is essential for the life of the red blood cells. It acts as an antioxidant for polyunsaturated fatty acids in tissue fats and it protects other nutrients such as vitamin A from oxidation. It is largely destroyed by freezing.

A.D.I. 0.15–2 mg/kg body weight*

*The lower value represents the daily dietary allowance recommended by the USA National Academy of Sciences/National Research Council. The upper value represents the maximum value for the A.D.I.

Typical products
Dairy blend
Edible fats
Edible oils
Salad oils
Essential oils
Lard
Dripping
Margarine

307 α-Tocopherol (vitamin E; DL-α-tocopherol)

Origin Produced by chemical synthesis.

Function Antioxidant; vitamin. It is largely destroyed by freezing.

Effects Helps the supply of oxygen to the heart and muscles. It is essential for the life of the red blood cells. It acts as an antioxidant for polyunsaturated fatty acids in the tissue fats. It protects other nutrients such as vitamin A from oxidation.

A.D.I. 0.15–2 mg/kg body weight (see 306).

Typical products Many of those permitted to contain 306.

308 γ-Tocopherol (vitamin E; DL-γ-tocopherol)

Origin Produced by chemical synthesis.

Function   Antioxidant; vitamin; less effective than alpha tocopherol (306 and 307) as a biological antioxidant (i.e. in animals), but similar capacity in a non-biological system, e.g. a polyunsaturated fatty acid or in cell cultures. It is largely destroyed by freezing.

Effects   Helps the supply of oxygen to the heart and muscles. It is essential for the life of the red blood cells. It acts as an antioxidant for polyunsaturated fatty acids in the tissue fats. It protects other nutrients such as vitamin A from oxidation.

A.D.I. —

Typical products   Many of those permitted to contain 306.

309   δ-Tocopherol (vitamin E; DL-δ-tocopherol)

Origin   Produced by chemical synthesis.

Function   Antioxidant; vitamin. Delta-tocopherol is purported to be the most effective antioxidant (of all the tocopherols) in non-biological systems. It is largely destroyed by freezing.

Effects   Helps the supply of oxygen to the heart and muscles. It is essential for the life of the red blood cells. It acts as an antioxidant for polyunsaturated fatty acids in the tissue fats. It protects other nutrients such as vitamin A from oxidation.

A.D.I. —

Typical products   Many of those permitted to contain 306.

310   Propyl gallate (propyl 3,4,5,-trihydroxybenzoate)

Origin   Propyl ester of gallic acid. Gallic acid is produced from tannins extracted from the nut galls. Another method of production hydrolyses the enzyme tannase, which also occurs in spent fungal broths of *Aspergillus niger* and *Penicillium glaucum*.

Function   Antioxidant in oils and fats, often in combination with BHT (321) and BHA (320) on which it has a synergistic (see glossary) effect.

Propyl gallate is more effective in numerous types of fats than BHA (320), but loses much of its activity when used in baked goods, because it is unstable at high temperatures.

Effects   All alkyl gallates may cause gastric or skin irritation in some people, including those who suffer from asthma or are sensitive to aspirin.

Its use is not permitted in foods intended specifically for infants or young children.

Propyl gallate is sometimes added to inner packaging material of foods like breakfast cereals and potato flakes, so it is possible that its vapour could contaminate the food.

A.D.I.   0–2.5 mg/kg body weight.

Typical products & maximum permitted levels
Dairy blend, edible
  fats, edible oils,
  lard, dripping,
  margarine, salad oils   100 mg/kg*
Essential oils   1 g/kg*

*Singly or in combination with octyl or dodecyl gallates (311 & 312).

311 Octyl gallate

Origin Ester of gallic acid. Gallic acid is obtained by acid or alkaline hydrolysis of the tannins extracted from nut galls. Another method hydrolyses the tannase enzyme from spent fungal broths of *Aspergillus niger* and *Penicillium glaucum*.

Function Antioxidant.

Effects All alkyl gallates may cause gastric irritation and problems in some people including those who suffer from asthma or are sensitive to aspirin. Not permitted in foods intended for infants or young children.

A.D.I. No A.D.I. allocated.

Typical products & maximum permitted levels
Dairy blend, edible
    fats, edible oils,
    lard, dripping,
    margarine, salad oils   100 mg/kg
Essential oils   1 g/kg*
*Singly or in combination with propyl or dodecyl gallates (310 & 312).

312 Dodecyl gallate (dodecyl 3,4,5,-trihydroxybenzoate)

Origin Ester of gallic acid. Gallic acid is obtained by acid or alkaline hydrolysis of the tannins extracted from nut galls. Another method hydrolyses the tannase enzyme from spent fungal broths of *Aspergillus niger* or *Penicillium glaucum*.

Function Antioxidant.

Effects All alkyl gallates may cause gastric irritation and problems in some people including those who suffer from asthma or are sensitive to aspirin. Not permitted in foods intended for infants or young children.

A.D.I. No A.D.I. allocated.

Typical products & maximum permitted levels
Dairy blend, edible
    fats, edible oils,
    lard, dripping,
    margarine, salad oils   100 mg/kg*
Essential oils   1 g/kg*
*Singly or in combination with propyl or octyl gallates (310 & 311).

317 Erythorbic acid (iso-ascorbic acid)

Origin This substance has one-twentieth of the vitamin C activity of L-ascorbic acid (300) and is produced commercially from sucrose, by fermentation with the mould, *Penicillium sp*.

Function Antioxidant in pickling brine and meat products to accelerate colour fixing in curing; prevents browning in cut fruit and yellowing in frozen fish.

Effects Not harmful. The substance is well metabolised.

A.D.I. 0–5 mg/kg body weight.

Typical products Many of those permitted to contain ascorbic acid (300). See that entry.

318 Sodium erythorbate (sodium iso-ascorbate)

Origin Commercially manufactured salt of erythorbic acid (317).

Function Antioxidant, with a strong affinity for oxygen when in solution. It is used in the same or similar capacity to erythorbic acid, in pickling brine and in meat products and to accelerate colour fixing in curing. In practice ascorbic acid (300) is more effective than sodium erythorbate.

Effects Sodium erythorbate has no known toxicity.

A.D.I. 0–5 mg/kg body weight.

Typical products Many of those permitted to contain ascorbic acid (300). See that entry.

319 *tert*-Butylhydroquinone (TBHQ)

Origin Derived from petroleum.

Function Antioxidant, often used in combination with other antioxidants, such as BHA(320), BHT(321) and propyl gallate(310), because hydroquinone quickly turns brown when exposed to the oxygen in the air.

Effects Small amounts of TBHQ have caused nausea, vomiting, ringing in the ears, delirium, suffocating feelings and collapse. A fatal dose is 5g. TBHQ was last considered by JECFA in 1987. There was conflicting evidence that it caused genes in bacterial and mammalian cells to mutate, so they requested further genotoxicity studies and feeding studies to take into account the normal degradation products of TBHQ in foods, before they re-evaluate it in 1990.

A.D.I. 0–0.2 mg/kg body weight (temporary).

Typical products & maximum permitted levels
Dairy blend, edible
   fats, edible oils,
   lard, dripping,
   margarine, salad oils   200 mg/kg
Essential oils   1 g/kg

320 Butylated hydroxyanisole (BHA)

Origin A mixture of 2- and 3-tert-butyl-4-methoxy-phenol, prepared from p-methoxyphenol and isobutene.

Function Delays, retards or prevents the development of rancidity or other flavour deterioration in foods due to oxidation. BHA is the most widely-used antioxidant for oils and fats either alone or with a gallate (310–312) and a synergist (see glossary), e.g. citric acid (330) or phosphoric acid (380).

It is heat resistant, so effective in baked products. Antioxidants may be lost during processing, with crisps and snack foods losing up to 90 per cent, biscuits 35 per cent. Certain commonly used cooking oils, such as soya and rapeseed, add BHA to prevent early rancidity, but others such as sunflower and safflower contain enough naturally occurring antioxidant in the form of vitamin E. It is possible that the use of added vitamin E will replace BHA in such uses. Rancidity is substantially delayed by storing oil in opaque containers.

Effects BHA is not permitted in foods intended specifically for infants or young children, except to preserve added vitamin A.

There is a mass of evidence to support the safety of BHA at likely levels of intake. It even seems to be a protection against some carcinogens. On the other hand there are also many scientific reports which cast doubt on its safety. At high levels there are frequent reports of toxicity, particularly its ability at high doses to promote forestomach cancers in rats and male Syrian golden hamsters. The suggestion is that BHA promotes forestomach tumours by inhibiting communication between cells, especially growth regulatory signals, and not by damaging the genes. Man does not have a forestomach so in that sense we are not at risk, but we do have similar cells lining our mouth, throat and gullet. A recent (unpublished) study by the British Industrial Biological Research Association has confirmed that BHA causes genetic changes to the ovaries of Chinese hamsters.

Increasingly, as added vitamin E or better storage and packing allow manufacturers to do without BHA, there would seem to be good reason for limiting its use. Children who eat foods containing BHA are particularly likely to consume more than the average, so their parents may be wise to choose foods free from BHA.

Some people are allergic to BHA; one study in 1977 suggested that there may be an imbalance in their body's fat metabolism.

A.D.I. 0–0.3 mg/kg body weight (temporary).

Typical products & maximum permitted levels

Dried instant mashed potato (dry weight)	100 mg/kg
Dairy blend, edible fats, edible oils, lard, dripping, margarine, salad oils	200 mg/kg
Essential oils	1 g/kg
Masticatory confectionery gum bases	200 mg/kg
Polyethylene film for wrapping food (in food by absorption)	2 mg/kg
Walnut kernels, pecan nut kernels	70 mg/kg

321 Butylated hydroxytoluene (BHT)

Origin Does not occur in nature and is prepared synthetically from p-cresol and isobutylene. It was developed initally as an antioxidant for use with petroleum and rubber products.

Function BHT delays, retards or prevents the development of rancidity and flavour deterioration in foods due to oxidation of the polyunsaturated fats and oils they contain.

Effects Some people are sensitive to the presence of BHT and develop rashes; they can be the same people who demonstrate aspirin sensitivity. There is a recent report in the *Lancet* of BHT causing a violent skin rash in a young French woman.

When administered in fairly low doses BHT increased the incidence of lung tumours in mice and the incidence of tumours of the liver, bladder and possibly of the food canal in rats. Yet, when rats were given BHT before a substance known to cause cancer, it (BHT) seemed to enhance the detoxification of the substance and may have protected the rats from its effects. It also acted as a chemopreventive in rat mammary tumours. Conversely it promoted bladder tumours in rats given a different substance known to cause cancer, followed by BHT. The animals given carcinogen only showed cell changes but did not develop tumours. It is claimed to be a potent inactivator of various fat-containing viruses.

When rabbits were given 1 gram of BHT per day they developed muscle weakness and died within two weeks.

Various reports have linked this additive with possible reproductive

ures in experimental animals given
gh doses, yet rats exposed *in utero* to
gh levels of BHT produced young rats
ich survived better than those which
d not received BHT.

It is not permitted in foods intended
ecifically for infants and young
ildren.

.I. 0–0.125 mg/kg body weight
mporary).

pical products & maximum permitted levels
olyethylene film for
wrapping food (in food by
absorption) 2 mg/kg
'alnut kernels
pecan nut kernels 70 mg/kg

nly permitted food uses in Australia.

22 Lecithins

gin Lecithins are mixtures or
ctions of phosphatides
omponents of fat) obtained by
ysical procedures from animal or
getable foodstuffs. Most commerical
cithin is obtained from soya beans.
her sources are egg yolk and
guminous seeds, including peanuts
d maize. Lecithin is present in all
ing cells and is a significant
nstituent of nerve and brain tissues.

ction In plant and animal cells
cithin protects the cell membranes
d the polyunsaturated fats contained
thin the cells from oxygen attack. It
an invaluable emulsifier, lowering
e surface tension of water and
owing the combination of oils and
s with water in margarine,
ocolate, mayonnaise, ice cream and
ked goods. Lecithin employed as an
ulsifier in bread increases loaf
ume, softens the crumb and extends

the shelf life. In margarine it also
prevents water leakage and protects
vitamin A. Hydroxylated lecithin is a
defoaming component in yeast and
beet sugar production.

Effects Lecithin is nutritious and non-
toxic. It is used experimentally to treat
senile dementia and to mobilise fats in
the body.

A.D.I. Not limited.

Typical products & maximum permitted levels
A wide range of foods
    including —

Chocolate	—
Dried milk	5 g/kg
Margarine	—
Confectionery	—
Dessert mix	—
Chocolate biscuits	—
Malted milk powder	8 g/kg

325 Sodium lactate

Origin The sodium salt of lactic acid
(270).

Function Humectant and substitute for
glycerol; synergistic effect on other
substances by increasing antioxidant
effect; bodying agent.

Effects Could have a certain toxicity
because of lactose intolerance for very
young children. No toxicological
problems known with adults.

A.D.I. Not limited.

Typical products Many of those
permitted to contain lactic acid (270).

326 Potassium lactate

Origin The potassium salt of lactic
acid (270).

Function   Capable of increasing the antioxidant effect of other substances; buffer.

Effects   Could have a certain toxicity because of lactose intolerance for very young children. No toxicological problems known with adults.

A.D.I.   Not limited.

Typical products   Many of those permitted to contain lactic acid (270).

327   Calcium lactate

Origin   Calcium salt of lactic acid (270). Also available commercially in hydrated forms.

Function   Antioxidant; capable of increasing antioxidant effect of other substances; buffer; firming agent; inhibits discolouration of fruits and vegetables; improves properties of dry milk powders and condensed milk; yeast food; dough conditioner.

Effects   None known. In medical use given for calcium deficiency but may cause gastrointestinal disturbances.

A.D.I.   Not limited.

Typical products   Many of those permitted to contain lactic acid (270).

328   Ammonium lactate

Origin   Prepared commerically by neutralising DL-lactic acid with ammonia.

Function   Buffering agent; dough conditioner.

Effects   There is no indication that beyond infancy the salts of lactic aci are normally injurious to health. Ver young children and those who may b lactose-intolerant should avoid this additive.

A.D.I.   Not limited.

Typical products   Many of those permitted to contain lactic acid (270

329   Magnesium lactate

Origin   The magnesium salt of lactic acid.

Function   Buffering agent; dough conditioner; dietary supplement as a source of magnesium.

Effects   There is no indication that beyond infancy the salts of lactic aci are normally injurious to health. Ver young children and those who are lactose-intolerant should avoid this additive.

A.D.I.   Not limited.

Typical products   Many of those permitted to contain lactic acid (270

330   Citric acid

Origin   Occurs naturally in high concentrations in lemon and other citrus juices and many ripe fruits; prepared commercially by the fermentation of molasses with funga strains of *Aspergillus niger*. Smaller amounts are also isolated from pineapple by-products and low-grad lemons. It is available commercially the anhydrous or monohydrate form

Function As a synergist to enhance the effectiveness of antioxidants; prevents discolouration of fruit, development of 'off' flavours and retains vitamin C. Stabilises the acidity of food substances; sequestrant; flavouring; helps jam to set. Used in wine production to combine with free iron to prevent the formation of iron-tannin complexes and hence cloudiness, and in the malting process in brewing to reduce excess losses of sugars from the germinated barley.

Effects Citric acid taken in very large quantities may occasionally cause erosion of the teeth and have a local irritant action.

A.D.I. Not limited.

Typical products A wide range of foods including —
Biscuits
Ice cream
Packet cake mix
Packet soup mix
Sorbet mix
Cider
Jam
Cheese
Artificial sweetener base
Canned fish other than
    fish paste or fish spread
Fruit drinks
Fruit flavoured drinks
Fruit juice drinks
Fruit butter
Infant formula
Low sodium salt substitute
Mustard paste, prepared mustard
Soft drinks
Sweetened coconut
Uncooked fermented
    manufactured meat
Processed cheese
Cheese spread
Cream cottage cheese

331 Sodium citrates — sodium dihydrogen citrate (monosodium citrate)

Origin *Mono*sodium salt of citric acid (330) in the anhydrous or monohydrate form.

Function Synergistic effect on other antioxidants; buffer to control the acidity of gelatin desserts, jams, sweets and ice cream, and retain carbonation in beverages; emulsifying salt in ice cream, processed cheese, and evaporated milk; sequestrant; added to infant formula and invalid food to prevent formation of large curds. Prevents clogging of cream in aerosols and 'feathering' when cream is used in coffee.

Effects Can alter urinary excretion of other drugs, thus making those drugs either less effective or more toxic.

A.D.I. Not limited.

Typical products A wide range of foods including many of those permitted to contain citric acid (330) and —
Cheese spread
Whipped thickened
    reduced cream

331 Sodium citrates — disodium citrate

Origin Sodium salt of citric acid (330) with one-and-a-half molecules of water.

Function Antioxidant; synergistic effect on other antioxidants; buffer; emulsifying salt.

Effects No adverse effects are known.

A.D.I. Not limited.

Typical products A wide range of foods including many of those permitted to contain citric acid (330) and sodium dihydrogen citrate. (331)

331 Sodium citrates — trisodium citrate

Origin *Tri*sodium salt of citric acid in anhydrous, dihydrate or pentahydrate form.

Function Antioxidant; buffer; emulsifying salt; sequestrant; stabiliser; used along with polyphosphates (450) and flavours to inject into chickens before freezing.

Effects No adverse effects are known.

A.D.I. Not limited.

Typical products A wide range of foods including many of those permitted to contain citric acid (330) and sodium dihydrogen citrate (331).

332 Potassium dihydrogen citrate (*mono*potassium citrate)

Origin Anhydrous *mono*potassium salt of citric acid (330).

Function Buffer; emulsifying salt; yeast food.

Effects None known; potassium is rapidly excreted in the urine in healthy individuals.

A.D.I. Not limited.

Typical products A wide range of foods including many of those permitted to contain citric acid (330).

332 Potassium citrate (*tri*potassium citrate)

Origin A potassium salt of citric acid (330).

Function Antioxidant; buffer in confectionery and artificially sweetened jellies and preserves. Emulsifying salt; sequestrant.

Effects None in foods; in therapeutic amounts when it is employed as a urinary alkaliser and gastric antacid, may make the skin sensitive and cause mouth ulcers to develop.

A.D.I. Not limited.

Typical products A wide range of foods including many of those permitted to contain citric acid (330).

333 Mono-, di-, and tri-calcium citrates

Origin Monohydrated *mono*calcium, trihydrated *di*calcium and tetrahydrated *tri*calcium salts of citric acid (330).

Function Buffers to neutralise acids in jams, jellies and confectionery; firming agents; emulsifying salts; sequestrants; improve baking properties of flour.

Effects None in foods; in therapeutic amounts may induce the formation of mouth ulcers.

A.D.I. Not limited.

Typical products A wide range of foods including many of those permitted to contain citric acid (330).

334 Tartaric acid (L-(+) tartaric acid)

Origin   A widely occurring fruit acid, found in grapes and other fruits either free or combined with potassium, calcium or magnesium, and sometimes deposited as crystals in wine. Tartarus is the name the medical alchemists used. Most of the L-tartaric acid is manufactured as a by-product of the wine industry (acid potassium tartrate is converted to calcium tartrate which is hydrolysed to tartaric acid and calcium sulphate). It may also be extracted from tamarind pulp.

Function   Antioxidant; capable of increasing the antioxidant effect of other substances (synergist); to adjust acidity in frozen dairy products, jellies, bakery products, beverages, confectionery, dried egg whites, sweets, preserves and wines; sequestrant (see glossary); diluent for food colours; constituent of grape and other artificial flavours; acid in some baking powders.

Effects   Eighty per cent of the tartaric acid ingested by man is destroyed by bacteria in the intestine. The fraction absorbed into the bloodstream is excreted in the urine. Large amounts of tartaric acid have been used as a laxative without apparent harm, although strong solutions above those employed in food products are midly irritant and may cause gastro-enteritis.

A.D.I.   0–30 mg/kg body weight.

Typical products   A wide range of foods including —
confectionery
jam
fruit jelly
fruit drink
Soft drink
Fruit flavoured drink
Fruit juice drink

335 Sodium tartrate (monosodium L-(+)-tartrate and disodium L-(+)-tartrate)

Origin   Monohydrated monosodium salt and dihydrated disodium salt of tartaric acid (334).

Function   Antioxidant and capable of increasing the antioxidant effect of other substances (synergist); buffer; emulsifying salt; sequestrant.

Effects   No known toxicological risks.

A.D.I.   0–30 mg/kg body weight (as L-(+)-tartaric acid (334)).

Typical products   A wide range of foods including many of those permitted to contain tartaric acid (334).

336 Potassium acid tartrate (monopotassium L-(+)-tartrate; potassium hydrogen tartrate; cream of tartar)

Origin   The Romans were probably the first to identify this substance as a fine crystalline crust during the fermentation of grape or tamarind juice. It was incorrectly termed *faecula* (little yeast) by them. It is still manufactured as a by-product of the wine industry. Anhydrous *mono*potassium salt of L-(+)-tartaric acid (334).

Function   Acid; buffer especially for de-acidification of wine; emulsifying salt; raising agent for flour, often used with

500 (sodium bicarbonate) because it works slowly and gives a more prolonged evolution of carbon dioxide; inverting agent for sugar in boiled sweet manufacture.

Effects   None known; potassium salts are readily excreted by healthy kidneys. The only people at risk are those whose kidney or liver functions are impaired.

A.D.I.   0–30 mg/kg body weight (as L-(+)-tartaric acid (334)).

Typical products   A wide range of foods including many of those permitted to contain tartaric acid (334).

336   Potassium tartrate (dipotassium L-(+)-tartrate)

Origin   *Di*potassium salt of L-(+)-tartaric acid (334).

Function   Antioxidant and capable of increasing the antioxidant effect of other substances (synergist); buffer; emulsifying salt.

Effects   No known toxicological risks.

A.D.I.   0–30 mg/kg body weight (as L-(+)-tartaric acid (334)).

Typical products   A wide range of foods including many of those permitted to contain tartaric acid (334).

337   Potassium sodium tartrate (potassium sodium L-(+)-tartrate; sodium and potassium tartrate; Rochelle salt)

Origin   Derivative of L-(+)-tartaric acid (334); available commercially in the form of potassium sodium tartrate with four molecules of water of crystallisation.

Function   Buffer for confectionery and preserves; emulsifying salt; stabiliser; capable of increasing antioxidant effect of other substances (synergist).

Effects   No known toxicological problems. Used medically as a cathartic (bowel evacuation). The tartrates of the alkali metals are less readily absorbed than the citrates.

A.D.I.   0–30 mg/kg body weight (as L-(+)-tartaric acid(334)).

Typical products   A wide range of foods including many of those permitted to contain tartaric acid (334).

338   Phosphoric acid (orthophosporic acid)

Origin   There are two types of acid production, the so-called 'Wet Process' and the 'Thermal' method. 'Wet Process' involves the manufacture of phosphoric acid from phosphate ore, followed by intensive purification to meet food-grade specifications. The 'Thermal' method reduces the phospate ore to elemental phoshorus electrothermally. Phosphorus is then burnt in air to produce phosphorus pentoxide which is dissolved in dilute phosphoric acid to create concentrated solutions. Used in concentrated aqueous solution.

Function   Capable of increasing the antioxidant effect of other substances (synergist); acidulant and flavouring agent in soft drinks, jams, frozen dairy products and sweets; used in the manufacture of cheeses which rely on the direct acidification of milk for their formation and in the brewing industry in the malting process, to reduce excess losses of sugars from the germinated barley rootlets. At the brewery, phosphoric acid may be added to the malt slurry to compensate for variations in the water supply in order to arrive at a beer of consistent quality. Sequestrant for rendered animal fat or animal and vegetable fat mixtures.

Effects No adverse effects are known in food concentrations.

M.T.D.I. 70 mg/kg body weight (expressed as phosphorus from all sources)*

Typical products & maximum permitted levels

Cheese	—
Cottage cheese	—
Kola type soft drinks	570 mg/kg
Cream cheese,	—
Neufchatel cheese	—

*This figure represents the maximum tolerable daily intake (M.T.D.I.) of phosphates. It is not an A.D.I. The M.T.D.I. is expressed as phosphorus and it applies to the sum of phosphates naturally present in food and permitted phosphate additives. It also applies to diets that are nutritionally adequate in respect of calcium. However, if the calcium intake were high, the intake of phosphate could be proportionally higher, and the reverse relationship would also apply. Since phosphorus (as phosphate) is an essential nutrient an M.T.D.I. (see glossary) is more appropriate than an A.D.I.

339 Sodium phosphate, monobasic (sodium dihydrogen orthophosphate)

Origin Prepared from phosphoric acid.

Function To improve texture and prevent seepage of serum from foods; to speed penetration of brine; anti-oxidant synergist; buffer; nutrient; gelling agent; stabiliser; anti-caking agent; sugar-clarifying agent.

Effects High dietary intakes of phosphorus as phosphates may upset the calcium/phosphorus equilibrium.

M.T.D.I. 70 mg/kg body weight (expressed as phosphorus from all sources). See phosphoric acid (338).

Typical products & maximum permitted levels
A wide variety of foods including —

Canned fish products	2.2 g/kg
Canned meat products	1.3 g/kg
Cheese spread	30 g/kg
Cocoa and milk, chocolate and milk	1.3 g/kg
Cured meat, corned meat, pickled meat, salted meat	1.3 g/kg
Frozen fish	1.3 g/kg
Manufactured meat	1.3 g/kg
Pressed corned meat, pressed cured meat, pressed pickled meat, pressed salted meat	1.3 g/kg
Processed cheese	30 g/kg
Reduced fat cheese spread	30 g/kg
Reduced fat processed cheese	30 g/kg
Sausage meat	1.3 g/kg

339 Sodium phosphate, dibasic (disodium hydrogen orthophosphate)

Origin Prepared from phosphoric acid.

Function To improve texture and prevent seepage of serum from foods; to speed penetration of brine; antioxidant synergist; buffer; nutrient; gelling agent; stabiliser; anti-caking agent; sugar-clarifying agent.

Effects High dietary intakes of phosphorus as phosphates may upset the calcium/phosphorus equilibrium.

M.T.D.I. 70 mg/kg body weight (expressed as phosphorus from all sources). See phosphoric acid (338)

Typical products Many of those permitted to contain sodium phosphate, monobasic.

339 Sodium phosphate, tribasic (trisodium orthophosphate)

Origin Prepared from phosphoric acid.

Function To improve texture and prevent seepage of serum from foods; to speed penetration of brine; antioxidant synergist; buffer; nutrient; gelling agent; stabiliser; anti-caking agent; sugar-clarifying agent.

Effects High dietary intakes of phosphorus as phosphates may upset the calcium/phosphorus equilibrium.

M.T.D.I. 70 mg/kg body weight (expressed as phosphorus from all sources). See phosphoric acid (338).

Typical products Many of those permitted to contain sodium phosphate, monobasic (339).

Note: the mono-, di- and tribasic sodium salts of phosphoric acid (338) are all classified as 339.

340 Potassium phosphate, monobasic (potassium dihydrogen orthophosphate)

Origin Prepared from phosphoric acid.

Function Buffer; sequestrant; emulsifying salt; antioxidant synergist.

Effects Phosphorus (as phosphate) is an essential nutrient. High dietary intakes of phosphorus as phosphates, however, may upset the calcium/phosphorus equilibrium.

M.T.D.I. 70 mg/kg body weight (expressed as phosphorus from all sources). See phosphoric acid (338).

Typical products and maximum levels
Many of those products permitted to contain sodium phosphate, monobasic (339)

Beverage whitener	20 g/kg
Low sodium salt substitute	40 g/kg

340 Potassium phosphate, dibasic (dipotassium hydrogen orthophosphate)

Origin *Di*potassium salt of phosphoric acid (338).

Function Buffer; emulsifying salt; antioxidant synergist; yeast food; sequestrant.

Effects Phosphorus (as phosphates) is essential for healthy parathyroid, bone, digestive and kidney metabolism. The body can use it most efficiently if it is present in a constant ratio with calcium, so it is important that the calcium/phosphorus balance is maintained. Too much phosphorus, as phosphate, could upset the balance and cause a deficiency of both minerals. In view of the concern expressed JECFA, in 1982, recommended that further studies should be carried out on the implications of high dietary intakes of phosphorus.

M.T.D.I. 70 mg/kg body weight (expressed as phosphorus from all sources). See phosphoric acid (338).

Typical products Many of those permitted to contain sodium phosphate, monobasic and potassium phosphate, monobasic.

340 Potassium phosphate, tribasic (tripotassium orthophosphate)

Origin *Tri*potassium salt of phosphoric acid (338).

Function Emulsifying salt; antioxidant synergist; buffer; sequestrant. Phosphorus (as phosphates) is essential for healthy parathyroid, bone, digestive and kidney metabolism.

Effects None known.

M.T.D.I. 70 mg/kg body weight (expressed as phosphorus from all sources). See phosphoric acid (338).

Typical products Many of those permitted to contain sodium phosphate, monobasic (339) and potassium phosphate, monobasic (340).

Note: the mono-, di- and tribasic potassium salts of phosphoric acid (338) are all classified as 340.

341 Calcium phosphate, monobasic (monocalcium orthophosphate; acid calcium phosphate; ACP)

Origin Calcium phosphate (apatite) occurs naturally; the pulverised rock is treated with sulphuric or phosphoric acid. The food-grade product of commerce is prepared directly from high-purity phosphoric acid. *Mono*basic calcium phosphate is available commercially in anhydrous form or as the monohydrate.

Function Improving agent in yeast-leavened bakery products; buffer; firming agent; emulsifying salt; sequestrant; yeast food; aerator-acidulant component of self-raising flours and some baking powders; antioxidant synergist; texturiser.

Effects No adverse effects known. Phosphorus (as phosphates) is essential for healthy parathyroid, bone, digestive and kidney metabolism.

M.T.D.I. 70 mg/kg body weight (expressed as phosphorus from all sources). See phosphoric acid (338).

Typical products & maximum permitted levels
Many of those permitted to contain sodium phosphate, monobasic and —

Flour for bread making	7 g/kg
Flour products prepared with yeast other than bread	7g/kg
Low sodium salt substitute	—
Whipped thickened reduced cream	6 g/kg

341 Calcium phosphate, dibasic (calcium hydrogen orthophosphate)

Origin Manufactured directly from phosphoric acid.

Function Firming agent; yeast food; nutrient mineral supplement in cereals and other foods; antioxidant synergist; dough conditioner.

Effects No adverse reactions are known, particularly as calcium phosphate is used as a calcium replenisher, dietary supplement and antacid.

M.T.D.I. 70 mg/kg body weight. (expressed as phosphorus from all sources) see phosphoric acid (338).

Typical products Many of those permitted to contain sodium phosphate, monobasic.

341 Calcium phosphate, tribasic (tricalcium orthophosphate)

Origin Prepared chemically from naturally derived calcium phosphate.

Function Anti-caking agent in icing sugar, instant (powdered) beverages, seasoning mixes and instant (powdered) soups; nutrient yeast food; diluent for vegetable extracts; clarifying agent for sugar syrups.

Effects Phosphates are essential for healthy parathyroid, bone, digestive and kidney metabolism, but in balance with calcium.

M.T.D.I. 70 mg/kg body weight (expressed as phosphorus from all sources). See phosphoric acid (338).

Typical products & maximum levels
Many of those permitted to contain sodium phosphate, monobasic and —
Artificial sweeteners
  of granular or
  powdered form   —
Icing mixture   4.4 g/kg
Table salt   20 g/kg

Note: the mono-, di- and tribasic potassium salts of phosphoric acid (338) are all classified 341.

343 Magnesium phosphate, dibasic (magnesium hydrogen phosphate: magnesium hydrogen orthophosphate trihydrate)

Origin This magnesium salt occurs in nature as the minerals newberyite and phosphor-roesslerite.

Function Dietary supplement; mineral nutrient.

Effects Phosphorus is an essential mineral nutrient, particularly important in the structure of bones and teeth and necessary for many biochemical body processes. Magnesium is essential too, necessary for functioning of many enzyme systems, for some B vitamins to function properly and for growth and repair of body tissues.

M.T.D.I. 70 mg/kg body weight (expressed as phosphorus from all sources). See phosphoric acid (338).

Typical products
Salt substitutes

343 Magnesium phosphate, tribasic ('neutral' magnesium phosphate)

Origin The octahydrate occurs in nature as the mineral bobierrite. Usually manufactured by reacting magnesium hydroxide or magnesium carbonate with phosphoric acid.

Function Dietary supplement; mineral nutrient; anticaking agent.

Effects Phosphorus is an essential mineral nutrient, particularly important in the structure of bones and teeth and necessary for many biochemical body processes. Magnesium is essential too, necessary for functioning of many enzyme systems, for some B vitamins to function properly and for growth and repair of body tissue.

M.T.D.I. 70 mg/kg body weight (expressed as phosphorus from all sources). See phosphoric acid (338).

Typical Products
Salt substitutes

Note: the di- and tribasic magnesium salts of phosphoric acid (338) are both classified as 343.

350 DL-Sodium malate

Origin A sodium salt of malic acid (296).

Function Buffer; seasoning agent.

Effects No adverse effects are known.

A.D.I. Not specified.

Typical products A wide range of foods including many of those products permitted to contain malic acid (296)
Fruit butter

Fruit drink
Fruit flavoured drink
Fruit juice drink
Low sodium salt substitute
Mustard paste,
    prepared mustard
Soft drinks
Sweetened coconut

350 DL-Sodium hydrogen malate

Origin A sodium salt of malic acid (296).

Function Buffer.

Effects No adverse effects are known.

A.D.I. Not specified.

Typical products Many of those products permitted to contain malic acid (296) and sodium malate (350).

351 DL-Potassium malate

Origin The potassium salt of malic acid (296).

Function Buffer.

Effects No adverse effects are known.

A.D.I. Not specified.

Typical products Many of those products permitted to contain malic acid (296) and sodium malate (350).

352 DL-Calcium malate

Origin A calcium salt of malic acid (296).

Function Buffer; firming agent; seasoning agent.

Effects None known.

A.D.I. Not specified.

Typical products Many of those products permitted to contain malic acid (296) and sodium malate (350).

352   Calcium hydrogen malate

Origin A calcium salt of malic acid (296).

Function Firming agent.

Effects No adverse effects are known.

A.D.I. Not specified.

Typical products Many of those products permitted to contain malic acid (296) and sodium malate (350).

353   Metatartaric acid

Origin Prepared from tartaric acid (334).

Function Sequestrant, especially in wine, for precipitating excess calcium.

Effects No adverse effects are known.

A.D.I. Not specified.

Typical products Wine

355   Adipic acid (hexanedioic acid)

Origin An organic acid which occurs in many living cells and especially in beet juice. Prepared synthetically for commercial use by oxidising cyclohexanol with concentrated nitric acid.

Function Acidulating agent; buffer; buffer neutralising agent.

Effects No adverse effects are known.

A.D.I. 0–5 mg/kg body weight (basis on free acid).

Typical products Reduced sodium salt mixture
Low sodium salt substitutes
(These are the only permitted uses in food in Australia.)

357   Potassium adipate

Origin The potassium salt of adipic acid.

Function Buffering agent; neutralising agent.

Effects No adverse effects are known.

A.D.I. 0-5 mg/kg body weight (based on free acid).

Typical products Low sodium salt substitutes only in Australia (only permitted use in Australia.)

E363   Succinic acid

Origin Occurs naturally in fossils, fungi and lichens, but prepared for commercial use from acetic acid.

Function Acid; buffer; neutralising agent.

Effects No adverse effects are known.

A.D.I. —

Typical products Not permitted in Australia

365 Sodium fumarate (monosodium fumarate)

Origin Sodium salt of fumaric acid (297).

Function Buffering agent; acidifier; seasoning agent; helps the strength of gelatine gels and liberates calcium in alginate preparations. Antioxidant and acidifying agent when sodium benzoate (211) is the preservative. It may be used for enhancing the whipping qualities of gelatine and egg whites contained in some products.

Effects No adverse effects are known.

A.D.I. 0–6 mg/kg body weight (based on fumaric acid).

Typical products
Fruit juice drinks
Gelatine desserts
Pie fillings
Refrigerated biscuit doughs
Edible coatings for sweets
Cheese
Jams
Jellies
Marmalade

366 Potassium fumarate

Origin Potassium salt of fumaric acid (297).

Function To maintain the pH (degree of acidity) of jams and jellies at between 2.8 and 3.5. Also helps the strength of gelatine gels and liberates calcium in alginate preparations. Antioxidant and acidifying agent when sodium benzoate is the preservative. It may be used for enhancing the whipping qualities of gelatine and egg whites contained in some products.

Effects No adverse effects are known.

A.D.I. No A.D.I. allocated.

Typical products
Many of those permitted to contain sodium fumarate (365).

367 Calcium fumarate

Origin Calcium salt of fumaric acid (297).

Function To maintain the pH (degree of acidity) of preserves at between 2.8 and 3.5. Also helps the strength of gelatine gels and liberates calcium in alginate preparations. Antioxidant and acidifying agent when sodium benzoate is the preservative. It may be used for enhancing the whipping qualities of gelatine and egg whites contained in some products.

Effects No adverse effects are known.

A.D.I. No A.D.I. allocated.

Typical products
Many of those permitted to contain sodium fumarate (365).

E370 1,4-Heptonolactone

Origin Prepared in the laboratory; a gamma lactone made from hydroxycarboxylic acid.

Function Acid; sequestrant.

Effects No adverse effects are known.

A.D.I. Not specified.

Typical products Not permitted in Australia.

375   Niacin (nicotinic acid; nicotinamide)

Origin Occurs naturally in yeast, liver, legumes, rice polishings and lean meats, although it is prepared for commercial use by the oxidation of nicotine with concentrated nitric acid.

Function B vitamin; colour protector.

Effects Nutrient essential for the conversion of food into energy; and aiding the maintenance of a normal nervous system. Nicotinic acid can dilate the blood vessels and, if given in therapeutic doses, it may produce flushing of the face, and pounding in the head and a sensation of heat. It is perfectly safe in normal food use.

A.D.I. Not specified.

Typical products
Bread
Flour
Breakfast cereals

380   Triammonium citrate

Origin The salt of citric acid (330), which dissolves easily in water, releasing free acid.

Function Buffer; emulsifying salt to blend pasteurised processed cheese and cheese foods; softening agent for cheese spreads.

Effects Citrates may interfere with the results of laboratory tests, including tests for pancreatic function, abnormal liver function and blood alkalinity-acidity.

A.D.I. Not limited.

Typical products A wide range of foods including processed cheeses.

381   Ammonium ferric citrate (ferric ammonium citrate)

Origin Prepared from citric acid (330).

Function Dietary iron supplement; used medically for raising the level of red blood cells.

Effects Iron is an essential mineral nutrient, preventing anaemia.

A.D.I. No A.D.I. allocated.

Typical products
Formula dietary foods
Breakfast cereals

381   Ammonium ferric citrate, green

Origin Prepared from citric acid (330).

Function Dietary iron supplement; anti-caking agent.

Effects Iron is an essential mineral nutrient, preventing anaemia.

A.D.I. No A.D.I. allocated.

Typical products —

E385   Calcium disodium ethylenediamine-tetraacetate (calcium disodium EDTA)

Origin Prepared synthetically.

Function Traces of free metal ions of aluminium, copper, zinc, iron, manganese or nickel are likely to occur in any manufactured food which has come into contact with machinery.

Positively charged, these ions are likely to combine with substances in the food to spoil it by discolouration, cloudiness, rancidity or unpleasant smells. EDTA acts as a 'chelating agent', attracting the positively charged ions by trapping them in its own negatively charged ones and rendering them inactive. EDTA is soluble in water but not in oil, so it can only be used in water-based foods or oil-water mixtures. In some senses it functions as an antioxidant.

Effects Intravenous injections of EDTA are a long established moderately successful treatment for lead poisoning, but oral administration of large amounts of EDTA in excess of that normally used in foods has caused vomiting, diarrhoea, abdominal cramps, kidney damage and blood in urine. It is important that the manufacturer adds only enough EDTA to bind the metal impurities *in the food*, as excess EDTA could combine with the body's essential metallic elements such as iron, zinc and copper, and prevent their utilisation.

A.D.I. 0–2.5 mg/kg body weight (as calcium disodium EDTA; no disodium EDTA to remain in foods).

Typical products Not permitted in Australia.

400–492   Vegetable Gums, Emulsifiers, some Anti-caking Agents, Humectants and Mineral Salts

400   Alginic acid

Origin   Extracted from brown seaweeds, the most widely used being species of *Laminaria* (British Isles, France, Norway, North America, Japan), *Macrocystis* (USA(and *Ascophyllum* (British Isles).

The alginate (or algin as it is sometimes called) is present in seaweed as a mixed sodium, potassium, calcium and magnesium salt of alginic acid. The seaweed is dried and then macerated and broken down with a dilute alkaline solution to extract the alginate. The alginate is precipitated from solution as the insoluble calcium salt, and further treated and purified to produce alginic acid — from which all the other alginates (401–405) are made. The basic extraction method has changed little since alginate was first isolated in about 1880. Commercial utilisation in the food industry began in 1934.

Function   Classed as a vegetable gum. Stabiliser and thickening agent.

Effects   This is a natural product which produces no known toxicological risks. In common with other soluble fibres, very large quantities, greater than those likely in any normal diet, can inhibit the absorption of certain nutrients, especially minerals and trace elements.

A.D.I.   0–50 mg/kg body weight.

Typical products   A wide range of foods including —
Ice cream (as
   stabilising colloid)
   ensuring creamy
   texture and
   preventing growth
   of ice crystals
Dessert mix
Yoghurt
Custard mix
Flavoured milk
Flavoured skim milk
Frozen food glazes
Thickened cream
Flavoured cordial
Fruit drink
Fruit juice drink
Ice confection

401   Sodium alginate

Origin   Extracted from brown seaweeds, especially *Laminaria*, and

duced as part of the manufacture of
inic acid (400) of which it is the
lium salt.

ction Stabliser, suspending agent
d thickening agent. Also used, in
mbination with a source of calcium,
a gelling agent. Classed as a
getable gum.

ects This is a natural product which
oduces no known toxicological
ks. In common with other soluble
res, very large quantities, greater
n those likely in any normal diet,
n inhibit the absorption of certain
trients, especially minerals and trace
ments.

.I. 0–50 mg/kg body weight
lculated as alginic acid (400)).

ical products A wide range of foods
cluding many of those permitted to
ntain alginic acid (400) and
eese spread
coa and milk
ocessed cheese

02   Potassium alginate

gin Prepared from alginic acid
0) derived from native brown
aweeds. The potassium salt of
jinic acid (400).

iction Emulsifier; stabiliser; boiled
ter additive; gelling agent. Classed
a vegetable gum.

ects This is a natural product which
oduces no known toxicological
ks. In common with other soluble
res, very large quantities, greater
an those likely in any normal diet,
n inhibit the absorption of of certain
trients, especially mineral and trace
ments.

A.D.I. 0–25 mg/kg body weight
(calculated as alginic acid (400)).

Typical products Many of those
permitted to contain alginic acid (400).

403   Ammonium alginate

Origin Prepared from alginic acid
(400) derived from native seeweeds. It
is the ammonium salt of alginic acid
(400).

Function Emulsifier; stabiliser; diluent
for colouring matter; thickener.
Classed as a vegetable gum.

Effects This is a natural product
which produces no known
toxicological risks. In common with
other soluble fibres, very large
quantities, greater than those likely in
any normal diet, can inhibit the
absorption of certain nutrients,
especially mineral and trace elements.

A.D.I. 0–50 mg/kg body weight
(calculated as alginic acid (400)).

Typical products Many of those
permitted to contain alginic acid (400).

404   Calcium alginate

Origin Prepared from alginic acid
(400) derived from native brown
seaweeds. The calcium salt of alginic
acid (400).

Function The addition of calcium to
algin solutions produces gels which
are very stable, so calcium alginate is a
useful emulsifier, stabiliser, thickener
and gelling agent. It is also added to
jam to prevent it oozing out of oven-
baked pastry foods. Classed as a
vegetable gum.

Effects This is a naturally derived product which produces no known toxicological risks. In common with other soluble fibres, very large quantities, greater than those likely in any normal diet, can inhibit the absorption of certain nutrients, especially minerals and trace elements.

A.D.I. 0–25 mg/kg body weight (calculated as alginic acid (400)).

Typical products Many of those permitted to contain alginic acid (400).

405 Propylene glycol alginate (propane-1, 2-diol alginate)

Origin The propylene glycol ester of alginic acid (400) derived from native brown seaweeds. It varies in composition according to its degree of esterification and the percentage of free and neutralised carboxyl groups in the molecule.

Function Emulsifier or stabiliser, especially in ice cream, water ices and salad dressings; thickener; solvent for extracts, flavours or spices; foam stabilising agent (helps to maintain a stable 'head' on light lagers and ales to compensate for loss of hops and malts or degradation of proteins by proteolytic enzymes added to prevent haze formation). It is stable below pH 3. Classed as a vegetable gum.

Effects None known.

A.D.I. 0–25 mg/kg body weight.

Typical products & maximum permitted levels
Many of those permitted to contain alginic acid (400)
Beer 100 mg/L

406 Agar (agar-agar; Japanese isinglass)

Origin 'Agar-agar' is a Malay word a describes the mucilage produced fro a red seaweed. In the last century, Japan was the only exporter of agar, but it has now been joined by Spain, Morocco and Portugal, New Zealand Korea, South Africa and the USA. *Gelidium amansii* was the original seaweed used to produce agar; othe members of the Gelidiaceae family a also used today and members of the Sphaerococcaceae and related red algae Rhodophyceae. The algae are dried and bleached on the shore and then pounded, washed and boiled. T extract is filtered through linen, cooled, pressed to remove water, dri and milled. It is sold in strips or powder form. Not to be confused wit isinglass which is the swim bladders fish.

Function A colloidal carbohydrate, agar produces rather firm, brittle gels which are not as effective in foods as carrageenan (407) or gelatin. It is use as a thickening agent, stabiliser and gelling agent, and as a humectant for icings on cakes. Classed as a vegetat gum.

Effects Agar is not digested; large quantities of it may temporarily increase flatulence and distension o cause intestinal obstruction, but it is likely that amounts in food are too small to produce these effects. In common with other soluble fibres, ve large quantities, greater than those likely in any normal diet, can inhibit the absorption of certain nutrients, especially minerals and trace elements. It is used medically as a bu laxative.

A.D.I.   Not limited.

Typical products   A wide range of foods
including —
Ice cream
Manufactured meat
Desserts
Canned galantine meat
Canned tongues
Canned trotters

407   Carrageenan (Irish moss)

Origin   'Irish moss' is another name for
carrageenan and the Irish have used a
seaweed extract in milk puddings, food
and medicine for some 600 years. It
was not produced commercially,
however, until the Second World War
when an alternative to (Japanese) agar
(406) was sought. Until the 1950s it
was mainly extracted on a commercial
scale in the USA, but expanding
demand extended industrial
production to Scandinavia and France.

It occurs in about 22 species of red
seaweeds belonging to the
Gigartinaceae, Solieriaceae,
Hypnaceae and Furcellariaceae
families and is recovered commercially
from *Chondrus* seaweed in the United
States and *Chondrus crispus* and
Gigartina sp. in Europe.

The seaweeds are dried
mechanically or are left on the shore to
be alternately bleached and soaked,
and then dried. They are then washed
to remove salts and debris before the
extraction process using alkaline hot
water. The resulting dried mucilage is
translucent and swells in cold water,
partially dissolving to produce a jelly.
The extract is concentrated to about 3
per cent carrageenan before alcohol is
added to precipitate it.

'Carrageenan' describes a number of
complex hydrocolloids rather than a
single substance. It consists of varying
amounts (depending on the processing
methods) of the ammonium, calcium,
magnesium, potassium or sodium salts
of sulphate esters of galactose and
3,6-anhydro-galactose copolymers.
The sulphate ester content of
carrageenan ranges from 18–40 per
cent. The principal copolymers are
designated *kappa-*, *lambda-* and *iota-*
and these three copolymers differ in
structure and in their gelling ability.
They are termed 'native' carrageenan,
or 'undegraded' carrageenan, meaning
that the long polysaccharide molecules
of carrageenan have not been sub-
divided or split. The carrageenan used
in food has a high molecular weight (1
to 8 000 000). 'Degraded' carrageenan
has a very low molecular weight (20–
30 000) and no gelling properties.

Food-grade carrageenan *must*
comprise the long-chain molecules
and must not be degraded.

Function   Stabilising, thickening,
suspending and gelling agent. It
imparts the desired body and texture to
foods, especially dairy products. It is
used in concentrations of 0.01–1.0 per
cent. It also has many uses in the fields
of drugs and cosmetics as well as
having wider industrial applications.
Classed as a vegetable gum.

Effects   Some confusion has arisen
because *degraded* carrageenan (the
kind which is *not* permitted in food
use) has induced ulcerative colitis in a
wide range of laboratory animals, and
tumours of the colon and rectum. To
ensure that degraded carrageenan is
never used in food, the current EEC
statutory specification for purity
requires that 'carrageenan shall not be

hydrolysed or otherwise be chemically degraded' and seeks to ensure this by imposing a minimum viscosity requirement on a solution of the material treated under standardised conditions.

The complex polysaccharide may be degraded a little in the acid environment of the stomach, but not enough to cause any harm. The question of whether more degradation occurs during rigorous food processing conditions of acid pH and high temperatures has not been satisfactorily resolved.

Native (undegraded) carrageenan on its own and administered in the diets of laboratory animals did not cause tumours to develop. When it was fed to rats with azomethane or N-nitrosomethylurea, all the rats fed carrageenan *plus one of these substances* developed colon tumours, whereas only *some* of the controls fed *no carrageenan but one or other of the substances* developed tumours.

When six patients with malignant colon disease were given 5 g degraded carrageenan daily for ten days before having a colectomy, there were no signs of any ulceration nor of absorption of the carrageenan. No pathological effects were seen in rhesus monkeys fed 500 mg/kg a day for seven and a half years, but they had soft stools and diarrhoea.

Guinea pigs, rabbits and mice showed changes in the mucous membranes of the caecum, colon and rectum resembling those found in ulcerative colitis in man when they were fed concentrations of undegraded carrageenan ranging from 0.1 per cent to 1 per cent in the drinking water.

It was therefore surprising that when the Joint Expert Committee on Food Additives in 1984 reviewed the A.D.I. for carrageenan which had previously been 75 mg/kg body weight, they allocated it the most favourable standing of 'A.D.I. not specified'. This evaluation means that the total daily intake of carrageenan, arising from its use at the levels necessary to achieve the desired effect and from its acceptable background in food, does not represent a hazard to health. We believe that until further relevant trials prove otherwise the intake of large regular amounts of carrageenan has not been shown to be totally safe.

A.D.I. Not specified.

Typical products A wide range of foods including —
Ice cream
Dessert mix
Jelly mix
Confectionery
Pastries
Biscuits
Cream cheese,
    Neufchatel cheese
Thickened cream
Sauce
Formula dietary foods
Evaporated milk

410 Locust bean gum (carob bean gum)

Origin The Locust or Carob tree (*Ceratonia siliqua*) is an evergreen tree belonging to the Leguminoseae or pea family native to the Mediterranean region. It produces pods which bear shiny brown seeds and it is the endosperm or stored food in the seeds which constitutes the carob bean gum. Carob powder (the chocolate substitute) is manufactured from the od of the same plant. Carob bean gum was used by the ancient Egyptians for mummy binding and the sugary pods, rich in protein, have been eaten since biblical times (St John's Bread). They are used for stock feed today. Locust bean gum is a high molecular weight polysaccharide composed of galactopyranose and mannopyranose units and known as galactomannan.

Function   Gelling agent; stabiliser for ice creams; emulsifier; thickening agent for soups, salad dressings and pie fillings; texture modifier in cheeses, cake and biscuit doughs. It helps to make carrageenan (407) gels softer and more palatable.

Effects   None known. Two American reports, one from the University of Minnesota, suggest that locust bean gum may lower blood cholesterol levels. In common with other soluble fibres very large quantities, greater than those likely in any normal diet, can inhibit the absorption of certain nutrients, especially minerals and trace elements.

A.D.I.   Not specified.

Typical products & maximum permitted levels
A wide range of foods including —

Artificial sweetener base	—
Chutney	—
Confectionery	—
Cream Cheese, Neufchatel cheese	5 g/kg*
Custard mix, dessert mix	—
Dried thickened cream, thickened cream powder	5 g/kg*
Egg white mix	5 g/kg*
Essences	—
Flavoured cordial, flavoured syrup, flavoured topping	5 g/kg*
Flour products other than bread	—
Formula dietary foods	—

Fruit drink	1 g/kg*
Fruit juice cordial, fruit juice syrup, fruit juice topping	5 g/kg*
Fruit juice drink	1 g/kg*
Imitation cordial, imitation syrup, imitation topping	5 g/kg*
Imitation cream	—
Imitation fruit	—
Jelly mix	—
Kernel paste, imitation almond paste, imitation marzipan	—
Low joule foods	—
Marzipan, almond paste, almond icing	—
Mayonnaise, salad dressing	—
Pickles	—
Precooked oatmeal	—
Sauce, catsup, ketchup, relish	—
Soups	—
Scrambled egg mix, frozen	5 g/kg*

*In total with other vegetable gums

412   Guar gum

Origin   A gum extracted from the stored food in the seeds of *Cyamopsis tetragonolobus*, or *C. psoraloides*, a member of the pea family native to India and the drier tropics and grown in the south-western areas of the USA as a cattle feed.

Function   Thickening agent; emulsion stabiliser; suspending agent; dietary bulking agent; helps diabetics control blood sugar levels.

Effects   Adverse effects only occur when excessively large quantities are consumed and can include nausea, flatulence and abdominal cramps. In common with other soluble fibres, very large quantities, greater than those likely in any normal diet, can inhibit the absorption of certain nutrients, especially minerals and trace elements. A positive effect is the reported reduction in blood cholesterol levels.

A.D.I. Not specified.

Typical products Many of those permitted to contain locust bean gum (410).

413 Tragacanth (gum tragacanth)

Origin Tragacanth gum exudes from the trunk and branches of *Astragalus gummifer* and other species of the same genera (pea family). It may flow naturally, but is more usually collected by incision — as rubber is — from small thorny bushes which grow sparsely in mountain locations in Iran, Iraq, Turkey, Russia and other parts of the Middle East. The exudate is a ribbon of soft tragacanth, varying in colour and quality according to the age of the bushes and the degree of burning received by the tops of the bushes. White or pale-yellow gum is used in pharmacy, while the amber, reddish or brown flakes are used in the food and textile industries. Powdered tragacanth is pale-yellow or white in colour. Chemically it consists mainly of high molecular weight polysaccharides composed of galacto-arabans and acidic polysaccharides containing galacturonic acid groups.

Function Emulsifier; stabiliser; thickener (especially in acidic foods); prevention of crystallisation in sugar confectionery; used in cake decorating in the home to convert royal icing to a paste which can be moulded with the fingers.

Effects Adverse reactions have only occurred rarely and contact dermatitis has been reported when tragacanth was used on the skin. Tragacanth has been used as an emulsifier since pre-Christian times and can be ingested in large amounts with impunity, although diarrhoea, flatulence or constipation may result.

When five healthy male volunteers consumed 9.9 g gum tragacanth daily for twenty-one days there were no adverse toxicological effects. The intestine transit time and the fat content of the stools increased in four of the men, but all the other parameters measured (blood cholesterol, urine analysis, glucose tolerance, etc.) were normal.

A.D.I. Not specified.

Typical products Many of those permitted to contain locust bean gum (410).

414 Acacia (gum arabic)

Origin The dried gum which flows from the stems and branches of *Acacia senegal* and related species (members of the pea family). It collects and dries in walnut-sized globules. After an incision has been made in the bark, the dried tears or globules are collected and exported without further processing apart from the removal of foreign objects. The most important region for gum arabic production is Kordofan in the Sudan, but the gum-yielding acacia trees grow along a 3,000 km wide band following the southern frontier of the Sahara desert from West Africa to the Middle East, and in India.

The Egyptians used acacia gum more than 4,000 years ago as an ingredient in paints. Chemically, it consists of high molecular weight polysaccharides mainly with their calcium, potassium and magnesium salts, which on hydrolysis yield arabinose, galactose, rhamnose and glucuronic acid.

Function To retard sugar crystallisation; thickener of sweets, jellies, glazes and chewing gum and to convert royal icing into a plastic paste in home cake decorating; emulsifier; stabiliser preventing chemical breakdown in food mixtures and maintaining the foam on beer and soft drinks; glazing agent; and used to help citrus and other oily flavours to be added to drinks. Gum arabic is the most readily water-soluble of all the vegetable gums.

Effects A few people have demonstrated hypersensitivity to gum arabic after breathing it in or eating it, but it is used medically as a demulcent to soothe irritations, especially of the mucous membranes, and has been shown to lower the cholesterol levels in the blood of rats.

When five healthy men ate 25 g gum arabic daily for twenty-one days there was no effect on glucose tolerance, stool weight or appearance. There was a slight reduction in cholesterol in the blood. It seems that gum arabic is largely degraded in the human colon.

The extensive data available from studies in animals and in man and the detailed chemical data available suggest gum arabic is one of the most extensively evaluated food additives.

No upper level limits were specified by the FAO/WHO Committee, reflecting its safety as a food additive.

A.D.I. Not specified.

Typical products Many of those permitted to contain locust bean gum (410).

415 Xanthan gum (corn sugar gum)

Origin Produced by the fermentation of a carbohydrate such as corn sugar with a bacterium called *Xanthomonas campestris* in the presence of nitrogen and mineral nutrients.

Function Stabiliser, thickener, and emulsifier for water-based foods such as dairy products and salad dressings. It can form a thick gel on standing, but is quite liquid when shaken, stirred or poured, so is a useful 'pseudoplasticiser' in salad dressings, helping them to pour well. Used in cake mixes to improve appearance and to allow fewer eggs or less water to be used without affecting the result. When xanthan gum and guar gum (412) are present together in the ratio 2:1 (xanthan to guar) gelation is enhanced.

Effects No adverse effects attributable to xanthan gum have been reported in toxicological tests on rodents.

When five male volunteers consumed xanthan gum in weights equal to fifteen times the pre-1987 A.D.I of 0–10 mg/kg body weight on each of twenty-three consecutive days their faecal weight increased, as did faecal transit time. Their blood and urine analyses remained the same and there was a moderate reduction in serum cholesterol, with an increase in faecal bile acids.

A.D.I. Not specified.

Typical products Many of those permitted to contain locust bean gum (410).

416 Karaya gum (Sterculia gum)

Origin An exudate from the trunk and stems of the tree *Sterculia urens* native to central India and Pakistan. The trees are tapped and the gum harvested twice a year. It collects in irregular-shaped masses which can weigh up to several pounds each and varies in colour and quality depending on the amount of impurities contained. The top grades are colourless and translucent.

Function Stabiliser; emulsifier; thickener; prevents ice-crystals from forming in ice cream. Used as a filler in lemon custard and as citrus and spice flavouring agent for beverages, ice creams and sweets. Karaya gum can attract and absorb sufficient water to multiply its original volume one hundred times.

Effects A few people are allergic to karaya gum which indicates that some of it is absorbed. It can function as a laxative, so little of it is digested, but it is not known how the presence of the substance in the gut affects the absorption of nutrients.

When five healthy male voluteers consumed 10.5 g of karaya gum (a very large amount in relation to the amount in foods) daily there was no toxic effect on intestinal transit time, faecal weight or composition, glucose tolerance,

serum cholesterol or any other of the parameters measured. Karaya gum had no metabolic action of any consequence.

A.D.I. 0–20 mg/kg body weight (temporary).

Typical products Many of those permitted to contain locust bean gum (410).

420 Sorbitol and sorbitol syrup

Origin A six-carbon sugar alcohol which was first discovered in the ripe fruits of Mountain ash (*Sorbus aucuparia*). It occurs in the fruits of other members of the same family (Rosaceae), notably in cherries, pears, plums and apples and also in seaweeds and other algae. It is metabolised in the body. Commercial sources are from glucose by high-pressure hydrogenation or electrolytic reduction. Sorbitol syrup is an aqueous solution of sorbitol and hydrogenated oligosaccharides.

Function Sweetening agent and substitute for glycerol. When added to syrups containing sucrose it reduces the tendency to deposit crystals on storage extending the product's shelf-life. Sorbitol masks the bitter after-taste of saccharin in drinks and helps to maintain the physical texture of chewy sweets. Also used as a humectant, stabiliser and texturiser.

Effects Sorbitol is converted to sugar in the bloodstream, but it is only absorbed slowly, making it a useful source of sugar for diabetics, and reducing the incidence of dental caries. The UK Food Standards

Committee in 1976 considered sorbitol to be an undesirable ingredient for general use in soft drinks since some people have low gastric tolerance for sorbitol. It was recommended that its use in soft drinks be limited to those intended for consumption by diabetics. Large amounts (30 g for children, 60 g for adults) could cause flatulence, abdominal distension or have a laxative effect, but it is well-tolerated. Sorbitol is not permitted in foods intended specifically for infants or young children.

A.D.I. Not specified.

Typical products
Confectionery
Pastries
Pre-packaged cakes
Mixed dried fruit
Carbohydrate modified foods
Low joule foods

421 Mannitol (manna sugar)

Origin Occurs naturally in the wood of coniferous trees. Generally prepared from seaweed or manna, the dried exudate of *Fraxinus ornus* (Manna ash) which grows in Sicily and the 'toe' of Italy. The French tamarisk (*Tamarix gallica var. mannifera*) which grows on the south coast produces a similar exudate to seal the bark when it has been attacked by scale insects. The biblical manna which fed the Israelites may have been the wind-blown dispersal of a lichen called *Lecanor esculenta* native to the Middle East and used by Arabs to produce a bread. Strong winds can tear it from its substrate and transport it considerable distances. Commercial mannitol is usually prepared by hydrogenation of invert sugar (glucose and fructose), monosaccharides and sucrose.

Function Texturising agent; dietary supplement; humectant; sweetener in sugar-free products; anti-caking agent; anti-sticking agent.

Effects Mannitol has been used for centuries as a sweetener with no adverse effects. About two-thirds of it is absorbed in the digestive tract of which some is excreted in the urine. Of the total intake only about half is assimilated, which reduces the relative calorific value of food sweetened with mannitol compared with sugar. It also reduces the incidence of dental caries. Hypersensitivity reactions have occurred occasionally and mannitol may cause nausea, vomiting and diarrhoea. It may also induce or exacerbate kidney disease. Not permitted in foods intended specifically for infants or young children.

A.D.I. Not specified.

Typical products
Carbohydrate modified foods
Low joule food

422 Glycerin (glycerol)

Origin Occurs naturally in many plant cells, synthesised by the plants themselves. It is an industrial by-product in the manufacture of soaps, candles and fatty acids from oils and fats. With the decline in the demand for soap and increasing use of detergents, other methods had to be found. Alternative methods synthesise glycerol from propylene or by fermentation from sugars.

Function Solvent for oily chemicals, particularly flavourings which are soluble in water; humectant (keeping foods moist) in marshmallows, pastilles and jelly-sweets; sweetener (about 0.6 times as sweet as cane sugar); bodying agent in combination with gelatins and edible gums; plasticiser in edible coatings for meat and cheese.

Effects Glycerol is a common substance in the body's biochemistry, as an energy source and is a component of more complex molecules. It is readily absorbed from the intestine and metabolised to carbon dioxide and glycogen (animal starch) or used in the synthesis of body fats. 'Binge' eating can produce effects such as headache, thirst, nausea and high blood sugar levels. It is mildly laxative.

A.D.I. Not specified.

Typical products
Liqueurs
Confectionery
Carbohydrate modified foods
Low joule foods
Vodka
Edible casings for sausages and
  manufactured meats
Crystallised pineapple
Dried fruit
Liquid coffee essence
Mustard paste, prepared mustard

E432 Polysorbate 20 (polyoxyethylene (20) sorbitan monolaurate; Tween 20)

Origin A complex mixture of partial lauric esters of sorbitol and its mono- and di-anhydrides condensed with ethylene oxide.

Function Emulsifier; stabiliser; dispersing agent. It is more hydrophilic (water-attracting) than polysorbate 60 (435) and polysorbate 80 (433).

Effects Polysorbate emulsifiers have been in use since the 1940s and because of their efficiency are only necessary in concentrations of 0.01 per cent. They may increase the absorption of liquid paraffin and other fat-soluble substances and have sometimes been used clinically to treat those with deficient fat absorption.

A.D.I. 0–25 mg/kg body weight.

Typical products Not permitted in Australia.

433 Polysorbate 80 (polyoxyethylene (20) sorbitan mono-oleate; Tween 80)

Origin A complex mixture of partial oleic esters of sorbitol and sorbitol anhydride copolymerised with ethylene oxide.

Function Emulsifier and defoamer in the production of sugar beet; stabiliser; keeps bread rolls and doughnuts moist; prevents oil leaking from artificial whipped cream; helps the solubility of non-dairy coffee whiteners.

Effects Polysorbate emulsifiers have been in use since the 1940s and, because of their efficiency, are only necessary in concentrations of 0.01 per cent. They may increase the absorption of liquid paraffin and other fat-soluble substances.

A.D.I. 0–25 mg/kg body weight.

Typical products A wide range of products including —
Bread
Chocolate
Fats and oils for frying
Confectionery
Vegetable fats and oils for use as shortening
Edible casings of animal origin
Mayonnaise
Cocoa and milk

E434 Polysorbate 40 (polyoxyethylene (20) sorbitan monopalmitate; Tween 40)

Origin A palmitate ester of sorbitol and sorbitol anhydride copolymerised with ethylene oxide.

Function Emulsifier; stabiliser; dispersing agent (especially of flavours); defoaming agent; wetting agent for powdered processed foods.

Effects Polysorbate emusliifiers have been in use since the 1940s and because of their efficiency are only necessary in concentrations of 0.01 per cent. They may increase the absorption of liquid paraffin and other fat-soluble substances.

A.D.I. 0–25 mg/kg body weight.

Typical products Not permitted in Australia.

435 Polysorbate 60 (polyoxyethylene (20) sorbitan monostearate; Tween 60)

Origin A complex mixture of partial stearic acid esters of sorbitol and its mono- and di-anhydrides condensed with ethylene oxide.

Function Emulsifier; stabiliser — especially in frozen desserts to prevent the oil and water separating out and creating wetness; prevents oil leaking from aritificial whipped cream and flavour oils leaking from sweets; keeps bread and doughnuts moist; wetting and dispersing agent for powdered processed foods like non-dairy coffee whiteners; added to chocolate coatings to prevent the fat used as a substitute for cocoa fat from tasting greasy; foaming agent in non-alcoholic beverage mix to be added to alcoholic beverages.

Effects Polysorbates may increase the absorption of liquid paraffin and other fat-soluble substances. The US Food and Drug Administration has asked for further studies of this additive.

A.D.I. 0–25 mg/kg body weight.

Typical products Many of those permitted to contain polysorbate 80 (433).

436 Polysorbate 65 (polyoxyethylene (20) sorbitan tristearate; Tween 65)

Origin A stearic acid ester of sorbitol and sorbitol anhydride copolymerised with ethylene oxide.

Function Emulsifier, especially in frozen desserts, preventing the oil and water from separating out and creating wetness; prevents oil leaking out of artificial whipped cream and flavour oils leaking from sweets; stabiliser; keeps bread and doughnuts moist; wetting and solution agent for processed dehydrated foods like non-dairy coffee whiteners; defoaming agent; flavour dispersing agent.

Effects   Polysorbate emuslifiers have been in use since the 1940s and because of their efficiency are only necessary in concentrations of 0.01 per cent. No known toxicity. Polysorbates may increase the absorption of liquid paraffin and other fat-soluble substances and have sometimes been used clinically to treat those with deficient fat absorption.

A.D.I.   0–25 mg/kg body weight.

Typical products   Many of those permitted to contain polysorbate 80 (433).

440(a)   Pectin

Origin   Protopectin is a polysaccharide present within and between the cell walls of dicotyledenous plants, cementing the cells together. During the ripening process of acid fruits (especially apples, plums, bitter oranges and lemons) protopectin accumulates and, as the fruit matures, enzymes break down the protopectin to pectin and soften the texture of the fruit. Apple residues from cider-making and orange pith are the commercial sources of pectin. Pectin consists mainly of the partial methyl esters of polygalacturonic acid.

Function   Efficient thickening gelling agent in acid (pH 2.4–4.0) media; bodying agent for artificially sweetened beverages; to make syrups for frozen products; stabiliser.

Effects   No real toxicological risks. Large amounts may cause temporary flatulence or intestinal distension, but also reduce blood cholesterol levels.

A.D.I.   Not specified.

Typical products & maximum permitted levels
A wide range of products including —

Jam	5 g/kg
Fruit jelly	5 g/kg
Marmalade	5 g/kg
Dessert mix	—
Pastry cooks' filling	5 g/kg

E440(b)   Amidated pectin

Origin   Treatment of pectin (440a) with ammonia, under alkaline conditions, so that a proportion of the methyl esters are converted to primary amides.

Function   Emulsifier; stabiliser; gelling agent especially for low-sugar gels; thickener.

Effects   No adverse effects are known.

A.D.I.   Not specified.

Typical products   Not permitted in Australia.

441   Gelatine

Origin   Gelatine is obtained by boiling animal skin (usually cattle's or pig's), ligaments, bones, sinews, or any tissue that contains collagen (from the Greek *kolla*, meaning 'glue' and *gennan*, 'to produce'). The tissues are first placed in a weak alkaline solution for 7–10 days before being boiled. It comprises a mixture of water-soluble proteins with the exception of the amino acid, tryptophan. It dries into brittle transparent flakes which are soluble in hot water. Gelatine swells in water, absorbing 5–10 times its own weight of water and forms a gel when it cools below 35–40°C.

Function Suspending, thickening and stabilising agent; emulsifier. Gelatines of various pHs (degrees of acidity) can be mixed with other gums, such as agar (406), tragacanth (413) or acacia (414). Gelatine putrefies rapidly when it is moist or in solution so foods containing gelatine have a limited shelf-life, unless they are frozen.

Effects As a source of protein, gelatine is of some (albeit limited) nutritional benefit. It lacks the amino acid, tryptophan, but contains substantial amounts of the amino acid, lysine, which some cereals and other foods lack.

Some people are allergic to gelatine, experiencing histamine-like side effects and in others it has the effect of lowering their resistance to infection.

Sometimes gelatine has sulphur dioxide (220) added as a preservative, so asthmatics and those sensitive to sulphites may be advised to be wary of foods containing gelatine. Used as an additive in an ingredient it would not say on the label whether sulphur dioxide was present or not unless the finished product contained more than 25 mg/kg of sulphur dioxide.

A.D.I. Not limited.

Typical products A wide variety of foods including —
Jellies
Desserts
Ice creams and water ices
Manufactured meats
Canned tongues, trotters and galantine meats
Low joule foods
Sweets like pastilles, gums and marshmallows
Whipped thickened reduced cream
Thickened cream

442 Ammonium salts of phosphatidic acid (ammonium phosphatides; emulsifier YN)

Origin Prepared synthetically.

Function Stabiliser; emulsifier.

Effects None known.

A.D.I. 0–30 mg/kg body weight (to be included in the M.T.D.I. for phosphates).

Typical products Many of those permitted to contain polysorbate 80 (433).

450 Sodium acid pyrophosphate (disodium dihydrogen diphosphate; disodium dihydrogen pyrophosphate)

Origin A sodium salt of pyrophosphoric acid. It is prepared by the heat condensation of sodium orthophosphate (in turn made from phosphoric acid).

Function Buffer; sequestrant; emulsifier; raising agent (for use in conjunction with sodium bicarbonate in flour goods); colour improver; chelating agent (see glossary).

Effects Phosphorus, as phosphate, is an essential nutrient present in bones, teeth, blood and cells, and is necessary for fat and protein assimilation and B vitamin digestion. The body can use it most efficiently if it is present in a constant 1:1 ratio with calcium, so it is important that the calcium/phosphate balance is maintained.

In view of the concern expressed that high intakes of phosphates and polyphosphates may be upsetting this balance, in 1982 JECFA recommended that further studies should be carried out on the implications of high dietary intakes of phosphorus.

The main toxicological finding in feeding studies with high levels of phosphates is kidney stones, to which rats are highly susceptible.

M.T.D.I. 70 mg/kg body weight (expressed as phosphorus from all sources). See phosphoric acid (338).

Typical products Many of those permitted to contain sodium phosphate, monobasic (339). Baking powder

450 **Trisodium diphosphate**

Origin A sodium salt of pyrophosphoric acid.

Function Buffer; sequestrant; emulsifier; colour improver; chelating agent (see glossary).

Effects Phosphorus, as phosphate, is an essential nutrient present in bones, teeth, blood and cells, and is necessary for fat and protein assimilation and B vitamin digestion. The body can use it most efficiently if it is present in a constant 1:1 ratio with calcium, so it is important that the calcium/phosphorus balance is maintained.

In view of the concern expressed that high intakes of phosphates and polyphosphates may be upsetting this balance, JECFA in 1982 recommended that further studies should be carried out on the implications of high dietary intakes of phosphorus.

The main toxicological finding in feeding studies with high levels of phosphates is kidney stones, to which rats are highly susceptible.

M.T.D.I. 70 mg/kg body weight. (expressed as phosphorus from all sources). See phosphoric acid (338).

Typical products Many of those permitted to contain sodium phosphate, monobasic (339).

450 **Sodium pyrophosphate (tetrasodium diphosphate)**

Origin A sodium salt of pyrophosphoric acid.

Function Buffer; emulsifying salt; sequestrant; gelling agent; stabiliser. A special milk-gelling grade of this additive is often used to achieve the desired set body of a dessert whip. It is used to aid rehydration and stabilise colour in dehydrated foods.

Effects Phosphorus, as phosphate, is an essential nutrient present in bones, teeth, blood and cells, and is necessary for fat and protein assimilation and B vitamin digestion. The body can use it most efficiently if it is present in a constant 1:1 ratio with calcium, so it is important that the calcium/phosphorus balance is maintained.

In view of the concern expressed that high intakes of phosphates and polyphosphates may be upsetting this balance, JECFA in 1982 recommended that further studies should be carried out on the implications of high dietary intakes of phosphorus.

The main toxicological finding in feeding studies with high levels of phosphates is kidney stones, to which rats are highly susceptible.

M.T.D.I. 70 mg/kg body weight (expressed as phosphorus from all sources). See phosphoric acid (338).

Typical products Many of those permitted to contain sodium phosphate, monobasic (339).

450 Potassium pyrophosphate (tetrapotassium diphosphate)

Origin A potassium salt of pyrophosphoric acid.

Function Emulsifying salts; buffer; sequestrant; stabiliser.

Effects Phosphorus, as phosphate, is an essential nutrient present in bones, teeth, blood and cells, and is necessary for fat and protein assimilation and B vitamin digestion. The body can use it most efficiently if it is present in a constant 1:1 ratio with calcium, so it is important that the calcium/phosphorus balance is maintained.

In view of the concern expressed that high intakes of phosphates and polyphosphates may be upsetting this balance, JECFA in 1982 recommended that further studies should be carried out on the implications of high dietary intakes of phosphorus.
The main toxicological finding in feeding studies with high levels of phosphates is kidney stones, to which rats are highly susceptible.

M.T.D.I. 70 mg/kg body weight (expressed as phosphorus from all sources). See phosphoric acid (338).

Typical products Many of those permitted to contain sodium phosphate, monobasic (339).

450 Sodium tripolyphosphate (pentasodium triphosphate)

Origin A sodium salt of triphosphoric acid. Prepared by the heat condensation of sodium orthophosphates.

Function Emulsifying salt; texturiser; buffer; sequestrant; stabiliser. By using polyphosphates, manufacturers can incorporate water into meat products by enhancing the water-binding ability of muscle proteins (which explains why bacon often seems to disappear in the pan). Polyphosphates are also used for protein solubilisation (in conjunction with salt) in, for example, comminuted (finely chopped) meats.

Effects Phosphorus (as phosphate) is an essential nutrient, present in bones, teeth, blood and cells, and is necessary for fat and protein assimilation and B vitamin digestion. The body can use it most efficiently if it is present in an equal ratio with calcium, so it is important that the calcium/phosphorus balance is maintained. Too much phosphate could upset the balance and cause a deficiency of both minerals. When rats are given high levels of phosphates they develop kidney stones (nephrocalcinosis), but man is not considered to have anything approaching the rat's susceptibility.

M.T.D.I. 70 mg/kg body weight (expressed as phosphorus from all sources). See phosphoric acid (338).

Typical products Many of those permitted to contain sodium phosphate, monobasic (339).

450 Potassium tripolyphosphate (pentapotassium triphosphate)

Origin A potassium salt of triphosphoric acid. Prepared by the heat condensation of potassium orthophosphates.

Function Emulsifying salt; texturiser; buffer; sequestrant; stabiliser.

Effects Phosphorus (as phosphate) is an essential nutrient present in bones, teeth, blood and cells, and is necessary for fat and protein assimilation and B vitamin digestion. The body can use it most efficiently if it is present in an equal ratio with calcium, so it is important that the calcium/phosphorus balance is maintained. Too much phosphate could upset the balance and cause a deficiency of both minerals. When rats are given high levels of phosphates they develop kidney stones (nephrocalcinosis), but man is not considered to have anything approaching the rat's susceptibility.

M.T.D.I. 70 mg/kg body weight (expressed as phosphorus from all sources). See phosphoric acid (338).

Typical products Many of those permitted to contain sodium phosphate, monobasic (339).

450 Sodium polyphosphates

Origin Sodium salts of polyphosphoric acids.

Function Emulsifying salts; sequestrants; stabilisers; texturisers.

Effects Phosphorus (as phosphate) is an essential nutrient present in bones, teeth, blood and cells, and is necessary for fat and protein assimilation and B vitamin digestion. The body can use it most efficiently if it is present in a constant 1:1 ratio with calcium, so it is important that the calcium/phosphorus balance is maintained.

In view of the concern expressed that high intakes of phosphates and polyphosphates may be upsetting this balance, the JECFA in 1982 recommended that further studies should be carried out on the implications of high dietary intakes of phosphorus.

The main toxicological finding in feeding studies with high levels of phosphates is kidney stones, to which rats are highly susceptible.

M.T.D.I. 70 mg/kg body weight (expressed as phosphorus from all sources). See phosphoric acid (338).

Typical products Many of those permitted to contain sodium phosphate, monobasic (339).

450 Potassium polyphosphates

Origin Potassium salts of polyphosphoric acids prepared by the heat condensation of potassium orthophosphates.

Function Emulsifying salts; stabilisers; sequestrants.

Effects Phosphorus (as phosphate) is an essential nutrient present in bones, teeth, blood and cells, and is necessary for fat and protein assimilation and B vitamin digestion. The body can use it most efficiently if it is present in a constant 1:1 ratio with calcium, so it is important that the calcium/phosphorus balance is maintained.

In view of the concern expressed that high intakes of phosphates and polyphosphates may be upsetting this balance, JECFA in 1982 recommended that further studies should be carried out on the implications of high dietary intakes of phosphorus.

The main toxicological finding in feeding studies with high levels of phosphates is kidney stones, to which rats are highly susceptible.

M.T.D.I. 70 mg/kg body weight (expressed as phosphorus from all sources). See phosphoric acid (338).

Typical products Many of those permitted to contain sodium phosphate, monobasic (339).

450(a) Ammonium phosphate dibasic (secondary ammonium phosphate diammonium hydrogen phosphate)

Origin Manufactured by a crystallisation process neutralising phosphoric acid with ammonia solution at elevated temperatures. Crystals of ammonium phosphate are formed as the temperature falls.

Function Yeast nutrient for bread doughs, as a source of phosphorus and nitrogen, acidic constituent of baking powder, buffer, sugar purifying agent.

Effects Phosphorus, as phosphate, is an essential nutrient, present in bones, teeth and blood and is necessary for fat and protein assimilation. The body can use it most efficiently if it is present in a constant 1:1 ratio with calcium, as it is important that the calcium/phosphorus balance is maintained.

M.T.D.I. 70 mg/kg body weight (expressed as phosphorus from all sources). See phosphoric acid (338).

Typical products
Baking powder
Salt substitutes

Note: In Australia both the mono- and dibasic ammonium salts of phosphoric acid are classified as 450(a).

450a Ammonium phosphate monobasic (ammonium dihydrogen phosphate; primary ammonium phosphate)

Origin Commercially available as the anhydrous salt. Manufactured by a crystallisation process neutralising phosphoric acid with ammonia solution at elevated temperatures. Crystals of ammonium phosphate are formed as the temperature falls.

Function Baking powder in combination with sodium bicarbonate, in fermentations of yeast cultures as a yeast nutrient, providing phosphorus and nitrogen.

Effects Phosphorus, as phosphate, is an essential nutrient, present in bones, teeth and blood and is necessary for fat and protein assimilation. The body can use it most efficiently if it is present in a constant 1:1 ration with calcium, as it is important that the calcium/phosphorus balance is maintained.

M.T.D.I. 70 mg/kg body weight (expressed as phosphorus from all sources). See phosphoric acid (338).

Typical products
Baking compounds
Salt substitutes

460 Microcrystalline cellulose

Origin The cellulose walls of plant fibres which are chemically fragmented into microscopic crystals.

Function Non-nutritive bulking agent; binder; anti-caking agent; dietary fibre; hydration aid; emulsion stabiliser; heat stabiliser; alternative ingredient; binder and disintegrant for tablets; carrier and microdispersant for quick drying; cellulose component and for texture modification.

Effects No adverse effects are known.

A.D.I. Not specified.

Typical products
Artificial sweeteners
Fabricated collagen casings
Low joule foods

460 Powdered cellulose

Origin The cellulose component of plant cell walls which are disintegrated mechanically to form a pulp and then dried.

Function Bulking aid; anti-caking agent; binder; dispersant; thickening agent and filter aid; used to assist isinglass finings in clearing of beer, associating with the protein and causing it to flocculate or collect into larger particles and settle.

Effects None known.

A.D.I. Not specified.

Typical products Fabricated collagen casings

461 Methylcellulose (methocel; cologel)

Origin Prepared from cellulose by treatment with alkali and methyl chloride.

Function Emulsifier; stabiliser; thickener; bulking and binding agent; film former and a substitute for water soluble gums. Also used in foods for diabetics, coeliacs or people who are allergic to gluten, or on low calorie diets, or kosher diets. Can function as a fat barrier.

Effects Methylcellulose reacts and forms complexes in solution with methylhydroxybenzoate (218) and propylhydroxybenzoate (E217). Excessive amounts could cause flatulence, distension or intestinal obstruction. People with intestinal obstruction should avoid foods containing methylcellulose. It is not known how the presence of the substance in the gut affects the absorption of nutrients.

A.D.I. 0–25 mg/kg body weight.

Typical products Many of those permitted to contain locust bean gum (410).

E463 Hydroxypropyl-cellulose

Origin Synthetically prepared from cellulose by treatment with alkali and propylene oxide.

Function Stabiliser in foams and lotions; emulsifier; thickener; suspending agent.

Effects No adverse effects are known.

A.D.I. 0–25 mg/kg body weight.

Typical products Not permitted in Australia

464 Hydroxypropylmethyl-cellulose (hypromellose)

Origin Prepared from cellulose by treatment with alkali and methyl chloride and propylene oxide.

Function Gelling or suspending agent; emulsifier; stabiliser and thickening agent; can function as a fat barrier.

Effects No adverse effects are known.

A.D.I. 0–25 mg/kg body weight.

Typical products Many of those permitted to contain locust bean gum (410).

465 Methylethylcellulose (ethylmethylcellulose)

Origin Prepared from cellulose.

Function Emulsifier; foam stabiliser; thickener; suspending agent.

Effects No adverse effects are known.

A.D.I. 0–25 mg/kg body weight.

Typical products and maximum permitted levels Imitation ice cream   9 g/kg

466 Sodium carboxymethyl-cellulose (carmellose sodium; CMC)

Origin Prepared by treating cellulose with alkali and monochloroacetic acid.

Function Thickening agent; texture modification; stabiliser; moisture migration control; gelling agent; non-nutritive bulking agent; prevention of crystal growth; prevention of syneresis (the drawing together of particles in a gel); decreasing fat absorption; foam stabiliser.

Effects When five healthy male volunteers were given 15 g sodium carboxymethylcellulose (7.5 times the A.D.I.) for twenty-three days they experienced no adverse effects. It had no effect on the biochemistry of the blood plasma, red and white blood cells or haemoglobin, urine composition, glucose tolerance, blood cholesterol, etc. The intestine transit time decreased for four of the five and increased for the fifth. Faecal fat increased in four of the men. CMC passes through the food canal without being digested or absorbed into the bloodstream.

A.D.I. 0–25 mg/kg body weight.

Typical products Many of those permitted to contain locust bean gum (410).

469 Sodium caseinate (casein-sodium)

Origin The sodium salt of casein, the principal protein of cow's milk (the other proteins are lactoalbumin and lactoglobulin). Sodium caseinate is manufactured from acid casein curd, made soluble by the addition of food grade sodium hydroxide (E524). The solution is then spray-dried to produce a fine cream coloured powder.

Function Emulsifier; stabiliser; binder; whitener for beverages and for high fat meat products.

Effects   No adverse effects are known.

A.D.I.   Not limited.

Typical products & maximum permitted levels
Beverage whiteners   60 g/kg
Whipped thickened reduced
cream   2.5 g/kg
Dessert mixes   —

E470   Sodium, potassium and calcium salts of fatty acids (soaps)

Origin   Prepared from fatty acids.

Function   Emulsifiers; stabilisers; anti-caking agents.

Effects   No adverse effects are known.

A.D.I.   Not limited.

Typical products   Not permitted in Australia

471   Mono- and di-glycerides of fat-forming fatty acids

Origin   A normal product of digestion, but prepared for commercial use from glycerin and fatty acids.

Function   Used in cakes to retain the foaming power of egg protein in the presence of fat; emulsifier; stabiliser; thickening agent. It is the commonest surfactant in ice cream where fat is emulsified into a complex watery matrix.

Effects   No adverse effects are known.

A.D.I.   Not limited.

Typical products & maximum permitted levels
A wide range of foods including —

Beverage whitener	15 g/kg
Cocoa and milk, chocolate and milk	5 g/kg
Confectionery	—
Custard mix, dessert mix	—
Dairy blend	—
Dairy ice mix	14 g/kg
Dried thickened cream, thickened cream powder	20 g/kg
Dried instant mashed potato	5 g/kg dry weight
Essences	—
Flavoured milk	—
Flavoured skim milk	—
Flour products other than bread	—
Formula dietary foods	—
Frozen yoghurt, frozen yoghurt products	—
Ice confection	14 g/kg
Ice cream	14 g/kg
Imitation cream	—
Margarine	—
Mayonnaise, salad dressing	—
Peanut butter, peanut paste	30 g/kg
Precooked oatmeal	—
Soups	—
UHT cream mixture, UHT thickened cream	3 g/kg
Whipped thickened reduced cream	6 g/kg

472(a)   Acetic and fatty acid esters of glycerol

Origin   Prepared from esters of glycerol and acetic acid.

Function   Emulsifiers, stabilisers; coating agents; texture modifying agents; solvents and lubricants.

Effects   No adverse effects are known.

A.D.I.   Not limited.

Typical products   Many of those permitted to contain mono- and di-glycerides of fat-forming fatty acids (471).

472(b) Lactic and fatty acid esters of glycerol (lacyoglycerides)

Origin   Prepared from esters of glycerol and lactic acid.

Function   Emulsifiers; stabilisers.

Effects   No adverse effects are known.

A.D.I.   Not limited.

Typical products   Many of those permitted to contain mono- and di-glycerides of fat-forming fatty acids (471).

472(c) Citric and fatty acid esters of glycerol (citroglycerides)

Origin   Prepared from esters of glycerol and citric acid.

Function   Emulsifiers and stablisers.

Effects   No adverse effects are known.

A.D.I.   Not limited.

Typical products   Many of those permitted to contain mono- and di-glycerides of fat-forming fatty acids (471).

472(d) Tartaric and fatty acid esters of glycerol

Origin   Prepared from esters of glycerol and tartaric acid.

Function   Emulsifiers and stabilisers.

Effects   No adverse effects are known.

A.D.I.   Not limited.

Typical products   Many of those permitted to contain mono- and di-glycerides of fat-forming fatty acids (471).

472(e) Diacetyltartaric and fatty acid esters of glycerol

Origin   Prepared from esters of glycerol and tartaric acid.

Function   Emulsifiers and stabilisers.

Effects   No adverse effects are known.

A.D.I.   Not limited.

Typical products   Many of those permitted to contain mono- and di-glycerides of fat-forming fatty acids (471).

473 Sucrose esters of fatty acids

Origin   Prepared from esters of glycerol and sucrose.

Function   Emulsifiers and stabilisers.

Effects   No adverse effects are known.

A.D.I.   0–10 mg/kg body weight.

Typical products   Many of those permitted to contain mono- and di-glycerides of fat-forming fatty acids (471).

E474 Sucroglycerides

Origin Prepared by the action of sucrose on natural triglycerides (from lard, tallow, palm oil, etc.).

Function Emulsifiers and stabilisers.

Effects Sucroglycerides are hydrolysed in the food canal to normal dietary constituents prior to absorption. Long- and short-term studies revealed no adverse effects, neither did a study in dogs fed sucrose esters from beef tallow fatty acids.

A.D.I. 0–10 mg/kg body weight.

Typical products Not permitted in Australia

475 Polyglycerol esters of fatty acids

Origin Prepared in the laboratory.

Function Emulsifiers and stabilisers.

Effects No adverse effects are known.

A.D.I. 0–25 mg/kg body weight.

Typical products & maximum permitted levels

Cake	15 g/kg
Imitation cream	5 g/kg
Margarine	5 g/kg
Mayonnaise, salad dressing containing oil	20 g/kg
Vegetable fats and oils for use as shortenings	20 g/kg
Whipped thickened reduced cream	5 g/kg

476 Polyglycerol esters of interesterified ricinoleic acid (polyglycerol polyricinoleate)

Origin Prepared from caster oil and glycerol esters.

Function Emulsifiers; stabilisers; when used with lecithin improve the fluidity of chocolate for coating, reducing the amount of expensive cocoa butter necessary, allowing a thinner coating of chocolate.

Effects No adverse effects are known.

A.D.I. 0–7.5 mg/kg body weight.

Typical products & maximum permitted levels

Chocolate, chocolate paste, drinking chocolate, confectioners' chocolate, chocolate coating, chocolate powder	4 g/kg
Milk chocolate	4 g/kg
White chocolate	4 g/kg

E477 Propane- 1,2,-diol esters of fatty acids (propylene glycol esters of fatty acids)

Origin Prepared from propylene glycol.

Function Emulsifiers and stabilisers.

Effects No adverse effects are known.

A.D.I. 0–25 mg/kg body weight.

Typical products In Australia propylene glycol stearate is permitted to be used in vegetable fats and oils sold for use as shortenings but no code number has been allocated to it.

480   Dioctyl sodium sulphosuccinate (docusate sodium)

Origin   Dioctyl sodium sulphosuccinate is prepared by a reaction of alcohol with maleic anhydride followed by the addition of sodium bisulphite.

Function   Emulsifier; wetting agent with detergent and dispersant properties, especially for flavours in drinks. Used as a solubilising agent for materials which are hard to wet like cocoa and gums. It is also used for cleaning leafy vegetables and fruits. Pharmaceutically it is valued as a laxative and for dissolving ear wax.

Effects   Docusate sodium is absorbed from the gut and excreted by the liver and in breast milk. Data from studies of this substance in the horse, guinea pig and man were not adequate for JECFA to establish an A.D.I. and they are awaiting results of studies on foetuses and exposure of babies through breast milk in addition to studies on the blood system before establishing an A.D.I.

A.D.I.   No A.D.I. allocated.

Typical products & maximum permitted levels
Cordials and syrups	50 mg/kg
Soft drinks	10 mg/kg

481   Sodium stearoyl lactylate (sodium stearoyl-2-lactylate)

Origin   Prepared from lactic acid.

Function   Stabiliser; emulsifier.

Effects   No adverse effects known.

A.D.I.   0–20 mg/kg body weight (temporary).

Typical products
Flour for bread-making
Biscuits
Bread
Cakes

482   Calcium stearoyl lactylate (calcium stearoyl-2-lactylate)

Origin   Prepared from lactic acid.

Function   Emulsifier; stabiliser; whipping aid.

Effects   No adverse effects known.

A.D.I.   0–20 mg/kg body weight.

Typical products
Flour for bread-making
Biscuits
Bread
Cakes

E483   Stearyl tartrate

Origin   Prepared from tartaric acid.

Function   Stabiliser; emulsifier; flour treatment agent.

Effects   No adverse effects known.

A.D.I.   0– 500ppm.

Typical products   Not permitted in Australia

491   Sorbitan monostearate

Origin   Prepared synthetically from stearic acid and sorbitol.

Function   Emulsifier; stabiliser; glazing agent.

Effects   No adverse effects are known.

A.D.I.   0–25 mg/kg body weight (a group A.D.I. for the sum of the sorbitan esters of lauric, oleic, palmitic and stearic acids).

Typical products   Many of those permitted to contain mono- and diglycerides of fatty acids (471).

492   Sorbitan tristearate (Span 65)

Origin   Prepared synthetically from stearic acid.

Function   Emulsifier; stabiliser.

Effects   Polysorbates may increase the body's absorption of liquid paraffin and fat-soluble substances.

A.D.I.   0–25 mg/kg body weight (a group A.D.I. for the sum of the sorbitan esters of lauric, oleic, palmitic and stearic acids).

Typical products & maximum permitted levels
Compounded chocolate   10 g/kg
(this is the only permitted food use in Australia)

E493   Sorbitan monolaurate (Span 20)

Origin   Prepared from sorbitol and lauric acid.

Function   Emulsifier; stabiliser; antifoaming agent.

Effects   No adverse effects are known.

A.D.I.   0–25 mg/kg body weight (a group A.D.I. for the sum of the sorbitan esters of lauric, oleic, palmitic and stearic acids).

Typical products   Not permitted in Australia

E494   Sorbitan mono-oleate (Span 80)

Origin   Prepared synthetically from sorbitol and oleic acid.

Function   Emulsifier; stabiliser.

Effects   No adverse effects are known.

A.D.I.   0–25 mg/kg body weight (a group A.D.I. for the sum of the sorbitan esters of lauric, oleic, palmitic and stearic acids).

Typical products   Not permitted in Australia

E495   Sorbitan monopalmitate (Span 40)

Origin   Prepared from sorbital and palmitic acid.

Function   Oil-soluble emulsifier; stabiliser.

Effects   No adverse effects are known.

A.D.I.   0–25 mg/kg body weight (a group A.D.I. for the sum of the sorbitan esters of lauric, oleic, palmitic and stearic acids).

Typical products   Not permitted in Australia.

500-579 More Mineral Salts and Anti-caking Agents

500 Sodium carbonate

Origin Although naturally occurring as saline residues deposited from the water of alkaline lakes, sodium carbonate is cheaper to manufacture by the Solvay process or electrolytically from sea or saline lake waters.

Function Base; used in the malting process of beer-making to remove 'testinic acid' from barley in the steep liquor.

Effects No adverse effects are known in small doses. Large amounts can corrode the gut and cause gastric upsets and circulation problems.

A.D.I. Not limited.

Typical products A wide range of foods including —
Confectionery
Custard mix, dessert mix
Egg white mix
Flour products other
than bread
Fruit flavoured
spreads, fruit
flavoured fillings
Imitation cream
Imitation fruit
Formula dietary foods
Mayonnaise, salad
dressing
Scrambled egg mix,
frozen
Soups

500 Sodium bicarbonate (sodium hydrogen carbonate; baking soda; bicarbonate of soda)

Origin Prepared synthetically.

Function Base; aerating agent; diluent.

Effects There are no problems with this substance in normal use.

A.D.I. Not limited.

Typical products Many of those permitted to contain sodium carbonate (500) and —
Pastry cooks' filling
Fruit jelly
Jam
Malted milk powder
Seltzer water

500 Sodium sesquicarbonate

Origin Occurs naturally in saline residues with other minerals formed in the same way, in California, Mexico and Egypt. Prepared also commercially.

Function Base.

Effects No adverse effects are known.

A.D.I. Not specified.

Typical products Not commonly used in Australia.

501 Potassium carbonate and potassium hydrogen carbonate

Origin Potassium bicarbonate may be prepared by saturating a concentrated solution of potassium carbonate with carbon dioxide.

Function Base; alkali.

Effects None known. It is used medicinally for the treatment of gastric hyperacidity. After it has been absorbed, it helps to maintain the alkaline balance of the blood.

A.D.I. Not limited.

Typical products Many of those permitted to contain sodium carbonate (500) and —
Low sodium salt
  substitute
Soda water

503 Ammonium carbonate

Origin A mixture of ammonium bicarbonate and ammonium carbonate, obtained by subliming a mixture of ammonium sulphate and calcium carbonate.

Function Buffer; neutralising agent; leavening agent.

Effects Turns into carbon dioxide in the stomach. There may be some alteration of the acid-base balance and pH of the urine.

A.D.I. Not specified.

Typical products Many of those permitted to contain sodium carbonate (500) and —
Low sodium salt
  substitute

503 Ammonium bicarbonate (ammonium hydrogen carbonate)

Origin Prepared by passing an excess of carbon dioxide through concentrated ammonia water.

Function Alkali; buffer; aerating agent, raising agent.

Effects There may be some alteration of the acid-base balance and pH of the urine. It is irritant to mucous membranes and is used medically as an expectorant.

A.D.I. Not specified.

Typical products Many of those permitted to contain sodium carbonate (500) and —
Low sodium salt
  substitute

504 Magnesium carbonate (magnesite)

Origin Magnesite occurs naturally in serpentine deposits in Greece and

India and replacing dolomite and limestone in Austria, Manchuria, Washington and Quebec. It may be prepared by mixing boiling concentrated solutions of magnesium sulphate and sodium carbonate. The 'heavy' variety is a granular powder; the 'light' variety is a very light fine powder.

Function Alkali; anti-caking agent; acidity regulator; anti-bleaching agent.

Effects Magnesium carbonate is insoluble in water but soluble in dilute acids, and is used pharmaceutically as an antacid and laxative. In the small amounts in which it is used in food it is unlikely to affect the pH balance of the stomach, or produce diarrhoea.

A.D.I. Not limited.

Typical products Many of those permitted to contain sodium carbonate (500) and —
Low sodium salt
  substitute
Table salt

507 Hydrochloric acid

Origin Produced industrially by the interaction of sodium chloride and sulphuric acid. It is one of the chemicals produced in the stomach to assist the digestive process.

Function Acid; used in the malting process in beer-making to reduce excess losses of carbohydrate from the germinating barley rootlets, and at the brewery it may be added to the malt slurry to compensate for variations in the water supply to arrive at a beer of consistent quality.

Effects Although highly corrosive and poisonous in its natural state, used as a

processing aid this acid is not present in foods in amounts capable of causing harm.

A.D.I. Not limited.

Typical products
Cottage cheese
Cream cheese

508 Potassium chloride

Origin Occurs naturally as a saline residue associated with rock salt, and around volcanic vents.

Function Gelling agent; salt substitute; dietary supplement; may be added to the malt slurry at the brewery to compensate for variations in the water supply in order to arrive at a beer of consistent quality.

Effects No problems in food use. It can, in large doses, cause intestinal ulceration, sometimes with haemorrhage perforation. Gastric ulceration may occur with sustained release tablets. Unpleasant taste in solution can cause nausea and vomiting. Potassium salts may have a diuretic effect.

A.D.I. Not limited.

Typical products
Reduced sodium foods such as
  reduced sodium bread
Low sodium salt
  substitute

509 Calcium chloride

Origin Obtained as a by-product of the Solvay process and is also a product from natural salt brines.

Function   Sequestrant; firming agent. In brewing may be added to the malt slurry to compensate for variations in the water supply in order to arrive at a beer of consistent quality.

Effects   No adverse effects are known.

A.D.I.   Not limited.

Typical products
Cheese
Cottage cheese
Low sodium
   substitute
Pickles
Canned tomatoes
Seltzer water
Whey cheese

510   Ammonium chloride

Origin   Prepared synthetically.

Function   Yeast food, especially in the beer stages of the fermentation of the wort in brewing; flavour.

Effects   Ammonium chloride is readily absorbed by the food canal and may decrease the acidity of the urine. It should be avoided by people with imperfect liver or kidney functions.

A.D.I.   Not limited.

Typical products
Flour products
   prepared with
   yeast other than bread
Flour for
   breadmaking
Low sodium salt
   substitute

511   Magnesium chloride (magnesium chloride, hexahydrate)

Origin   Magnesium chloride is made from magnesium ammonium chloride hexahydrate in the presence of hydrochloric acid.

Function   Firming agent, colour retention agent, nutrient.

Effects   No adverse affects are known. Magnesium is an essential nutrient, maintaining the health of muscle and heart tissues and preventing painful periods. Magnesium chloride is sometimes used therapeutically to treat those suffering from magnesium deficiency, although more usually magnesium sulphate is given.

A.D.I.   Not limited.

Typical products
Infant formula (nutrient)
Salt substitutes

E513   Sulphuric acid

Origin   Prepared commercially by the 'contact' or 'chamber' process.

Function   Acid; used in the malting process in beer-making to reduce excess losses of carbohydrate from the germinated barley rootlets, and at the brewery sulphuric acid may be added to the malt slurry to compensate for variations in the water supply to arrive at a beer of consistent quality.

Effects   Used as a processing aid, although highly corrosive in its natural state, this acid is present in foods in such minute amounts that it is incapable of causing harm.

A.D.I.   No available information.

Typical products   Not permitted in Australia.

514   Sodium sulphate

Origin   Occurs naturally as thenardite and mirabilite. The USSR, Canada and the USA are the chief producers.

Function   Diluent; in brewing it may be added to the malt slurry to compensate for variations in the water supply to arrive at a beer of consistent quality.

Effects   Although the healthy body can adapt to a wide range of sodium intake daily, excessive sodium can be dangerous because it is closely linked to the body's water balance. Those at greatest risk are small babies and people suffering with kidney and heart complaints. It is an effective purgative.

A.D.I.   No available information.

Typical products   Permitted in Australia only as a diluent for colour powders.

515   Potassium sulphate

Origin   Occurs in nature as a triple sulphate of potassium, magnesium and calcium, particularly at Stassfurt in Germany.

Function   Salt substitute for dietetic use.

Effects   No adverse effects are known.

A.D.I.   Not specified.

Typical products
Low sodium salt substitute

516   Calcium sulphate

Origin   A naturally occurring mineral; commercial sources are primarily the USA and France, followed by Spain, Great Britain and Canada.

Function   Firming agent; sequestrant; nutrient; yeast food; inert excipient; may be added to the malt slurry at the brewery to compensate for variations in the water supply in order to arrive at a beer of consistent quality.

Effects   None known.

A.D.I.   Not limited.

Typical products
Acid phosphate
    powder
Baking powder
Canned tomatoes
Flour for
    breadmaking
Jelly mix
Flour products
    prepared with
    yeast other than
    bread

518   Magnesium sulphate (Epsom salts, epsomite)

Origin   Occurs in solution in sea- and mineral-waters and is deposited from the waters of saline lakes and as crusts in limestone caves.

Function   Dietary supplement; firming agent.

Effects   An effective laxative, magnesium is not absorbed to any large extent by the body so that toxicity is not a problem except to people whose kidneys are functioning imperfectly.

A.D.I. No available information.

Typical products
Infant formula (mineral nutrient)

519 Cupric sulphate (copper sulphate)

Origin Copper sulphate occurs in nature as the minerals chalcanthite and hydrocyanite, but is prepared industrially on a large scale by spraying hot dilute sulphuric acid on to scrap copper in a lead-lined tower. The copper sulphate salt is crystallised out when an adequate concentration has been achieved.

Function Antimicrobial preservative; colour fixative; mineral nutrient. It is also used in the production of azo dyes (see glossary).

Effects Copper is an essential nutrient, required for efficient functioning of many enzymic reactions, for connective tissue formation and for protecting body cells from oxidation, for the formation of red blood cells and absorption of iron from food, for healthy bones and white blood cells and consequent resistance to infection.

A normal diet contains 2–5 mg of copper, derived mainly from meat, offal, cereals and vegetables. Copper deficiency is rare except in premature babies or people with Menke's (kinky hair) syndrome, when copper sulphate may be used as a supplement. Large quantities of copper sulphate (more than would be the case from food) irritate the mucous membranes of the mouth, throat and stomach, followed by nausea, vomiting, a metallic taste, bloody diarrhoea, colic, hypotension and coma.

A.D.I. No A.D.I. allocated.

Typical products
Infant formula (mineral nutrient)

E524 Sodium hydroxide

Origin Manufactured by electrolysis from brine, or precipitated from sodium carbonate and lime solution (Gossage's method).

Function Base especially to neutralize free fatty acids in the manufacture of food oils, colour solvent; authorised in the manufacture of caramel; oxidising agent, especially of black olives; used in the malting process of beer-making to remove 'testinic acid' from barley in the steep liquor and, at the brewery, sodium hydroxide may be added to the malt slurry, to compensate for variations in the water supply in order to arrive at a beer of consistent quality.

Effects Used as a processing aid it is not used in amounts which would be caustic.

A.D.I. Not limited.

Typical products Not permitted in Australia.

E525 Potassium hydroxide

Origin Prepared industrially by electrolysis of potassium chloride.

Function Base; oxidising agent, especially of black olives.

Effects   Used as a processing aid, it is not used in amounts which would be caustic.

A.D.I.   Not limited.

Typical products   Not permitted in Australia.

526   Calcium hydroxide

Origin   Prepared by the hydration of lime.

Function   Firming agent; neutralising agent; nutrient; used in the malting process of beer-making to remove 'testinic acid' from barley in the steep liquor and, at the brewery, calcium hydroxide may be added to the malt slurry to compensate for variations in the water supply to arrive at a beer of consistent quality.

Effects   Used as a processing aid it is not used in amounts that would be caustic.

A.D.I.   Not limited.

Typical products
Infant formula (mineral nutrient)

E527   Ammonium hydroxide

Origin   Prepared from ammonia gas.

Function   Food colouring diluent and solvent; alkali.

Effects   Used as a processing aid, it is highly unlikely to be present in amounts that would be caustic.

A.D.I.   Not limited.

Typical products   Not permitted in Australia.

E528   Magnesium hydroxide

Origin   Occurs in nature as the mineral periclase. It is prepared commercially from magnesite ores.

Function   Alkali.

Effects   Used as a processing aid, it is not used in amounts that would be caustic.

A.D.I.   Not limited.

Typical products   Not permitted in Australia.

529   Calcium oxide

Origin   Prepared from limestone.

Function   Alkali; nutrient.

Effects   Used as a processing aid, it is not used in amounts that would be caustic.

A.D.I.   Not limited.

Typical products   Many of those permitted to contain sodium carbonate (500).

E530   Magnesium oxide

Origin   A naturally occurring mineral, particularly in rocks which have undergone change brought about by pressure and heat, and it is prepared commercially from magnesite ores. It then has to be specially prepared to be in the right form to absorb water and function as an anti-caking agent.

Function   Anti-caking agent; alkali.

Effects   None known.

A.D.I. Not limited.

Typical products Not permitted in Australia.

E535 Sodium ferrocyanide (sodium hexacyanoferrate II)

Origin Manufactured synthetically.

Function Anti-caking agent; crystal modifier.

Effects There is a very strong chemical bonding between the iron and cyanide groups which prevents ferrocyanides from being toxic (see 536).

A.D.I. 0–0.025 mg/kg body weight.

Typical products Not permitted in Australia.

536 Potassium ferrocyanide (potassium hexacyanoferrate II)

Origin Prepared on a commercial scale as a by-product in the purification of coal gas.

Function Anti-caking agent, especially in table salt. Used to remove excessive metals, especially iron and copper in white and rosé wine production. First a controlled amount of potassium ferrocyanide and then zinc sulphate heptahydrate are added which brings down a blue precipitate of the metals. The process is called 'blue finings'.

Effects Because the iron and cyanide groups are strongly bonded there is a very low level of toxicity. Nevertheless, ferrocyanides, like nitrates and nitrites (249–252), are 'metahaemoglobinants'

which means they are capable of converting the haemoglobin in the red blood corpuscles from the ferrous to the ferric states. In the ferric state the haemoglobin is incapable of transporting oxygen.

A.D.I. 0–0.025 mg/kg body weight (calculated as sodium ferrocyanide).

Typical products
Salt (other than table salt)
Wine

E540 Dicalcium diphosphate (calcium hydrogen phosphate)

Origin Occurs in nature as the mineral monetite, also prepared synthetically.

Function Neutralising agent, dietary supplement; buffering agent; yeast food.

Effects Little dicalcium diphosphate is absorbed by the intestines, and there is little danger of any adverse reaction.

M.T.D.I. 70mg/kg body weight (expressed as phosphorus from all sources). See phosphoric acid (338).

Typical products Not permitted in Australia.

541 Sodium aluminium phosphate, acidic

Origin Prepared from high-purity phosphoric acid.

Function Aerator, acidulant (raising agent) in flour confectionery.

Effects Sodium aluminium phosphate has been considered by the toxicological committees on the basis of its aluminium, rather than its phosphates component. Aluminium poses a problem because of the evidence that an accumulation of it in the cells of the nervous system could be potentially toxic, and responsible for Parkinson-type diseases and senile dementia. However, a high aluminium content may have adverse effects on the metabolism of phosphorus, calcium or fluoride and may induce or intensify skeletal abnormalities.

A.D.I. 0–0.6 mg/kg body weight (temporary, group A.D.I. for aluminium salts, expressed as aluminium).

Typical products
Acid phosphate powder, phosphate aerator.

E541 Sodium aluminium phosphate, basic

Origin Prepared from high-purity phosphoric acid.

Function Emulsifying salt in processed cheese manufacture in America.

Effects Sodium aluminium phosphate has been considered by the toxicological committees on the basis of its aluminium rather than its phosphate component. Aluminium poses a problem because of the evidence that an accumulation of it in the cells of the nervous system could be potentially toxic, and responsible for Parkinson-type diseases and senile dementia.

Sodium aluminium phosphate fed to rats in doses of up to 30 000 ppm caused no toxic effects nor significant aluminium deposits in the skeleton.

A.D.I. 0–0.6 mg/kg body weight (temporary, group A.D.I. allocated to aluminium salts, expressed as aluminium).

Typical products Not permitted in Australia.

542 Bone phosphate (edible bone phosphate)

Origin The degreased steam-extract from animal bones. It is calcium phosphate in an impure state, although the impurities do not affect its activity, being of biological origin.

Function Anti-caking agent; mineral supplement; filler in tablet making.

Effects None known.

M.T.D.I. 70mg/kg body weight (expressed as phosphorus from all sources). See phosphoric acid (338)

Typical products
Dried milk for drink machines.

E544 Calcium polyphosphates

Origin Calcium salts of polyphosphoric acids. Manufactured by the heat condensation of calcium orthophosphate.

Function Emulsifying salts — have an action on milk proteins which prevents processed cheeses from separating out; mineral supplements; calcium source in instant milk-based desserts; firming agents.

Effects Calcium and phosphorus are both essential nutrients present in bones and teeth, and as long as they are used in a constant ratio there should be no problem.

M.T.D.I. 70mg/kg body weight (expressed as phosphorus from all sources). See phosphoric acid (338).

Typical products Not permitted in Australia.

E545 Ammonium polyphosphates

Origin Ammonium salts of polyphosphoric acids.

Function Emulsifiers; emulsifying salts; sequestrants; yeast foods; stabilisers.

Effects Phosphorus as phosphate is an essential nutrient present in bones, teeth, blood and cells. It is necessary for fat and protein assimilation and B vitamin absorption. The body can use it most efficiently if it is present in a constant ratio with calcium.

In view of the concern expressed that high intakes of phosphates and polyphosphates may be upsetting this balance, JECFA, in 1982, recommended that further studies should be carried out on the implications of high dietary intakes of phosphorus.

M.T.D.I. 70mg/kg body weight (expressed as phosphorus from all sources). See phosphoric acid (338).

Typical products Not permitted in Australia.

551 Silicon dioxide (silica)

Origin Silicon dioxide is the commonest rock-forming mineral and sand is composed mainly of small grains of quartz or flint, both of which are silicon dioxide. For use in foods, quartz is further processed to produce a microcellular powder, a granular gel form and a colloidal form by further hydrolysis.

Function Suspending and anti-caking agent; thickener and stabiliser in suspensions and emulsions, including wine. Used to assist isinglass finings in clearing of beer by associating with the protein and causing it to flocculate and settle, and as a filtration aid when suspended yeast is filtered from 'green' beer.

Effects No adverse effects are known in food use because it is so inert.

A.D.I. Not specified.

Typical products & maximum permitted levels

Artificial sweetener	—
Beverage whitener	3 g/kg
Confectionery —	
hard tablet,	
hard pellet,	
hard roll type	5 g/kg
Drink machine dried milk	4 g/kg
Low sodium salt substitute	10 g/kg
Table salt	20 g/kg

552 Calcium silicate

Origin A naturally occurring mineral in impure limestones known as wollastonite. Many different forms of calcium silicate are known with various percentages of water or crystallisation. Commercial calcium silicate (*Micro-Cel Sil-Ca* and *Silene*) is prepared from lime and diatomaceous earth under carefully controlled conditions.

To be an effective anti-caking agent, a hydrated silicate has to be precipitated and subsequently dried to ensure an 'active' material that will attract moisture.

Function Anti-caking agent; in pharmacology as an antacid; glazing, polishing and release agent (sweets); dusting agent (chewing gum); coating agent (rice); suspending agent.

Effects No adverse effects are known. It is used pharmaceutically as an antacid.

A.D.I. Not specified.

Typical products
Table salt
Low sodium salt substitute.

E553(a) Magnesium silicate (synthetic) and magnesium trisilicate

Origin Magnesium silicate is a synthetic compound of magnesium oxide and silicon dioxide, or can be prepared from sodium silicate and magnesium sulphate. Magnesium trisilicate occurs in nature as the minerals meerschaum, parasepiolite and sepiolite.

To be an effective anti-caking agent, a hydrated silicate is precipitated and subsequently dried to ensure an 'active' material that will attract moisture.

Function Anti-caking agent and tablet excipient and as an antacid in pharmacology; glazing, polishing and release agent (sweets); dusting agent (chewing gum); coating agent (rice).

Effects Magnesium trisilicate is non-toxic even in very large doses. It has

absorbent and antacid properties and the action continues slowly for some time.

A.D.I. Not specified.

Typical products Not permitted in Australia.

553(b) Talc (French chalk)

Origin A naturally occurring mineral, worked in the USA, France, Italy, Canada, etc.

Function Release agent; anti-caking agent; chewing gum component; filtering aid and dusting powder.

Effects There have been reports of links between talc and stomach cancer.

A.D.I. Not specified.

Typical products & maximum permitted levels
Chocolate	2 g/kg
Confectionery	2 g/kg
Polished rice	5 g/kg

554 Sodium aluminosilicate (aluminium sodium silicate)

Origin Naturally occurring mineral, known as analcite and natrolite and also prepared synthetically by processes starting with quartz and gibbsite.

Function Anti-caking agent.

Effects Aluminium salts can be absorbed from the intestines and concentrated in various human tissues, including bone, the parathyroid and the brain. Aluminium has been shown to be neurotoxic (damaging nerves) in rabbits and cats, and high concentrations have been detected in the brain tissue of patients with Alzheimer's disease (senile dementia). Various reports have suggested that high aluminium intakes may be harmful to some patients with bone disease or kidney impairment.

A.D.I.   Not specified.

Typical products & maximum permitted levels

Beverage whitener	3 g/kg
Drink machine dried milk	4 g/kg
Table salt	20 g/kg

556   Calcium aluminium silicate (aluminium calcium silicate)

Origin   Naturally occurring mineral, known as scolecite and heulandite.

Function   Anti-caking agent.

Effects   Aluminium salts can be absorbed from the intestines and concentrated in various human tissues, including bone, the parathyroid and the brain. Aluminium has been shown to be neurotoxic (damaging nerves) in rabbits and cats, and high concentrations have been detected in the brain tissue of patients with Alzheimer's disease (senile dementia). Various reports have suggested that high aluminium intakes may be harmful to some patients with bone disease or kidney impairment.

A.D.I.   Not specified.

Typical products
Salt

558   Bentonite

Origin   A particular clay deposit occurring in thin beds in the western USA, believed to result from the decomposition of volcanic ash.

Function   Anti-caking agent; clarifying agent, especially of wine; filtration aid when suspended yeast is filtered from 'green' beer; suspending and emulsifying agent.

Effects   No adverse effects are known.

A.D.I.   —

Typical products
Wine

559   Kaolin (heavy) and kaolin (light)

Origin   Occurs in nature as an altered mineral in granite, particularly in Cornwall (UK), the USA, France, China and Malaysia. A puried clay consisting mainly of alumina, silica and water.

Function   Anti-caking agent; clarifying agent, especially of wine.

Effects   No adverse effects are known.

A.D.I.   Not specified.

Typical products
Wine

570   Stearic acid

Origin   Naturally occurring fatty acid found in all animal fats and vegetable oils. Prepared synthetically for commercial use.

Function   Anti-caking agent.

Effects No adverse effects are known.

A.D.I. —

Typical products
Artificial sweeteners
Confectionery — hard tablet,
   hard pellet or hard roll type

572   Magnesium stearate

Origin Prepared synthetically from commercial stearic acid.

Function Anti-caking agent; emulsifier; release agent.

Effects No adverse effects are known from the consumption of this additive, but accidental inhalation of the powder can be harmful.

A.D.I. Not limited.

Typical products
Artificial sweeteners
Confectionery — hard tablet,
   hard pellet or hard roll type.

575   Glucono delta-lactone (D-glucono-1,5-lactone)

Origin Prepared by oxidation of glucose.

Function Acid; sequestrant. In the dairy industry prevents milkstone formation (deposits of magnesium and calcium phosphates etc., when milk is heated to a high temperature); in breweries prevents beerstone formation.

Effects No adverse effects are known.

A.D.I. Not specified.

Typical products
Artificial sweetener base
Cottage cheese
Cream cheese, Neufchatel cheese
Cheese
Flour products other than bread
Gluten-free food
Manufactured meat

E576   Sodium gluconate

Origin Prepared synthetically; the sodium salt of gluconic acid.

Function Sequestrant; dietary supplement.

Effects No adverse effects are known.

A.D.I. 0–50 mg/kg body weight (calculated as gluconic acid from all sources).

Typical products Not permitted in Australia.

577   Potassium gluconate

Origin Prepared synthetically; the potassium salt of gluconic acid.

Function Sequestrant; nutrient.

Effects No adverse effects are known.

A.D.I. 0–50 mg/kg body weight (calculated as gluconic acid from all sources).

Typical products —

578   Calcium gluconate

Origin Prepared synthetically; calcium salt prepared from gluconic acid.

Function Buffer; firming agent; sequestrant; nutrient.

Effects No adverse effects are known.

A.D.I. 0–50 mg/kg body weight (calculated as gluconic acid from all sources).

Typical products
Infant formula (mineral nutrient)

579 Ferrous gluconate (iron gluconate)

Origin Prepared from barium gluconate and ferrous sulphate. It has a smell resembling caramel and a taste which is salty at first and then tastes slightly of iron.

Function Ferrous gluconate may be used as a yellowish-grey food colour, or as a flavouring agent. It is used in the UK in table olives to stabilise the colour of the olives darkened by oxidation. Nutrient. It is also used to treat iron-deficiency anaemia.

Effects Iron given in therapeutic doses causes problems in about 20 per cent of the population who may suffer from gastrointestinal discomfort, diarrhoea and vomiting. Others suffer constipation. Supplementation with iron may compete with the body's absorption of other mineral nutrients, such as zinc or copper.

A.D.I. Not specified.

Typical products
Infant formula (mineral nutrient)
Formula dietary food,
cereal based foods for infants and young children.

620 L-Glutamic acid

Origin A naturally occurring amino acid of great importance in the nitrogen metabolism of plants and animals, but prepared commercially by the fermentation of a carbohydrate solution by a bacterium, e.g. *Micrococcus glutamicus.* Several other methods exist.

Function Dietary supplement; flavour enhancer; salt substitute.

Effects In the same way as monosodium glutamate (621) was thought to cause 'Chinese restaurant syndrome', it was supposed that glutamic acid might cause similar problems and it is still considered inadvisable for young children.

A.D.I. 0–120 mg/kg body weight (included in the group A.D.I. for L-glutamic acid and its ammonium, calcium, sodium, magnesium and potassium salts, as glutamic acid, not applicable to infants under 12 weeks).

Typical products
Low sodium salt substitute

621 Monosodium glutamate (sodium hydrogen L-glutamate; Aji-no-moto; MSG)

Origin *mono*Sodium glutamate is the sodium salt of glutamic acid (620). It is an amino acid (several amino acids together make up a protein). The various forms of glutamic acid are referred to as 'glutamates'. Glutamate is a common substance widely found in plant and animal tissues. It occurs especially in foods such as meat, fish, poultry and milk. Human breast milk contains about 22 mg of glutamate per 100 ml milk, which is ten times as much as in cow's milk.

Early Japanese cooks learnt from experience that foods flavoured with stock made from a seaweed called *Laminaria japonica* tasted delicious. The active substance was isolated in 1908 by a professor at Tokyo University, Kikunae Ikeda, and found to be glutamic acid. He differentiated it from the other four basic tastes of sweet, sour, salty and bitter, and called it *'umami'*, roughly translated as 'deliciousness'.

Today 90 per cent is manufactured

by fermentation using molasses from cane or beet sugar, and 10 per cent in South-East Asia from sago and tapioca starch, or from plant proteins rich in glutamic acid such as wheat protein and sugar beet.

Function Interesting sensory work done in Japan shows that the *umami* taste is additional to the four basic tastes. Stocks made from fish or meat come closest to the *umami* taste, while stocks made from vegetables fall much closer within the sweet, sour, bitter or salty areas. When the two are combined there is a 'synergistic effect', the one enormously enhancing the other to a position close to the *umami* one. The interplay of the protein stock with the glutamic acid of the vegetables produces an increase in flavour up to eight times the properties of the ingredients.

MSG is widely used as a flavour enhancer to increase the palatability of proteinaceous foods. It may be a useful ingredient for those needing to reduce their sodium intake, since the larger the amount of monosodium glutamate used, the less salt is required, because sodium is about 13 per cent of MSG by weight but 40 per cent of table salt. Some Chinese take away meals contain MSG in quantities of 5–10 g.

Effects The 'Umami Information Centre' is confident that MSG is safe for human intake. It says that research on humans as well as laboratory animals, including mice, rats, hamsters, rabbits, dogs and monkeys, overwhelmingly indicates that MSG taken in reasonable amounts produces no cause for concern. In infant mice, the most susceptible species known, dietary feeding of about 10,000 times the equivalent daily intake level of man produced no harmful effects.

Glutamate does not cross the placenta to reach the developing foetus but once consumed by infants from breast milk it is readily metabolised. The link between monosodium glutamate and the 'Chinese Restaurant Syndrome' first decribed in 1968 by Dr Robert Ho Man Kwok now seems to be rather tenuous. The symptoms of the syndrome occur after eating meals and consist of a tightening of the jaw muscles, numbness of the neck, chest and hands, thirst and nausea, palpitations, dizziness, fainting, pounding, vice-like headache, and a cold sweat around the face and armpits. Yet, when people who said they suffered from CRS were given drinks with and without MSG they experienced symptoms each time. Orange juice, tomato juice and cold coffee were just as effective as MSG in inducing the reactions, and it is suggested that these people may have sensitive nerve endings in the gullet which transmit the stimulus to the arms and chest. Although uncomfortable, the symptoms are neither long-lasting nor serious.

Despite these safety assurances, experiments on young mice, rats, rabbits, guinea pigs, hamsters and rhesus monkeys showed that MSG caused damage to brain cells. This was true in both infant and adult animals, but adults were only susceptible in much higher doses. Another experiment showed that, whereas exposure to MSG caused mature but not young brain cells to die, the action was dependent on a lack of calcium.

It looks as though a consumption of not more than 2 g per day will cause no problems in all but the most sensitive people.

A.D.I. 0–120 mg/kg body weight (included in group A.D.I.). See L-glutamic acid (620).

Typical products Foods where flavourings or condiments are permitted such as —
Packet soup and quick soups
Flavoured noodles
Sauces
Note — In Australia MSG is not permitted to be used in foods manufactured specifically for infants and young children.

622 Monopotassium glutamate (potassium hydrogen L-glutamate)

Origin Prepared synthetically.

Function Flavour enhancer; salt substitute.

Effects Sometimes nausea, vomiting, diarrhoea and abdominal cramps may occur, although there is usually little toxicity of potassium salts when taken by mouth in healthy individuals, as potassium is rapidly excreted in the urine. Potassium could be harmful for those with impaired kidneys.

A.D.I. 0–120 mg/kg body weight (included in group A.D.I.). See L-glutamic acid (620).

Typical products
Low sodium salt substitute.

623 Calcium dihydrogen di-L-glutamate (calcium glutamate)

Origin Prepared synthetically.

Function Flavour enhancer; salt substitute.

Effects None known.

A.D.I. 0–120 mg/kg body weight (included in group A.D.I.). See L-glutamic acid.

Typical products Low sodium salt substitute.

624 Monoammonium L-glutamate

Origin Prepared synthetically.

Function Flavour enhancer; salt substitute.

Effects None known.

A.D.I. 0–120 mg/kg body weight (included in group A.D.I.). See L-glutamic acid (620).

Typical products
Low sodium salt substitute.

625 Magnesium di-L-glutamate

Origin Prepared synthetically.

Function Flavour enhancer; salt substitute.

Effects None known.

A.D.I. 0–120 mg/kg body weight (included in group A.D.I.). See L-glutamic acid (620).

Typical products
Low sodium salt substitute.

627 Disodium guanylate (guanosine 5'-(disodium phosphate))

Origin The sodium salt of 5' guanylic acid, a widely-occurring nucleotide (isolated from sardines and yeast extract), prepared synthetically for commercial use.

Function Flavour enhancer.

Effects No adverse effects are known, but prohibited in or on foods intended for infants or young children. People suffering from conditions such as gout, which require the avoidance of purines, are recommended to avoid this susbstance.

A.D.I. Not specified.

Typical products Foods where flavourings permitted except in infants' foods.

631 Disodium inosinate (inosine 5'-(disodium phosphate))

Origin The disodium salt of inosinic acid (muscle inosinic acid) which can be prepared from meat extract and dried sardines. It was originally isolated from Japanese bonito (a tuna-like fish), small dried flakes of which were often added to improve the flavour of soups.

Function Flavour enhancer.

Effects No adverse effects are known, but prohibited in or on foods specially made for infants and young children. People suffering from conditions such as gout which require the avoidance of purines, should avoid this substance.

A.D.I. Not specified.

Typical products Foods where flavourings permitted except in infants' foods.

E635 Sodium 5'ribonucleotide

Origin A mixture of *di*sodium guanylate (627) and *di*sodium inosinate (631).

Function Flavour enhancer.

Effects No adverse effects are known, but not permitted in foods specially prepared for infants or young children. People suffering from conditions such as gout, which require the avoidance of purines, should avoid this substance.

A.D.I. Not specified.

Typical products Not permitted in Australia.

636 Maltol

Origin A naturally occurring substance found in the bark of young larch trees, pine needles, chicory wood, tars, oils and roasted malt. Also obtained chemically by alkaline hydrolysis of streptomycin salt.

Function Flavouring agent, to impart a 'freshly baked' smell and flavour to bread and cakes. Synthetic flavouring agent for coffee, fruit, maple, nut and vanilla flavours.

Effects None known.

A.D.I. 0–1 mg/kg body weight.

Typical products Artificial sweeteners.

637   Ethyl maltol

Origin   Chemically prepared from maltol.

Function   Flavouring to impart a sweet taste and flavour-enhancer.

Effects   No adverse effects are known.

A.D.I.   0–2 mg/kg body weight.

Typical products
Artificial sweeteners
Essences
Flavours
Fruit flavoured drinks
Soft drinks

900-1202 Miscellaneous Additives including Bleaching Agents, Flour Treatment Agents and Propellants

900 Dimethylpolysiloxane (dimethicone)

Origin A chemically manufactured mixture of liquid dimethylpolysiloxane and silicon gel or silicon dioxide.

Function Water repellent; anti-foaming agent.

Effects No adverse effects known.

A.D.I. 0–1.5 mg/kg body weight (this A.D.I. applies only to compounds with a relative molecular mass in the range of 200–300).

Typical products & maximum permitted levels

Confectionery	10 mg/kg
Edible fats and edible oils used for frying	10 mg/kg
Flavoured cordial, flavoured syrup, flavoured topping	10 mg/kg
Fruit juice cordial, fruit juice syrup, fruit juice topping	10 mg/kg
Imitation cordial, imitation syrup, imitation topping	10 mg/kg
Soft drinks	10 mg/kg
Soluble coffee, instant coffee	10 mg/kg
Vinegar	10 mg/kg

901 Beeswax (white) and beeswax (yellow)

Origin A naturally occurring product from the bee honeycomb. White beeswax is the bleached and purified form.

Function Glazing and polishing agent; release agent; also used in fruit and honey flavourings for beverages, ice cream, baked goods and honey.

Effects Beeswax was formerly used to treat diarrhoea and has been used as a repository for slow-release tablets. Resins in the wax occasionally cause hypersensitivity reactions.

A.D.I. No available information.

Typical products & maximum permitted levels

Confectionery	500 mg/kg in total with carnauba wax (903)
Apples (waxed)	250 mg/kg in total with carnauba wax (903) and shellac (904)

903   Carnauba wax

Origin A yellow to light-brown wax obtained from the surface of leaves of *Copernicia cerifera,* the Brazilian wax palm. The crude wax is yellow or dirty green, brittle and very hard.

Function Glazing and polishing agent for sugar confectionery. It enhances the hardness of other waxes and increases their lustre.

Effects Skin sensitivity or irritation is infrequent.

A.D.I. No available information.

Typical products & maximum permitted levels
Confectionery   500 mg/kg in total with beeswax (901)
Apples (waxed)   250 mg/kg in total with beeswax (901) and shellac (904)

904   Shellac

Origin Shellac is a substance obtained from the resin produced by the lac insect *(Laccifer lacca,* a member of the *Lacciferidae)* related to mealy bugs and scale insects belonging to the *Coccoidea.* It is a native of India. Four commercial grades are produced by different chemical processes. One method mixes shellac resin with small amounts of arsenic trisulphide (for colour) and rosin. White shellac is free of arsenic.

Function Glazing agent.

Effects No significant reports of adverse effects, although it may cause skin irritation.

A.D.I. No available information.

Typical products & maximum permitted levels
Confectionery   1 g/kg in total with permitted modifying agents
Apples (waxed)   250 mg/kg in total with beeswax (901) and carnauba wax (903)

905   Mineral oil, white (petrolatum)

Origin Distillates of petroleum.

Function Polishes, glazing agents, sealing agents; in confectionery, ingredient for chewing gum; defoaming agent in processing of sugar beet and yeast; lubricant and binder for capsules and tablets supplying small amounts of flavour, spice, condiments and vitamins. Lubricant in food-processing equipment and meat-packing plants.

Effects May inhibit absorption of digestive fats and fat-soluble vitamins, and has a mild laxative effect. There has been some suspicion that liquid paraffin may be partly responsible for bowel cancer. Excessive dosage may result in anal seepage and irritation.

A.D.I. Not specified.

Typical products & maximum permitted levels
Dried fruit (to prevent sugaring of berries and clouding of film bags)   3 g/kg
Confectionery   2 g/kg
Fabricated collagen casings for sausages and manufactured meats   50 g/kg

E907 Refined microcrystalline wax

Origin Prepared by solution of the heavy fraction of petroleum by dewaxing or de-oiling methods.

Function Chewing gum ingredient; polishing and release agent; stiffening agent and used for tablet coating.

Effects The unrefined form is a possible human carcinogen and the refined form used as a food additive may also be carcinogenic.

A.D.I. No available information.

Typical products Not permitted in Australia.

920 L-cysteine hydrochloride and L-cysteine hydrochloride monohydrate

Origin A diamer of L-cysteine, a naturally occurring amino acid, and manufactured from animal hair and chicken feathers. In China it is made from human hair.

Function Improving agent for flour, other than wholemeal. Flavour, especially chicken flavour.

Effects None known.

A.D.I. No available information.

Typical products
Flour for breadmaking.

924 Potassium bromate

Origin Prepared synthetically.

Function Flour-maturing or improving agent. It has an effect on the proteins which make up the gluten in the wheat flour. When the wheat flour is mixed with water the potassium bromate is activated and helps the proteins retain the carbon dioxide gas generated by the yeast during fermentation. The result is a softer, lighter loaf with a good eating quality.

In the UK used in the malting process in beer-making to reduce excess losses of carbohydrate from the germinated barley rootlets. An additional function of the potassium bromate is to control protein degradation within the malting barley and thus reduce the levels of nitrogen in the wort.

Effects In strong concentrations can cause nausea, vomiting, severe abdominal pain, diarrhoea and even convulsions, but, used as a processing aid, even the detectable residue left in beer would not have serious consequences.

A.D.I. 0–75 mg/kg body weight (temporary).

Typical products & maximum permitted levels
Flour products prepared with yeast other than bread	30 mg/kg
Flour for breadmaking	30 mg/kg

925 Chlorine

Origin Found in the earth's crust and in seawater, it is a greenish-yellow gas with a suffocating odour. Produced on a large scale by electrolysis.

Function Antibacterial and antifungal preservative; bleaching, ageing and oxidising agent.

Effects A powerful irritant, which is dangerous to inhale. Bleaching of flour has never been demonstrated to be 100 per cent safe. The process takes its toll of flour nutrients and destroys much of the vitamin E content. The chlorine used in drinking water often contains carcinogenic carbon tetrachloride, a contaminant formed during the production process. Chlorination has also been found to sometimes form undesirable carbon 'ring' compounds in water, such as toluene, xylene and styrene, the suspected carcinogen observed in drinking-water treatment works in the mid-West of the USA.

Use in flour 2.5 g/kg flour acceptable.

Typical products
Flour (only permitted use in food in Australia)

926 Chlorine dioxide

Origin Prepared synthetically by one of a number of methods: from chlorine and sodium chlorite; from potassium chlorate and sulphuric acid; or by passing nitrogen dioxide through a column of sodium chlorate.

Function Bleaching and improving agent for flour; bleaching agent for fats and oils, beeswax, etc.; purification of water; taste and odour control of water; oxidising agent; bactericide and antiseptic.

Effects The gas is highly irritating to the mucous membranes of the respiratory tract but, because it is a processing aid, there are only harmless tiny residues remaining in the flour. Bleaching of flour has never been demonstrated to be 100 per cent safe. It takes its toll of flour nutrients and destroys much of the vitamin E.

A.D.I. 0–30 mg/kg body weight (conditional).

Typical products
Flour (only permitted use in food in Australia).

E927 Azodicarbonamide (azoformamide)

Origin Prepared synthetically.

Function Flour-improving or -maturing agent to improve the tolerance of bread dough under a wide range of fermentation conditions.

Effects No adverse effects are known.

A.D.I. 0–45 ppm

Typical products Not permitted in Australia.

928 Benzoyl peroxide (dibenzoyl peroxide)

Origin Benzoyl peroxide is prepared by an interaction between benzoyl chloride and cooled sodium peroxide.

Function Bleaching agent for flours. Unlike some other bleaching agents, it does not have the dual function of 'improving' flours. It has some antimicrobial activity.

Effects During the process of flour bleaching, most of the benzoyl peroxide is converted to benzoic acid (210), so that little benzoyl peroxide remains as a residue in the flour, and still less in the baked product.

A.D.I. 0–40 mg/kg body weight.

Typical products
Flour

931 Nitrogen

Origin Nitrogen constitutes nearly 80
per cent of the earth's atmosphere and
is an essential constituent of all living
organisms. It is prepared industrially
by the fractional distillation of liquid
air, by the removal of oxygen by
combustion or by the reduction of
ammonia.

Function Its main use is in food
freezing processes, for gas-packed
foods and for food dressings. In air-
tight packaging, nitrogen prevents
deterioration of food by oxidation.

Effects Nitrogen is an inert gas which
is unlikely to react with food
components. In 1980 JECFA agreed
that as long as nitrogen met the
Committee's food grade specification,
there would be no toxicological hazard
in its use as a food additive. There is no
reason to doubt this statement.

A.D.I. Not specified.

Typical products
Foods packed in pressurised
containers.

932 Nitrous oxide (Laughing gas)

Origin Present in the earth's
atmosphere, nitrous oxide contributes
0.00005 per cent by volume. It is
prepared industrially by the thermal
decomposition of ammonium nitrate.

Function Whipping agent for whipped
cream; propellant in aerosol cans for
cream and frothy toppings in use for
almost 30 years.

Effects Nitrous oxide is very stable
and chemically inert at room
temperature. References to its effects
on individuals are limited to its
inhalation in dental or analgesic use
when it is administered with oxygen,
when doubts have been expressed
about its safety. The only known
danger in food use is to food workers,
who should handle it carefully. There
is no evidence that the low levels in
use as a food additive cause any
problems.

A.D.I. No A.D.I. allocated.

Typical products
Creams and whipped creams in
    aerosol cans
Desserts
Sauces
Toppings

965 Hydrogenated glucose syrup

Origin Hydrogenated glucose syrup
covers a range of products from syrups
to crystals, but they all originate from
starch from various sources,
decomposed with digestive enzymes
and water. The starch molecules start
off in long chains, but on being broken
down, glucose and oligosaccharides,
followed by maltitol and sorbitol (420)
are formed. Maltitol constitutes 50–90
per cent of the preparations for which
specifications are available.

Function Some manufacturers use
glucose syrup as a substitute for
refined sugar (sucrose), although it is

not quite as sweet, or because it forms smaller crystals on freezing.

Effects Hydrogenated glucose syrup produces a laxative effect at high concentrations in the same way as do sorbitol (420), mannitol (421), glycerin (422) and xylitol (967). Manufacturers should take this into account when considering levels of usage of one of these substances alone or in combination with one of the others.

Most hydrogenated glucose syrups are broken down in the gastro-intestinal tract to glucose and sorbitol, with only tiny amounts of maltitol remaining unchanged to be absorbed into the bloodstream. Intestinal bacteria attack any residual maltitol. JECFA removed the A.D.I. in 1986 because hydrogenated glucose syrups are metabolised to natural body constituents and are therefore harmless.

A.D.I. Not specified

Typical products
Carbohydrate modified —
    confectionery
    chocolate
    jam
    ice cream
Dried fruits
Low joule foods

967   Xylitol

Origin Xylitol is a naturally occurring 5-carbon polyalcohol found in a few fruits (raspberries and plums) and vegetables (lettuce and endives) and in the human body as the metabolite of some carbohydrates. It has about the same sweetness as sugar. Formerly obtained from birchwood, xylitol is now produced commercially as a waste product from the pulp industry.

Function Sweetener, especially in diabetic foods for insulin-dependent diabetics, as it is an insulin-independent carbohydrate source; humectant; useful because it adds extra body to calorie-reduced and carbohydrate-modified foods, is less likely to cause cooked foods to turn brown and, unlike sugar, which browns, is stable at high temperatures. It is much more expensive than refined sugar.

Effects Reported to have diuretic effects on and produce kidney stones in some rats, but JECFA in 1983 decided these reports could not be applied to human beings and could have been caused by physiological disturbances. In human subjects consumption of xylitol has been shown not to be associated with kidney stone formation.

Xylitol does not cause tooth decay and an experiment in Canada with 433 eight-year old children of low socio-economic class showed xylitol actually arrested the rate of tooth decay. The children were given 15 per cent or 65 per cent xylitol chewing gum three times a day at school and those who chewed the gum had a smaller proportion of decayed, missing and filled teeth than the group which did not. 65 per cent xylitol chewing gum was more effective than 15 per cent. There was no difference between children who chewed gum and the control group when asked about stomach pain.

Xylitol can be used as the sole carbohydrate source to maintain growth and normal physiological functions. An experiment in Texas showed that daily doses of xylitol, ranging from 30 g in 3 doses to 100 g in two doses along with a regulated diet could be fairly well tolerated by healthy people, although all suffered diarrhoea at the beginning. A maximum dose of 30 g per day was recommended. In some people xylitol causes an imbalance of tissue metabolites and uric acid production, but this is not thought to be significant.

A.D.I. Not specified. However, JECFA in 1983 recommended that controls be exercised to limit the consumption of polyols from all sources to levels below those at which they induce diarrhoea.

Typical products
Carbohydrate modifed —
  ice cream
  chocolate
  confectionery
  jam
Note: In Australia carbohydrate modified foods must carry in the label the following advice: 'Excess Consumption may have a Laxative Effect.'

1200   Polydextrose

Origin   Developed by Pfizer Inc in the 1970s, polydextrose was approved for use in foods by the US Food and Drug Administration in 1981 and by the National Health and Medical Research Council in Australia in 1985. It is made from glucose, sorbitol and citric acid. Three forms exist — polydextrose A, the acid form, polydextrose N, which is neutralised with potassium hydroxide and polydextrose K, neutralised with potassium bicarbonate.

Contributing only 4 kJ/gram it has one-quarter of the energy value of sugar and only one-tenth of that of fats.

Function   Reduced-calorie bulking agent that can replace all or part of the sugar and some of the starch and fats and consequently reduce the energy value by up to 50 per cent. It is also used to adjust the texture, thickness and moisture content of food products, where substituting artificial sweeteners has thinned out the food and drink.

Polydextrose can improve the flavour of many foods by removing excessive sweetness or it can be used in foods to reduce their sweetness and will not promote tooth decay.

Effects   Polydextrose, like dietary fibre, is only partially digested and provides little energy. It does not interfere with the uptake of vitamins, minerals or amino acid, nor promote tooth decay, or cause plaque formation on teeth.

At very high doses, polydextrose A and N produce diarrhoea in human subjects. The neutralised form produces the greatest laxative effect, probably because the potassium content exacerbates the problem. Similar results pertained in experiments with rats, dogs and monkeys. Rats fed up to 20 per cent polydextrose A showed no effects with regard to birth defects nor on infant growth.

It does not significantly affect blood glucose nor insulin levels and can be used safely by diabetics.

A.D.I.   0–70 mg/kg body weight.

Typical products
Low joule foods
Carbohydrate modified foods —
  chocolate
  confectionery
  jams
  ice cream

Note: In Australia, carbohydrate modified foods are required to include in their labels the following advice: 'Excess Consumption may have a Laxative Effect.'

1201 Polyvinylpyrrolidone (povidone)

Origin It is a yellow solid resembling albumin in appearance. Produced commercially by a complex method involving acetylene, formaldehyde, hydrogen and ammonia.

Function Stabiliser; suspending and bodying agent; dispersing agent. Binder, diluent and/or coating agent for tablets and carrier for drugs.

Effects Povidone is inert and non-toxic and is used in tablets over prolonged periods without any harmful effects.

A.D.I. 0–50 mg/kg body weight.

Typical products Artificial sweeteners

1202 Polyvinyl polypyrrolidone (Insoluble polyvinylpyrrolidone)

Origin This substance is the insoluble form of polyvinylpyrrolidone, with a very high relative molecular mass.

Function Clarifying agent for wine.

Effects Insoluble polyvinylpyrrolidone does not seem to produce any adverse effects in short-term feeding studies in dogs and rats. When the substance was tested with a radio-isotope form to ascertain the extent of its absorption in the gut, it was hardly absorbed at all. The slight amount that did occur was probably due to traces of the soluble form in the material.

A.D.I. Not specified.

Typical products Used in course of manufacture of wine

1400–1450   Thickeners (Modified Starches)

Modified starches —
1400 Dextrins
1403 Bleached starch
1404 Oxidised starch
1405 Enzyme-treated starches
1410 Monostarch phosphate
1412 Distarch phosphate esterified with sodium trimetaphosphate
1412 Distarch phosphate esterified with phosphorus oxychloride
1413 Phosphated starch phosphate
1414 Acetylated distarch phosphate
1420 Starch acetate esterified with acetic anhydride
1421 Starch acetate esterified with vinyl acetate
1422 Acetylated distarch adipate
1440 Hydroxypropyl starch
1442 Hydroxypropyl distarch phosphate
1450 Starch sodium octenylsuccinate

Origin   Starch is the main storage form of energy of many plants. Commercially important sources include potatoes, cereals like wheat, maize, rice and barley, or roots like cassava. Starch in one form or another is the main constituent of the staple diet. Unmodified or native starch occurs in the form of minute granules.

The granules are visible to the naked eye and their size and shape are characteristic of the plant from which the starch was obtained. When intact, the grains are insoluble in cold water. The molecules of starch are held together in the granule by hydrogen bonds which weaken as the temperature of the water rises. As the bonds weaken, they allow the granules to take in water, to swell and thicken. However, such dispersions are fairly unstable as the swollen granule is unable to withstand mechanical breakdown or very high or low temperatures.

Modified starches are food starches which have one or more of their original characteristics altered by various treatments in accordance with good manufacturing practice. (See individual modified starches.) Modified starches expand the usefulness of starch.

Function   Thickener, stabilisers, binders.

A.D.I.   Not specified.

1400 Dextrins

Origin Dextrins are white or yellow powders produced by dry heating of unmodified starches alone or in the presence of suitable food grade acids and buffers. Corn (maize) and tapioca are the main starches used. Dextrins occur in malt and during food processing. Dextrin is produced, for example, when bread is toasted.

Function Foam stabiliser for beer; diluting agent for dry extracts and pills, in polishing cereals; preparation of emulsions; thickener and binder. Tapioca dextrins form very transparent films and are used as extenders for delicately flavoured foods and as carriers for flavours and colours. Corn dextrins are useful as general purpose extenders for pasta and pizza doughs.

Dextrins are also used in postage-stamp glue.

Effects No adverse effects are known.

A.D.I. Not specified.

Typical products A wide variety of foods including —
Artificial sweetener bases
Essences
Soluble coffee and chicory extracts
Flour products other than bread
Confectionery

1403 Bleached starch

Origin Bleached starch is obtained by treating native starch with peracetic acid and/or hydrogen peroxide or sodium hypochlorite, or sodium chlorite, or sulphur dioxide or alternative permitted forms of sulphites, or potassium permanganate, or ammonium persulphate.

Function Stabiliser; thickener; binder. It is used particularly to reduce viscosity in cooked products like casseroles and batter mixes and in confectionery in combination with gelatine and gum arabic.

Effects No adverse effects are known, unless sulphur dioxide or other sulphiting agents were used in the bleaching process, when residual sulphur dioxide up to a maximum of 50 mg/kg may be present. In such circumstances the product could present a danger to asthmatics.

A.D.I. Not specified.

Typical products A wide variety of foods including —
Casserole mixes
Batter mixes
Confectionery like jelly sweets and wine gums

1404 Oxidised starch

Origin Oxidised starch is obtained by treating native starch with sodium hypochlorite.

Function Emulsifier; thickener; binder. It is used in similar situations to bleached starch, to reduce the viscosity of batters and cooked casseroles and in confectionery in combination with gelatine and gum arabic.

Effects Residual sulphur dioxide, up to a maximum of 50 mg/kg could cause this substance to present a problem to asthmatics.

A.D.I. Not specified.

Typical products Many of those permitted to contain bleached starch (1403)

1405 Enzyme-treated starches

Origin When corn starch is subjected to acid-enzyme treatment, glucose, maltose and higher oligosaccharides are produced. The degree of conversion of the starch is measured in terms of the dextrose equivalent (DE). DE is defined as the percentage of reducing sugars as dextrose on a dry weight basis. Products with a DE of less than 20 are maltodextrins whilst those with a DE of greater than 20 are corn syrups. (Pure dextrose has a DE of 100.) Currently enzyme-treated starches with the code number 1405 are not being used in Australia.

Function Thickener, binder, stabiliser.

Effects Naturally occurring in the body, enzyme-treated starches are of nutritive value and are readily digestible with a calorie value equal to sugar.

A.D.I. Not specified.

Typical products —

1410 Monostarch phosphate

Origin Monostarch phosphate is a crosslinked modified starch, where the ruptured hydrogen bonds are esterified or in a sense 'spot-welded' with orthophosphoric acid, sodium or potassium orthophosphate, or sodium tripolyphosphate. The crosslinking treatment strengthens the relatively tender waxy starches, imparting enhanced viscosity.

Function Stabiliser; thickener; binder. This modified starch tends not to have a lot of food applications. It is used to optimise viscosity in chilled and instant dairy products.

Effects Crosslinked food starches are readily metabolised and in *in vitro* studies there is so little difference between the digestibility of monostarch phosphates compared with native starch as to be insignificant. Monostarch phosphates are comparable to unmodified control starches in caloric value.

A.D.I. Not specified.

Typical products Many of those permitted to contain bleached starch (1403) and chilled and instant dairy products.

1412 Distarch phosphate esterified with sodium trimetaphosphate

Origin This distarch phosphate is a crosslinked modified starch, where the ruptured hydrogen bonds are reinforced or in a sense 'spot-welded' with sodium trimetaphosphate. The crosslinking treatment strengthens the relatively tender waxy starches, imparting enhanced viscosity and resistance to severe agitation and extended cooking times, which could cause chemical or mechanical breakdown. It is only necessary to replace about one in 1000 'anhydroglucoside units' to produce an effective crosslinked starch.

Function Stabiliser; thickener; binder;

provides a smooth or pulpy moist texture in baked pies and tarts; provides instant thickening in dry dessert mixes and can thicken without lumping and aid blending in soup mixes. It is also used to provide a crisp coating to chips and as an internal binder in extruded chips. In frozen dairy products it restricts swelling and it gives a creamy texture to mayonnaise and salad dressings.

Effects Crosslinked food starches are readily metabolised and in *in vitro* studies there is so little difference between the digestibility of distarch phosphates compared with native starch as to be insignificant. Distarch phosphates are comparable to unmodified control starches in caloric value.

A.D.I. Not specified.

Typical products
Fruit pie fillings
Instant puddings and
    desserts
Chips
Mayonnaise and salad
    dressings
Baked pies and tarts
Soup mixes
Frozen dairy products
Sauces and ketchups

1412 Distarch phosphate esterified with phosphorus oxychloride

Origin In the case of this crosslinked modified starch the distarch phosphate crosslinks or 'spot-weldings' are reinforced and stabilised with phosphorus oxychloride, imparting resistance to thermal, mechanical or chemical breakdown to the dispersion. It is only necessary to replace about 1 in 1000 'anhydroglucoside units' to produce an effective crosslinked starch.

Function Stabiliser; thickener; binder. Not as much used as distarch phosphate esterified with sodium trimetaphosphate except in situations of more stringent processing, because the crosslinking is stronger.

Effects Crosslinked food starches are readily metabolised and in *in vitro* studies there is so little difference between the digestibility of distarch phosphates compared with native starch as to be insignificant. Distarch phosphates are comparable to unmodified control starches in caloric value.

A.D.I. Not specified.

Typical products Some of those permitted to contain distarch phosphate esterified with sodium trimetaphosphate.

1413 Phosphated distarch phosphate

Origin In phosphated distarch phosphate some of the hydrogen bonds are both crosslinked or 'spot-welded' with phosphate to reinforce them and dually modified or stabilised with a 'monosubstituent group' of phosphate. The level of monosubstituent groups introduced in the production of modified starch is relatively low: the maximum level for phosphates is 0.4 per cent phosphorus, which corresponds to one phosphate group for roughly 47–48 anhydroglucoside units. This further stabilises the suspension, preventing gelling or 'weeping' on cooling and giving further resistance to extremes of temperature, especially freeze-thawing regimes.

Function Stabilising agent, especially in circumstances of repeated freezing and thawing in combination with other types of starches, such as waxy maize, tapioca and potato starches. Thickening agent; binder.

Effects Modified starches containing monosubstituent groups in combination with crosslinks may show slightly lower rates of digestion, depending on the level of substitution. This is of little or no significance at the levels of daily intake found in the normal human diet. Monosubstituent modified food starches rarely exceed 5–6 per cent concentration in food, contributing only 1 per cent of the daily intake.

A.D.I. Not specified.

Typical products
Flavoured yoghurts and
    products heat-treated
    after fermentation
Ice cream
Hydrolysed protein-based
    and soy-based infant
    formulas
Canned foods for infants
    and young children
Cereal-based foods for
    infants and young
    children

1414 Acetylated distarch phosphate

Origin In acetylated distarch phosphate some of the hydrogen bonds are both crosslinked or

'esterified' with a phosphate (either sodium trimetaphosphate or phosphorus oxychloride) to reinforce them and then stabilised with a 'monosubstituent group' of acetate (acetic anhydride). The level of monosubstituent groups introduced in the production of modified starch is relatively low: the maximum level for acetates is 2.5 per cent which corresponds to one acetate group for roughly every 10–11 anhydroglucoside units. This further stabilises the suspension, preventing gelling or 'weeping' on cooling and giving further resistance to extremes of temperature, while still maintaining a good texture.

Function Stabilising agent, providing good freeze-thaw stability, resisting high temperatures and low pHs, this starch is advantageous under fairly severe food processing conditions such as light canning. It is not used a great deal except under acid conditions, as the acetate tends to turn into acetic acid and make the product taste of vinegar. Thickener; emulsifier.

Effects Modified starches containing monosubstituent groups in combination with crosslinks may show slightly lower rates of digestion, depending on the level of substitution. This is of little or no significance at the levels of daily intake found in the normal human diet. Monosubstituent modified food starches rarely exceed 5–6 per cent concentration in food, contributing only 1 per cent of the daily intake.

A.D.I. Not specified.

Typical products
Thin canned soups
Canned foods for infants
    and young children

Cereal-based foods for
infants and young
children
Canned fruit pie fillings
Hydrolysed protein-based
and soy-based infant
formulas

1420 Starch acetate esterified with acetic anhydride

Origin In this starch acetate some of
the hydrogen bonds are both
crosslinked by treating starch with a
mixed anhydride of adipic and acetic
anhydride to reinforce them and then
stabilised with 'monosubstituent
groups' of acetate. The level of
monosubstituent groups introduced in
the production of modified starch is
relatively low: the maximum level for
acetates is 2.5 per cent which
corresponds to one acetate group for
roughly every 10–11 anhydroglucoside
units. This further stabilises the
suspension, preventing gelling on
cooling and giving further resistance to
extremes of temperature.

Function Stabilising agent, especially
in circumstances of repeated freezing
and thawing and rarely on its own,
sometimes with 1421 or in
combination with other types of
starches, such as waxy maize, tapioca
and potato starches. Thickener; binder.

Effects Modified starches containing
monosubstituent groups in
combination with crosslinks may show
slightly lower rates of digestion,
depending on the level of substitution.
This is of little or no significance at the
levels of daily intake found in the
normal human diet. Monosubstituent
modified food starches rarely exceed

5–6 per cent concentration in food,
contributing only 1 per cent of the daily
intake.

A.D.I. Not specified.

Typical products
Confectionery
Yoghurts
Fruit flavoured fillings
Egg white mix

1421 Starch acetate esterified with vinyl acetate

Origin In this starch acetate the
hydrogen bonds have been stabilised
by treatment of the starch with
monosubstituent groups of vinyl
acetate. The level of monosubstituents
in the production of food starches is
relatively low: the maximum level of
substitution in acetates is 2.5 per cent,
corresponding to one acetate group for
roughly 10-11 anhydroglucoside units.

Function Stabilising agent, especially
in circumstances of repeated freezing
and thawing in combination with other
types of starches, such as waxy maize,
tapioca and potato starches.
Thickener; binder.

Effects Modified starches containing
monosubstituent groups in
combination with crosslinks may show
slightly lower rates of digestion,
depending on the level of substitution.
This is of little or no significance at the
levels of daily intake found in the
normal human diet. Monosubstituent
modified food starches rarely exceed
5-6 per cent concentration in food,
contributing only 1 per cent of the daily
intake.

A.D.I. Not specified.

Typical products Many of those
permitted to contain 1420.

1422 Acetylated distarch adipate

Origin Acetylated distarch adipate is a crosslinked modified starch where the ruptured hydrogen bonds are reinforced with a mixed anhydride of adipic and acetic anhydride, imparting resistance to thermal, chemical and mechanical breakdown to the dispersions. It is only necessary to replace about one in a thousand anhydroglucoside units to produce an effective crosslinked starch.

Function Stabiliser; thickener; binder. Provides texture, cling and imparts body and 'mouthfeel' to tinned soups, sauces, custards and gravies and is very resistant to breakdown under acid conditions (down to pH4.5) in tinned fruit pie fillings and in frozen fruit pies it provides cuttability. It imparts body and mouthfeel to dry pie fillings and helps water absorption. In addition, it gives a short dry texture to hot extruded snacks, gives a good suspension of particulates in pickles, and relishes and imparts a longer shelf-life and moisture to dry cake mixes.

Effects In the laboratory there is so little difference in the digestibility of acetylated distarch adipate compared with native starch as to be insignificant, even when the starch has been treated 20 per cent more than normal. Laboratory animals metabolize acetylated distarch adipate very well.

A.D.I. Not specified.

Typical products
Canned fruit pie fillings
Frozen fruit pies and toppings
Frozen savoury pies and sauces
Sauces, ketchups, pickles
    and relish
Dry pie fillings
Dry cake mixes
Yoghurts
Canned foods for infants
    and young children
Cereal-based foods for
    infants and young
    children

1440 Hydroxypropyl starch

Origin Hydroxypropyl starch is a chemically modified starch by the introduction of the stabilising hydroxypropyl group. The level of substitution introduced is relatively low: propylene oxide treatment level for hydroxypropyl starches varies, but is generally no greater than a 1 in 5 replacement of anhydroglucoside units. This treatment further stabilises the starch, preventing gelling and 'weeping' on cooling, providing further resistance to extremes of temperature, and maintaining textural appearance.

Function Stabilising agent, especially in circumstances of repeated freezing and thawing in combination with other types of starches, such as waxy maize, tapioca and potato starches. Thickener; binder. Gives a glossy appearance and prevents weeping but is not resistant to processing and is little used in the food industry.

Effects Hydroxypropyl starches are not readily digested nor assimilated and rats fed hydroxypropyl starch egested 95 per cent of it through the faeces. The greater the degree of modification of the starch, the less well it is broken down in the gut or digested.

A.D.I. Not specified.

Typical products Many of those permitted to contain 1442.

1442 Hydroxypropyl distarch phosphate

Origin In hydroxypropyl distarch phosphate some of the hydrogen bonds are both crosslinked or 'spot-welded' with phosphate to reinforce them and stabilised with a monosubstituent hydroxyl group. The level of substitution is relatively low: propylene oxide treatment level for hydroxypropyl starches varies but is generally no greater than a 1 in 5 replacement of hydrogen bonds. This treatment further stabilises the starch, preventing gelling and 'weeping' on cooling, providing further resistance to extremes of temperature and maintaining textural appearance.

Function Used especially in UHT canned puddings, imparting a cuttable creamy body, and to impart a texture, cling and mouthfeel in canned soups, sauces and gravies; gives good freeze-thaw stability, clarity and texture to frozen pies and toppings, where it also provides cuttability and it improves the shelf-life of frozen desserts. It is used in sauces, pickles and ketchups because it is stable at low pHs (acid conditions) and it holds the particles well in suspension. Improving 'mouthfeel' and extending shelf-life, it is employed in some instant pudding, dessert and cake mixes and it helps to give a 'home-made' appearance to instant gravies. It is more expensive than other modified starches. Thickener.

Effects Hydroxypropyl starches are not readily digested nor assimilated and rats fed hydroxypropyl starch excreted 95 per cent of it through the faeces. The greater the degree of modification of the starch, the less well it is broken down in the gut or digested.

A.D.I. Not specified.

Typical products
Canned soups,
   sauces and gravies
Frozen fruit pies and toppings
Frozen desserts
Sauces and ketchups
Instant pudding, dessert
   and cake mixes
Instant gravy and sauce mixes

1450 Starch, sodium octenylsuccinate

Origin Starch sodium octenylsuccinate is native starch chemically modified or stabilised through the introduction of an octenylsuccinate half ester monosubstituent group. The level of substitution is very low with at most about one anhydroglucoside unit in 50 being exchanged for a monosubstituent, and this introduces new or added functionality into the starch molecules, especially emulsion-stabilising properties.

Function Stabilising agent, especially in circumstances of repeated freezing and thawing with other types of starch such as waxy maize, tapioca and potato starches; thickener; binder.

Effects No adverse effects are known.

A.D.I. Not specified.

Typical products
Essences
Salad dressings
Beverage whiteners
Dry drink bases

1505–1520 More Miscellaneous Additives

1505 Triethyl citrate (ethyl citrate)

Origin A bitter oily liquid which is soluble in water and can be mixed with alcohol.

Function Sequestrant, preventing rancidity; carrier solvent.

Effects Triethyl citrate is hydrolysed to citrate and ethanol in man. Rats can tolerate triethyl citrate up to 2.0g/kg body weight. Several studies show triethyl citrate does not cause the genes of bacteria to mutate.

A.D.I. 0–20 mg/kg body weight.

Typical products & maximum permitted levels
Egg white, liquid and dried
liquid 1.25 g/kg
Smoke flavour

1510 Ethyl alcohol (ethanol)

Origin Manufactured by the fermentation of starch, sugar or other carbohydrates or from ethylene, acetylene, liquors from waste sulphites, by hydrolysis of ethyl sulphate or by the oxidation of methane.

Function Alcoholic beverages in various dilutions; extraction solvent and carrier.

Effects JECFA decided in 1970 that its use as an additive was self-limiting and sufficiently safe that no quantitive restrictions were required. Overdoses are notoriously poisonous — nausea, vomiting, flushing, mental excitement or depression, drowsiness, impaired co-ordination and perception, stupor, coma. Ethyl alcohol is not acceptable to some religious groups but as there is no legal requirement to name additive carriers, there is no way of establishing its presence or absence.

A.D.I. Limited by GMP.

Typical products
*Alcoholic beverages
Artificial sweetener bases
Essences
Some food colours in liquid form

*In Australia alcoholic beverages are required to carry in their labels a statement of the percentage by volume of ethanol at 20°C present in the form — '× % ALCOHOL BY VOLUME' or '× % ALC/VOL'.

1517 Glycerol diacetate (diacetin)

Origin The commercial diacetin is probably a mixture of glycerol 1, 2- and 1, 3-diacetates.

Function Solvent/carrier solvent.

Effects —

A.D.I. Not specified.

Typical products & maximum permitted levels
Confectionery 100 mg/kg
Essences —

1518 Triacetin (glycerol triacetate)

Origin Prepared by the acetylation of glycerol, it is a colourless oily liquid which has a fatty smell and a bitter taste.

Function Solvent, used to dilute and carry food flavours. It can also be used as a humectant. In the USA it is used as a coating for vegetables and fruits. It is used therapeutically because of its anti-fungal effect.

Effects Glycerol triacetate is well metabolised and is not thought to present a hazard to human health. Rats given diets of 50 per cent triacetin had no problems in tolerating it.

A.D.I. Not specified.

Typical products
Essences

1520 Propylene glycol

Origin Prepared industrially from propylene or by heating glycerol with sodium hydroxide, or by reacting propylene oxide with water.

Function Solvent, dissolving many essential oils, and flavours, wetting agent and humectant in shredded coconut. Used in cosmetics a great deal because it is cheaper than glycerin and permeates the skin better.

Effects In low doses propylene glycol seems to be well tolerated over a range of laboratory animals, whereas at high doses it becomes extremely toxic causing depression of the central nervous system and kidney failure.

A.D.I. 25 mg/kg body weight.

Typical products & maximum permitted levels
Artificial sweetener bases —
Essences —
Sweetened coconut 22.5 g/kg

Alphabetical List of Additives and their Code Numbers

Note — The additives in this list which have a number bearing an 'E' prefix are not permitted in Australia.

414	Acacia	554	Aluminium sodium silicate
260	Acetic acid	123	Amaranth
472(a)	Acetic and fatty acid esters of glycerol	E440(b)	Amidated pectin
1422	Acetylated distarch adipate	264	Ammonium acetate
1414	Acetylated distarch phosphate	403	Ammonium alginate
142	Acid Brilliant Green BS	503	Ammonium bicarbonate
341	Acid calcium phosphate	503	Ammonium carbonate
450	Acid sodium pyrophosphate	510	Ammonium chloride
222	Acid sodium sulphite	381	Ammonium ferric citrate
341	ACP	381	Ammonium ferric citrate; green
355	Adipic acid	503	Ammonium hydrogen carbonate
406	Agar	E527	Ammonium hydroxide
406	Agar agar	328	Ammonium lactate
621	Aji-no-moto	450(a)	Ammonium phosphate dibasic
404	Algin	450(a)	Ammonium phosphate monobasic
405	Alginate ester	442	Ammonium phosphatides
400	Alginic acid	E545	Ammonium polyphosphates
129	Allura red AC		
E173	Aluminium	442	Ammonium salts of phosphatidic acid
556	Aluminium calcium silicate		

147

160(b)	Annatto extracts		302	Calcium ascorbate
163	Anthocyanins		302	Calcium L-ascorbate
160(e)	β-Apo-8'-carotenal		213	Calcium benzoate
160(e)	β-8'-Apocarotenal		E227	Calcium bisulphite
160(f)	β-Apo-8'-carotenoic acid, ethyl ester		170	Calcium carbonate
			509	Calcium chloride
300	Ascorbic acid		509	Calcium chloride; anhydrous
304	Ascorbyl palmitate		333	Calcium citrates — mono, di and tri
E927	Azodicarbonamide			
E927	Azoformamide		E238	Calcium formate
122	Azorubine		367	Calcium fumarate
500	Baking soda		578	Calcium gluconate
162	Beet Red		623	Calcium glutamate
901	Beeswax, white		623	Calcium dihydrogen di-L-glutamate
901	Beeswax, yellow			
558	Bentonite		352	Calcium hydrogen malate
210	Benzoic acid		341	Calcium hydrogen orthophosphate
928	Benzoyl peroxide			
162	Betanin		E540	Calcium hydrogen phosphate
320	BHA			
321	BHT		E227	Calcium hydrogen sulphite
500	Bicarbonate of soda		526	Calcium hydroxide
E230	Biphenyl		327	Calcium lactate
161(b)	Bixin		352	DL-Calcium malate
151	Black PN		529	Calcium oxide
1403	Bleached starch		341	Calcium phosphate, monobasic
542	Bone phosphate, edible			
151	Brilliant Black BN		341	Calcium phosphate, dibasic
151	Brilliant Black PN			
133	Brilliant Blue FCF		341	Calcium phosphate, tribasic
124	Brilliant Scarlet 4R			
E154	Brown FK		E544	Calcium polyphosphates
155	Brown HT		282	Calcium propionate
320	Butylated hydroxyanisole		E470	Calcium salts of fatty acids
321	Butylated hydroxytoluene		552	Calcium silicate
263	Calcium acetate		E385	Calcium disodium EDTA
404	Calcium alginate			
556	Calcium aluminium silicate			

E385	Calcium disodium ethylenediamine tetra-acetate
203	Calcium sorbate
482	Calcium stearoyl-2-lactylate
516	Calcium sulphate
E226	Calcium sulphite
161(g)	Canthaxanthin
E160(c)	Capsanthin
E160(c)	Capsorubin
150	Caramel
153	Carbon black
290	Carbon dioxide
466	Carboxymethylcellulose, sodium salt
466	Caramellose sodium
120	Carmine of Cochineal
120	Carminic acid
122	Carmoisine
903	Carnauba wax
410	Carob bean gum
160(a)	Carotenes — α, β, γ
407	Carrageenan
469	Casein-sodium
460	Cellulose, microcrystalline
460	Cellulose, powdered
170	Chalk
251	Chile saltpetre
925	Chlorine
926	Chlorine dioxide
140	Chlorophyll
155	Chocolate brown HT
330	Citric acid
472(c)	Citric and fatty acid esters of glycerol
472(c)	Citroglycerides
331	Citrosidine
466	CMC

120	Cochineal
461	Cologel
E141	Copper complexes of chlorophyll and chlorophyllins
E141	Copper phaeophytins
519	Copper sulphate
415	Corn sugar gum
336	Cream of tartar
161	Cryptoxanthin
519	Cupric sulphate
100	Curcumin
920	L-cysteine hydrochloride
920	L-cysteine hydrochloride monohydrate
1400	Dextrins
1517	Diacetin
472(e)	Diacetyltartaric and fatty acid esters of glycerol
928	Dibenzoyl peroxide
333	Dicalcium citrate
E540	Dicalcium diphosphate
900	Dimethicone
900	Dimethylpolysiloxane
480	Dioctyl sodium sulphosuccinate
E230	Diphenyl
340	Dipotassium hydrogen orthophosphate
336	Dipotassium L-(+)-tartrate
331	Disodium citrate
450	Disodium dihydrogen diphosphate
339	Disodium hydrogen orthophosphate
450	Disodium dihydrogen pyrophosphate
627	Disodium guanylate
631	Disodium inosinate

223	Disodium pyrosulphite
335	Disodium L-(+)-tartrate
1412	Distarch phosphate
480	Docusate sodium
312	Dodecyl gallate
312	Dodecyl 3,4,5-trihydroxybenzoate
542	Edible bone phosphate
442	Emulsifier YN
1405	Enzyme treated starches
518	Epsom salts
317	Erythorbic acid
127	Erythrosine
1510	Ethanol
1510	Ethyl alcohol
1505	Ethyl citrate
160(f)	Ethyl ester of β-Apo-8'-carotenoic acid
E214	Ethyl-4-hydroxybenzoate
E214	Ethyl para-hydroxybenzoate
E215	Ethyl-4-hydroxybenzoate, sodium salt
637	Ethyl maltol
465	Ethylmethylcellulose
133	FD and C Blue 1
132	FD and C Blue 2
129	FD and C Red 40
110	FD and C Yellow 6
381	Ferric ammonium citrate
579	Ferrous gluconate
161	Flavoxanthin
142	Food Green S
E154	Food Brown
E236	Formic acid
553(b)	French chalk
297	Fumaric acid
160(a)	Gamma-carotene
441	Gelatine

575	Glucono delta-lactone
575	D-Glucono-1, 5-lactone
620	L-glutamic acid
422	Glycerol
1517	Glycerol diacetate
1518	Glycerol triacetate
E175	Gold
142	Green S
627	Guanosine 5'-(disodium phosphate)
412	Guar gum
414	Gum arabic
413	Gum tragacanth
503	Hartshorn
E370	1,4-Heptonolactone
E239	Hexamine
E239	Hexamethylenetetramine
355	Hexandioic acid
507	Hydrochloric acid
965	Hydrogenated glucose syrup
E231	2-Hydroxybiphenyl
E463	Hydroxypropylcellulose
464	Hydroxypropylmethylcellulose
1442	Hydroxypropyl distarch phosphate
1440	Hydroxypropyl starch
464	Hypromellose
132	Indigo carmine
132	Indigotine
631	Inosine 5'-(disodium phosphate)
407	Irish moss
172	Iron hydroxides
172	Iron oxides
317	Iso-ascorbic acid
406	Japanese isinglass
559	Kaolin (heavy and light)

416	Karaya gum
E154	Kipper Brown
270	Lactic acid
472(b)	Lactic and fatty acid esters of glycerol
101	Lactoflavin
472(b)	Lactoglycerides
E478	Lactylated fatty acid esters of glycerol and propane 1,2-diol
322	Lecithins
620	L-glutamic acid
142	Lissamine Green
E180	Lithol Rubine BK
410	Locust bean gum
161	Lutein
E160(d)	Lycopene
504	Magnesite
504	Magnesium carbonate
511	Magnesium chloride
343	Magnesium hydrogen orthophosphate trihydrate
343	Magnesium hydrogen phosphate
E528	Magnesium hydroxide
329	Magnesium lactate
E530	Magnesium oxide
343	Magnesium phosphate, dibasic
343	Magnesium phosphate, tribasic
E553(a)	Magnesium silicate synthetic
E553(a)	Magnesium trisilicate
572	Magnesium stearate
518	Magnesium sulphate
296	DL-Malic acid
636	Maltol
421	Manna sugar

421	Mannitol
353	Metatartaric acid
461	Methocel
461	Methylcellulose
465	Methylethylcellulose
218	Methyl 4-hydroxybenzoate
218	Methylparaben
218	Methyl *para*-hydroxybenzoate
E219	Methyl 4-hydroxybenzoate, sodium salt
460	Microcrystalline cellulose
E907	Microcrystalline wax, refined
905	Mineral oil, white
341	Monocalcium orthophosphate
472(e)	Mono- and diacetyltartaric acid esters of mono- and diglycerides of fatty acids
471	Mono- and diglycerides of fat-forming fatty acids
333	Monocalcium citrate
332	Monopotassium citrate
622	Monopotassium glutamate
336	Monopotassium L-(+)-tartrate
331	Monosodium citrate
365	Monosodium fumarate
621	Monosodium glutamate
335	Monosodium L-(+)-tartrate
1410	Monostarch phosphate
621	MSG
235	Natamycin
375	Niacin
375	Nicotinamide
375	Nicotinic acid
234	Nisin
931	Nitrogen

932	Nitrous oxide	E430	Polyoxyethylene (8) stearate
160(b)	Norbixin	E431	Polyoxyethylene (40) stearate
216	n-Propyl p-hydroxybenzoate	E544	Polyphosphates, calcium
311	Octyl gallate	E545	Polyphosphates, ammonium
338	Orthophosphoric acid	450	Polyphosphates, potassium and sodium
E231	Orthophenylphenol		
1404	Oxidised starch	E432	Polysorbate 20
304	Palmitoyl-L-ascorbic acid	E434	Polysorbate 40
E131	Patent blue V	435	Polysorbate 60
440(a)	Pectin	436	Polysorbate 65
450	Pentapotassium triphosphate	433	Polysorbate 80
		1202	Polyvinylpolypyrrolidone
450	Pentasodium triphosphate	1201	Polyvinylpyrrolidone
905	Petrolatum	124	Ponceau 4R
1413	Phosphated distarch phosphate	261	Potassium acetate
		336	Potassium acid tartrate
338	Phosphoric acid	357	Potassium adipate
E180	Pigment Rubine	402	Potassium alginate
235	Pimaricin	303	Potassium ascorbate
1200	Polydextrose	212	Potassium benzoate
475	Polyglycerol esters of fatty acids	228	Potassium bisulphite
		924	Potassium bromate
476	Polyglycerol esters of interesterified ricinoleic acid	501	Potassium carbonate
		508	Potassium chloride
		332	Potassium citrates — mono and tri
476	Polyglycerol polyricinoleate		
		536	Potassium ferrocyanide
E430	Polyoxyl 8 stearate	366	Potassium fumarate
E431	Polyoxyl 40 stearate	577	Potassium gluconate
E432	Polyoxyethylene (20) sorbitan monolaurate	536	Potassium hexacyanoferrate (II)
433	Polyoxyethylene (20) sorbitan mono-oleate	501	Potassium hydrogen carbonate
E434	Polyoxyethylene (20) sorbitan monopalmitate	332	Potassium dihydrogen citrate
435	Polyoxyethylene (20) sorbitan monostearate		
		622	Potassium hydrogen L-glutamate
436	Polyoxyethylene (20) sorbitan tristearate		

340	Potassium dihydrogen orthophosphate
228	Potassium hydrogen sulphite
336	Potassium hydrogen tartrate
E525	Potassium hydroxide
326	Potassium lactate
351	Potassium malate
224	Potassium metabisulphite
252	Potassium nitrate
249	Potassium nitrite
224	Potassium pyrosulphite
240	Potassium phosphate monobasic
340	Potassium phosphate, dibasic
340	Potassium phosphate, tribasic
450	Potassium tripolyphosphate
450	Potassium polyphosphates
283	Potassium propionate
450	Potassium pyrophosphate
E470	Potassium salts of fatty acids
337	Potassium sodium tartrate
337	Potassium sodium L-(+)-tartrate
202	Potassium sorbate
515	Potassium sulphate
225	Potassium sulphite
336	Potassium tartrate
450	Potassium tripolyphosphate
1201	Povidone
460	Powdered cellulose
405	Propane -1, 2-diol alginate
E477	Propane -1, 2-diol esters of fatty acids
280	Propionic acid
1520	Propylene glycol
405	Propylene glycol alginate
E477	Propylene glycol esters of fatty acids
310	Propyl gallate
310	Propyl 3,4,5-trihydroxybenzoate
216	Propyl 4-hydroxybenzoate
216	Propylparaben
216	Propyl para-hydroxybenzoate
E217	Propyl 4-hydroxybenzoate, sodium salt
E104	Quinoline yellow
E128	Red 2G
E907	Refined microcrystalline wax
161	Rhodoxanthin
101	Riboflavin
101	Riboflavin-5'-phosphate sodium
337	Rochelle salt
E180	Rubine
161	Rubixanthin
252	Saltpetre
904	Shellac
551	Silica
551	Silicon dioxide
E174	Silver
262	Sodium acetate
450	Sodium acid pyrophosphate
401	Sodium alginate
541	Sodium aluminium phosphate, acidic
E541	Sodium aluminium phosphate, basic
554	Sodium aluminosilicate
301	Sodium ascorbate

211	Sodium benzoate
500	Sodium bicarbonate
E232	Sodium biphenyl-2-yl oxide
222	Sodium bisulphite
500	Sodium carbonate
466	Sodium carboxymethyl-cellulose
469	Sodium caseinate
331	Sodium citrates — mono, di and tri
262	Sodium diacetate
331	Sodium dihydrogen citrate
318	Sodium erythorbate
E215	Sodium ethyl *para*-hydroxybenzoate
E535	Sodium ferrocyanide
E237	Sodium formate
365	Sodium fumarate
E576	Sodium gluconate
627	Disodium guanylate
E535	Sodium hexacyanoferrate (II)
500	Sodium hydrogen carbonate
262	Sodium hydrogen diacetate
621	Sodium hydrogen L-glutamate
350	DL-Sodium hydrogen malate
339	Sodium dihydrogen orthophosphate
222	Sodium hydrogen sulphite
E524	Sodium hydroxide
631	Sodium inosinate
318	Sodium iso-ascorbate
325	Sodium lactate
350	DL-Sodium malate
223	Sodium metabisulphite
E219	Sodium methyl *para*-hydroxybenzoate
251	Sodium nitrate
250	Sodium nitrite
E232	Sodium orthophenylphenate
339	Sodium phosphate, monobasic
339	Sodium phophate, dibasic
339	Sodium phosphate, tribasic
450	Sodium polyphosphates
337	Sodium potassium tartrate
281	Sodium propionate
E217	Sodium propyl *para*-hydroxybenzoate
450	Sodium pyrophosphate
E635	Sodium 5'-ribonucleotide
E470	Sodium salts of fatty acids
500	Sodium sesquicarbonate
201	Sodium sorbate
481	Sodium stearoyl-2-lactylate
514	Sodium sulphate
221	Sodium sulphite
335	Sodium tartrate
450	Sodium tripolyphosphate
200	Sorbic acid
E493	Sorbitan monolaurate
E494	Sorbitan mono-oleate
E495	Sorbitan monopalmitate
491	Sorbitan monostearate
492	Sorbitan tristearate
420	Sorbitol
E493	Span 20
E495	Span 40
492	Span 65
E494	Span 80
1403	Starch, bleached
1405	Starch, enzyme treated
1404	Starch, oxidised

1420	Starch acetate esterified with acetic anhydride	309	δ-Tocopherol
1421	Starch acetate esterified with vinyl acetate	306	Tocopherols concentrate, mixed
1450	Starch, sodium octenyl succinate	413	Tragacanth
570	Stearic acid	380	Triammonium citrate
E483	Stearyl tartrate	333	Tricalcium citrate
416	Sterculia gum	341	Tricalcium orthophosphate
E363	Succinic acid	1505	Triethyl citrate
E474	Sucroglycerides	332	Tripotassium citrate
473	Sucrose esters of fatty acids	340	Tripotassium orthophosphate
220	Sulphur dioxide	331	Trisodium citrate
E513	Sulphuric acid	450	Trisodium diphosphate
110	Sunset yellow FCF	339	Trisodium orthophosphate
553(b)	Talc	500	Trona
181	Tannic acid	100	Turmeric
181	Tannins	E432	Tween 20
334	Tartaric acid	E434	Tween 40
472(d)	Tartaric and fatty acid esters of glycerol	435	Tween 60
102	Tartrazine	436	Tween 65
319	TBHQ	433	Tween 80
319	*tert*-Butylhydroquinone	153	Vegetable carbon
450	Tetrapotassium diphosphate	161	Violoxanthin
450	Tetrasodium diphosphate	375	Vitamin B
E233	Thiabendazole	101	Vitamin B_2
E233	2-(Thiazol-4-yl) benzimidazole	300	Vitamin C
171	Titanium dioxide	306	Vitamin E (natural)
307	α-Tocopherol	E907	Wax, refined, microcrystalline
308	γ-Tocopherol	415	Xanthan gum
		161	Xanthophylls
		967	Xylitol
		107	Yellow 2G

Food Additive Class Names approved in Australia

A listing of some Australian approved food additives by functional class name. Some food additives can perform more than one function and consequently may appear in more than one class.

An approved food additive which does not belong to one of the above functional classes must be declared in a statement of ingredients by its full name and not by its code number, e.g. the sodium and potassium nitrates and nitrites.

Anti-caking agents

170	Calcium carbonate	554	Aluminium sodium silicate
460	Microcrystalline cellulose	556	Aluminium calcium silicate
460	Powdered cellulose		
536	Potassium ferrocyanide	558	Bentonite
542	Edible bone phosphate	559	Kaolin
551	Silicon dioxide	570	Stearic acid
552	Calcium silicate	572	Magnesium stearate
553(b)	Talc		

Antioxidants

300	Ascorbic acid	317	Erythorbic acid
301	Sodium ascorbate	318	Sodium erythorbate
304	Ascorbyl palmitate	319	tert-Butylhydroquinone
306-309	Tocopherols	320	Butylated hydroxyanisole
310	Propyl gallate	321	Butylated hydroxytoluene
311	Octyl gallate	322	Lecithins
312	Dodecyl gallate		

Artificial Sweetening Substances

These substances have not been allocated code numbers and therefore must be identified in ingredient lists by their full names.

Acesulphame K

Aspartame

Cyclamate (cyclohexyl sulphamic acid or its sodium or calcium salt)

Saccharin

Thaumatin

Bleaching agents

925	Chlorine
926	Chlorine dioxide
928	Benzoyl peroxide

Colours

100	Curcumin
100	Turmeric
101	Riboflavin
101	Riboflavin-5′-phosphate
102	Tartrazine
107	Yellow 2G
110	Sunset yellow FCF
120	Cochineal
122	Azorubine
123	Amaranth
124	Ponceau 4R
127	Erythrosine
129	Allura red AC
132	Indigotine
133	Brilliant blue FCF
140	Chlorophyll
142	Green S
150	Caramel
151	Black BN
153	Carbon black
155	Brown HT
160(b)	Annatto extracts
161	Xanthophylls
161(g)	Canthaxanthin
162	Beet red
163	Anthocyanins
171	Titanium dioxide
172	Iron oxides; iron hydroxides

Emulsifiers

322	Lecithins
433	Polysorbate 80
435	Polysorbate 60
436	Polysorbate 65
442	Ammonium salts of phosphatidic acid
471	Mono- and di-glycerides of fat forming fatty acids
472(a)	Acetic and fatty acid esters of glycerol
472(b)	Lactic and fatty acid esters of glycerol

Emulsifiers cont.

472(c) Citric and fatty acid esters of glycerol

472(d) Tartaric and fatty acid esters of glycerol

472(e) Diacetyltartaric and fatty acid esters of glycerol

473 Sucrose esters of fatty acids

491 Sorbitan monostearate

Flavour enhancers

620 Glutamic acid
621 Monosodium glutamate
627 Disodium guanylate
631 Disodium inosinate

636 Maltol
637 Ethyl maltol
— Thaumatin

Flour treatment agents

223 Sodium metabisulphite
300 Ascorbic acid
481 Sodium stearoyl lactylate
482 Calcium stearoyl lactylate

510 Ammonium chloride
516 Calcium sulphate
920 L-cysteine hydrochloride
924 Potassium bromate

Food Acids

260 Acetic acid
261 Potassium acetate
262 Sodium acetate

263 Calcium acetate
264 Ammonium acetate
270 Lactic acid

Food Acids cont.

296	Malic acid		335	Sodium tartrate
297	Fumaric acid		336	Potassium tartrates
325	Sodium lactate		337	Potassium sodium tartrate
326	Potassium lactate		350	Sodium malates
327	Calcium lactate		351	Potassium malate
328	Ammonium lactate		352	Calcium malate
330	Citric acid		354	Calcium tatrate
331	Sodium citrates		365	Sodium fumarate
332	Potassium citrates		366	Potassium fumarate
333	Calcium citrate		367	Calcium fumarate
334	Tartaric acid		380	Tri ammonium citrate

Humectants

420	Sorbitol		1200	Polydextrose
422	Glycerin			
965	Hydrogenated glucose syrups			

Mineral Salts

500	Sodium bicarbonate		529	Calcium oxide
500	Sodium carbonate		336	Potassium acid tartrate
501	Potassium bicarbonate		339	Sodium orthophosphates
501	Potassium carbonate		340	Potassium orthophosphates
503	Ammonium bicarbonate		341	Calcium orthophosphates
503	Ammonium carbonate		450	Sodium and potassium metaphosphates, polyphosphates and pyrophosphates
504	Magnesium carbonate			
170	Calcium carbonate			
509	Calcium chloride			

Preservatives

200	Sorbic acid	221	Sodium sulphite
201	Sodium sorbate	222	Sodium bisulphite
202	Potassium sorbate	223	Sodium metabisulphite
203	Calcium sorbate	224	Potassium metabisulphite
210	Benzoic acid	225	Potassium sulphite
211	Sodium benzoate	234	Nisin
212	Potassium benzoate	280	Propionic acid
213	Calcium benzoate	281	Sodium propionate
216	Propylparaben	282	Calcium propionate
218	Methylparaben	283	Potassium propionate
220	Sulphur dioxide		

Propellants

290	Carbon dioxide	—	Butane
931	Nitrogen	—	Isobutane
932	Nitrous oxide	—	Octafluorocyclobutane
—	Propane		

Thickeners

1400	Dextrins	1414	Acetylated distarch phosphate
1403	Bleached starch		
1404	Oxidised starch	1420	Starch acetate
1405	Enzyme-treated starches	1422	Acetylated distarch adipate
1410	Monostarch phosphate	1440	Hydroxypropyl starch
1412	Distarch phosphate	1442	Hydroxypropyl distarch phosphate
1413	Phosphated starch phosphate		

Vegetable Gums

400	Alginic acid	414	Acacia
401	Sodium alginate	415	Xanthan gum
402	Potassium alginate	416	Karaya gum
403	Ammonium alginate	440(a)	Pectin
404	Calcium alginate	461	Methylcellulose
405	Propylene glycol alginate	464	Hydroxypropylmethyl cellulose
406	Agar		
407	Carrageenan	466	Sodium carboxymethyl cellulose
410	Locust bean gum		
412	Guar gum	1450	Starch sodium octenylsuccinate
413	Tragacanth		

Vitamins

101	Vitamin B$_2$	306-9	Vitamin E
300	Vitamin C	375	Niacin

Appendix I

Food Legislation in Australia

Under the Australian Federal system, food administration is the individual responsibility of each State and Territory. In Australia there is no single legislative authority responsible for food legislation as, for example, there is in New Zealand. Each State has its own Pure Food Act or equivalent legislation. However, the food regulations of the States and the Northern Territory are all based on food standards recommended by the National Health and Medical Research Council (NHMRC) on advice from its Australian Food Standards Committee (AFSC) and its expert subcommittees. The subcommittees that provide expert advice to the AFSC are the Food Analysis Subcommittee, the Food Microbiology Subcommittee and the Food Science and Technology Subcommittee.

The Food Science and Technology Subcommittee inquires into matters of food science and technology including the technological need for and safety of food additives, specifications for the identity and purity of food additives, and the use of colouring substances in food and oral pharmaceuticals. It also looks into contaminants in food such as aflatoxins and heavy metals. The Food Science and Technology Subcommittee in its evaluation of food additives uses the procedures laid down by the World Health Organisation and endorsed by the NHMRC (see Appendix II).

In 1986 the Commonwealth of Australia, the States and the Northern Territory signed an agreement for the adoption of uniform food standards. The purpose of the Agreement was to provide for the adoption of a code of uniform food standards developed by the NHMRC into the food legislation of each State and Territory of the Commonwealth following the publication of that code in the Commonwealth of Australia Gazette. In April 1987 the National Food Standards Council endorsed the NHMRC Food Standards Code and agreed that it would be incorporated into the legislation of each State and Territory to take effect on 1 September 1987. A great step towards the attainment of uniform food law throughout Australia had thus been taken.

The NHMRC Food Standards Code is a compilation of the food standards that have been developed by the Food Standards Committee of NHMRC and is divided into parts as follows:

Part A   prescribes general standards relating to the labelling, advertising and date marking of packaged food. It also prescribes standards for permitted food additives, vitamins and minerals as well as maximum residue limits for pesticides, agricultural chemicals and other contaminants that apply to all foods.

Parts B to R   prescribe standards for specific foods.

Part S   contains miscellaneous food provisions.

The code was published in the Commonwealth of Australia Gazette No. P 27 on 27 August 1987 and will be amended periodically by the inclusion of amendments to existing standards and new food standards determined in either case by the NHMRC and approved by the National Food Standards Council. Amendment No. 1 to the code was published in Commonwealth of Australia Gazette No. P 19 on 15 July 1988, the amendments therein to begin on 1 February 1989.

Appendix II

The Regulation of Food Additives in Australia

Tom Heyhoe

The regulation of and attitude to the use of food additives varies from country to country. In Australia, regulatory authorities probably have a more restrictive view than comparable bodies in many other countries. This is evidenced by the fact that an additive may not be incorporated in any food in Australia unless its use in that food is *specifically* permitted in the National Health and Medical Research Council's (NHMRC) Food Standards Code and corresponding State legislation.

Approval of Food Additives
Approvals for food additives will usually fall into three categories:
approval to increase the amount of an additive in a food where that additive's use is already permitted;
approval of an additive for use in a specific food or class of foods where that additive is already permitted in some other foods;
approval of an additive which has not previously been permitted in Australia.
An approval typical of the first category would be for an increase in the permitted level of a preservative in a food. This would be based on the necessity of the preservative but its lack of efficacy at the currently permitted level. Approvals for such a variation in the Food Standards Code are rarely sought and rarely given.

Category two approvals are often sought where an additive has proved particularly useful in meeting a technological need in one class of foods and it can be seen that it would have application in another. Both category one and category two approvals are given only after submission of a formal application and a thorough multi-stage review process.

The third category, that for additives not previously permitted, is one in which approvals can be sought for a newly developed food additive or for an additive already in wide use overseas. In the case of the latter, it may be that the particular food in which it is used has not previously been manufactured in Australia but is now going to be. Approvals in the third category undergo the same process of review as the other two but much more information must be provided.

The Need for Food Additives

The principles which are used by the NHMRC in evaluating the desirability or otherwise of approving the use of an additive are clearly stated in the NHMRC's Supplement to the Food Standards Code. This statement, 'Principles for the Evaluation of Food Additives' is as follows:

1 The use of a food additive is justified only when it serves one or more of the following purposes:
    to maintain or improve the nutritional quality of a food;
    to improve the palatability, or appearance of a food or to render the food more appetising;
    to improve the storage life of a food;
    to provide aids in producing, manufacturing, packing, processing, preparing, treating, packaging, transporting, holding, or storing foods;
    as a preservative only when necessary because there is no alternative practicable means of preservation of the food.
2 The use of a food additive is *not* justified:
    if the proposed level of use constitutes a hazard to the health of the consumer;
    if it causes an appreciable reduction in the nutritive value of a food;
    if it disguises the faulty or inferior qualities of a product or the use of processing and handling techniques which are not permitted;

    if it deceives the purchaser or consumer;

    if the desired effect can be obtained by another method of processing which is economically and technologically feasible.

3 Approval for the use of a food additive should be based on anticipated intake in relation to consumption patterns of the community. Special regard should be given to vulnerable groups with special diets such as infants and the elderly.

4 Where it is necessary to use a food additive for any purpose, the purpose must be specific and in the best interests of the consumer. It must be established that there are no alternative means of achieving the purpose more consistent with the best interests of the consumer.

5 Approval for the use of a food additive shall not be general but shall be limited to specific foods for specific purposes under specific conditions, unless otherwise determined.

6 A food additive must be:

    used in the minimum amount necessary to effect the intended purpose under good manufacturing practice;

    acceptable at the level approved on toxicological grounds.

7 A food additive must be in conformity with an acceptable standard of purity.

8 (a) All food additives proposed for use shall have had adequate toxicological evaluation;

  (b) Permitted food additives are subject to continuing observation and are reappraised in the light of changing conditions of use and new scientific information.

9 Incidental food additives shall not exceed the lowest levels that are technologically feasible.

Extracted from the National Health Medical Research Council's Supplement to the Food Standards Code, 1988.

Application Format

For a food additive to be approved in Australia formal application for its use must be made.

The application format used is in two parts. Part A must be completed for all food additive applications. Part B is required for previously unapproved food additives, i.e. those previously described under category three.

The key information required under Part A includes:

the specific type of food in which use of the additive is requested;

the proposed maximum level of use of the additive;

the purpose of the additive together with evidence that it will achieve the intended effect;

the probable daily intake of the additive in the diet;

evidence of approval or rejection by any other body, e.g. the Joint Expert Committee on Food Additives of the Food and Agriculture Organisation/World Health Organisation;

a recognised standard of purity for the additive, e.g. Food Chemicals Codex;

the advantages which will accrue to the consumer from the use of the additive;

requests from manufacturers of the food or foods in which the additive is proposed to be used establishing the need for it;

analytical methods to determine the amount of the additive in the foods in which it is proposed to be used.

The major part of the information required in Part B relates to the safety of the food additive. Necessary are full details of toxicological and pharmacological investigations which must have been carried out under internationally recognised procedures.

The Approval Process

The approval process for food additive applications is complex and time-consuming. It involves sequential review by a series of committees. At any stage of this review process the application can be rejected or modified or further information can be requested from the applicant.

The first step is that of lodging the application with the Food Science and Technology Subcommittee (FST) of the NHMRC. This committee is composed of independent experts, including three toxicologists.

FST makes its recommendations to the Australian Food Standards Committee (AFSC). AFSC is comprised of 19 members drawn as follows:

Commonwealth Government Departments (4);

State Government Representatives (8 — one from each of the six States and two Territories);

consumers (2);

industry (3);

university/research (2).

AFSC considers the FST recommendation and, if it approves, it converts the application to food standard format. AFSC may call for public comment on the proposal. After review of this it forwards its recommendation to the Public Health Committee (PHC). The PHC is an advisory committee to the NHMRC and its membership centres around those Commonwealth and State public servants with direct administrative responsibility for public health.

PHC then passes its recommendation to the National Food Standards Council (NFSC). The NFSC consists of the Commonwealth Minister for Consumer Affairs and the Ministers for Health of the six States and the Northern Territory. Endorsement by the NFSC of the additive application in the form of a new or altered food standard is a mechanism for ensuring national uniformity.

At this stage, the NFSC approval of the new food additive use is grouped with other amended or new standards for publication in the Commonwealth of Australia Gazette. Because food laws are administered at State and Territory level, recognition by them is required. In some of these this recognition is by reference, i.e. automatic on publication in the Commonwealth Gazette. In others, separate regulation is required and this can delay the nationwide adoption of any new standard.

The whole process will typically take two years or more.

Other Aspects

There is another side to the question of food additives: this is the review, modification and/or deletion of additive approvals. The NHMRC also monitors the use of food additives in Australia, estimates changes in consumer intake levels, and reviews evidence related to new toxicology studies.

While it is uncommon, any of the above can lead to reduction in the permitted maximum level of use of a food additive or, indeed, withdrawal of approval for its use.

Appendix III

Colourings and Flavourings

Tom Heyhoe

Colourings and flavourings are amongst the most widely used food additives. They are also the additives about which many questions are raised by consumers. The questions raised typically relate to the safety of particular colours and flavours, the advantages of natural over artificial chemicals, and the necessity of using them at all.

Safety

All colours added to food are classed as food additives and must undergo the same scrutiny before permission is given for their use. The procedures followed for this are dealt with in Appendix II, The Regulation of Food Additives in Australia.

Colours permitted in food are covered in Part A of the Standard A5 of the NHMRC Food Standards Code (see Appendix I). Those allowed include some naturally derived colours, principally plant extracts, their chemically identical synthetic duplicates, and purely artificial colours such as tartrazine. For this last category Standard A5 specifies the maximum overall amounts which may be used in foods.

Colours used in food must also conform to specifications for identity purity laid down in Standard all of the NHMRC Food Standards Code. For the majority of colours, the specification is contained in the Food and Agriculture Organisation's 1984 Food and Nutrition Paper 31/1, 'Specifications for identity and purity of food colours'.

The safety of flavourings is not controlled in the same way as that of colourings. It basically relies on the general provisions of State Food Acts that nothing injurious to health may be added to food and on flavour manufacturers using only flavours and flavour components which are internationally recognised as safe.

Natural vs artificial

Permitted colourings fall into three classes: natural; synthesised duplicates of naturally occurring materials; and chemically synthesised compounds which have not been found in nature. Flavourings may also be classified in this way as natural, nature identical, and artificial.

There is no reason to believe that naturally occurring chemicals are inherently safer than those made in the laboratory. However, Australian consumers appear to have expressed a preference for more 'natural' foods and foods using only natural ingredients are becoming more and more common on supermarket shelves.

The Need for Colours and Flavours

The addition of colouring to food is not a modern invention but has been practised for well over a thousand years. Much experimental work has shown that the colour of a food affects our perception of its flavour. Therefore, colours are routinely added to those foods for which the addition of colour is permitted in order to enhance its appearance and appeal.

Flavourings such as spices have been added to food probably since the advent of cooking. Food is an essential source of nutrients but should also be enjoyed. The addition of flavourings is part of increasing this enjoyment.

The National Health and Medical Research Council recognises this in its Principles for the Evaluation of Food Additives. One of the principles for justification of the use of a food additive is to improve palatability, appearance or appetite appeal. However, such justification must be balanced against others of these principles which state that an additive should *not* be used if it disguises the faulty or inferior quality of a food or where it deceives the consumer.

Glossary of Additive Terms

Acid Acids are added to foods either to impart a sour or sharp flavour or for technological reasons, to control the level at which other substances in the food can function. The degree of acidity can thus be controlled in jams and preserves to regulate the optimum level of setting that can be achieved by the pectin in the fruit. Substances which neutralise acids are called alkalis or bases such as sodium, calcium and ammonium hydroxide, and substances which can hold the acid-alkali balance at a constant level are known as buffers.

A.D.I. The full acceptable daily intake (A.D.I.) for man, expressed on a body weight basis (mg/kg body weight) is the amount of food additive that can be taken daily in the diet, over a lifetime, without risk. It is allocated only to substances for which the available data include either the results of adequate short-term and long-term toxicological investigations or satisfactory information on the biochemistry and metabolic fate of the compound, or both.

The Joint WHO/FAO Expert Committee on Food Additives (JECFA) may allocate a full A.D.I. in cases where they are satisfied no further data are required, or a temporary A.D.I. in cases where some additional data are thought to be desirable. They must indicate to industry the time period within which the data must be submitted. If the data required are not submitted then the temporary A.D.I. may be withdrawn. In practice, however, this rarely happens.

Other A.D.I. classifications include:
- 'A.D.I. not specified' or 'A.D.I. not limited'
  An ADI without an explicit indication of the upper limit of intake may be assigned to substances of very low toxicity, especially those that are food constituents or that may be considered as

foods or normal metabolites in man. This means that, on the basis of available data (chemical, biochemical and toxicological), the total daily intake of the substance arising from its uses at levels necessary to achieve the desired effect and from its acceptable background in food, does not represent a hazard to health. The establishment of an acceptable daily intake expressed in mg/kg body weight for these substances is not deemed necessary.

• 'A.D.I. not allocated'
Where the available information is not sufficient to establish the safety or when the specifications for identity and purity of the substance are not adequate. The fact that an A.D.I. for an additive has not been established should not be interpreted as casting doubt on its safety nor should it necessarily be considered as a reason for its withdrawal from use.

• Group A.D.I.
An acceptable daily intake established for a group of compounds that display similar toxic effects, thus limiting their cumulative intake.

Allergy A reaction in which the body cannot effectively deal with a substance, usually a protein. We have an immune response to most foreign substances which enables our antibodies to remove them from the body by forming antigen/antibody complexes. Common foods which cause this kind of reaction are fish, eggs, shellfish, wheat, cow's milk and nuts, and recent work has shown that tartrazine (102) increases plasma histamine levels in normal (non-sensitive) people as may certain other colours and preservatives.

Anti-caking agents These are substances which are added to foods such as icing sugar or salt or powdered milk to help them to flow freely and prevent the particles sticking together.

Anti-foaming agents These are substances added to a food either to prevent excessive frothing on boiling or to reduce the formation of scum or to prevent boiling over. Dimethylpolysiloxane (900), an inert silicone substance, is an example of an antifoaming agent.

Antioxidants Under normal circumstances fats and oils slowly become oxidised when they are exposed to the oxygen in the atmosphere. The process is accompanied by the development of a rancid 'off' flavour. If 'off' fats and oils are eaten, they can cause sickness. The addition of antioxidants to the fats prevents the process of oxidation. Antioxidants are also added to other non-fat foods such as cut fruits to prevent discolouration brought about by oxidation.

Artificial Sweetening Substances These are substances, other than sugar, capable of producing a sweet taste. The following are permitted artificial sweetening substances in Australia. They do not possess code numbers:

Acesulfame potassium (Acesulfame K), a non-nutritive chemical, two hundred times as sweet as sugar.

Aspartame Prepared from two amino acids, phenylalanine and aspartic acid with about two hundred times the sweetness of sugar. It is safe except for people with phenylketonuria (PHK) because like many natural foods, *Aspartame* contains phenylalanine.

Cyclamate (cyclohexylsulphamic acid or its calcium or sodium salts)

Saccharin made from o-sulfamoylbenzoic acid.

Thaumatin protein obtained by extraction from the fruit of *Thaumatococcus daniellii*, a tropical plant found in Sierra Leone, Zaire, Sudan and Uganda. It has a liquorice after-taste.

In Australia artificial sweetening substances may only be used in brewed soft drinks, low joule foods and carbohydrate modified chewing gum. They do not have code numbers.

Azo Dyes An azo dye has a particular chemical structure of the atoms in its molecule. It could be this 'azo' construction within the molecule to which a proportion of the population is sensitive, or it might be because of impurities. About a fifth of people who are sensitive to aspirin (usually middle-aged adults and more commonly women than men) are also sensitive to azo dyes. Other groups which may be affected are asthmatics and people who suffer from eczema.

The kinds of reactions that occur in sensitive people are contractions of the bronchi — the tubes allowing air into the lungs — (and asthmatic attacks), nettle rash, watering eyes and nose, blurred vision, swelling of the skin with fluid and in extreme cases shock and reduction in blood platelets with the production in the blood of anti-platelet antibodies. (The blood platelets are involved in blood clotting to seal wounds).

It has been suggested by the late Dr Ben Feingold that azo dyes are among those substances which could trigger off the hyperactivity syndrome in children (see pages 14–16). The following are azo dyes:

102	Tartrazine
107	Yellow 2G
110	Sunset yellow FCF
122	Carmoisine
123	Amaranth
124	Ponceau 4R
E128	Red 2G
E154	Brown FK
155	Chocolate brown HT
151	Black PN
E180	Pigment rubine

'Coal tar dye' refers to dyes which were once made from coal tar but nowadays are made synthetically. They may have the 'azo' configuration, or they may not. It includes the above plus:

E104	Quinoline yellow
127	Erythrosine
E131	Patent blue V
132	Indigo carmine
133	Brilliant blue FCF

Bases Bases are added to foods to increase their alkalinity or reduce their acidity. Sometimes they are added to react with acids to give off carbon dioxide gas for operating purposes.

BIBRA British Industrial Biological Research Association.

Bleaching Agents Substances employed to artificially bleach and whiten flour.

Buffers Buffers are chemical substances which can resist considerable changes in the acid/alkali balance of solutions. The scale along which acid or alkali levels are measured is called the pH. Buffers (usually salts of weak acids) can maintain the pH at a predetermined level despite the addition of further acid or alkali.

Bulking Aids Food additives which add to the bulk of the food but do not add to the calorific or energy value. The bulking aids are of value in slimming foods but they also help to 'pad out' or simulate more expensive ingredients.

Chelating Substances When the acid/alkali ratio exceeds a particular limit or the ratio of traces of metal to one another exceeds a particular level, the trace metals may be precipitated out. The addition of a chelating substance such as EDTA (E385) retains the trace elements in the food solution, by bonding them on to an amino acid.

Coal Tar Dye See azo dye. 'Coal tar' is not synonymous with 'azo' dye.

Codex Alimentarius Commission The Commission was formed in 1962 to implement the Joint FAO/WHO Food Standards Programme. The Commission is an intergovernmental body made up of more than 120 Member Nations, the delegates of whom represent their own countries. The Commission's work of harmonising food standards is carried out through various committees, one of which is the Codex Committee on Food Additives (CCFA). JECFA serves as the advisory body to the Codex Alimentarius Commission on all scientific matters concerning food additives.

Colour Index (C.I.) Numbers These colour reference numbers are allocated in the *Colour-Index of the Society of Dyers and Colourists* (3rd Edition with 1975 revisions).

Colourings Water- or oil-soluble substances (or insoluble substances) which are produced artificially or are naturally occurring. Sometimes the colouring is permitted only on the outside of foods, especially confectionery, but usually it is permitted throughout the food.

Diluents Substances which are used to dilute other additives or to dissolve them.

Double-blind Trials These are methods of testing drugs or additives without the subject knowing whether they are receiving the drug or not. If not, they would receive a placebo. The true effects of the drug can then be assessed.

Double-blind Crossover Trials During the double-blind test (see above) the code-holder crosses over the drug and the placebo (page 178) without the knowledge of the experimenter or subject.

Emulsifiers These are substances which can bring together oil, which is water-hating (hydrophobic), and water, which is lypophobic (fat-hating), and mix them so that they do not separate out into layers. Some emulsifiers are vegetable gums, some are chemicals and others are synthetically produced derivatives of natural products.

Emulsifying Salts A mixture of salts such as citrates, phosphates and tartrates which is added to cheese when it is melted as part of its processing to prevent the 'stringiness' which normally happens when cheese is cooked.

Enzymes Natural protein catalysts which are responsible for most metabolic reactions in the living cell.

Excipients This is normally a pharmacological term for 'inactive' powdered substances which are used to bind an 'active' drug into a tablet. The term is also applied in the baking industry to denote a carrier substance for additives used in bread.

FAC Food Advisory Committee (UK).
Advises the Ministry of Agricultures, Fisheries and Food (MAFF) on the composition, labelling and advertising of food. It was formed in 1983 by the amalgamation of the Food Additives and Contaminants Committee and the Food Standards Committee.

Firming Agents Calcium and magnesium salts are employed to retain the natural firmness or crispness of fruits and vegetables and to prevent their softening during the processing period.

Flavour Modifiers or Enhancers These are substances used to enhance or reduce the taste or smell of a food without imparting any flavour of their own, so they are not 'flavours' as such.

Food Intolerance This is not to be confused with food allergy (see Allergy) which involves an immune response. It is also known as food idiosyncracy and pseudo-allergy.

One explanation is that the individual is deficient in the enzyme capable of metabolising the food substance or ingredient. This may help to explain why young children may be more susceptible to some foods or ingredients: their metabolic activity is not developed. Substances such as *mono*Sodium glutamate (621) or caffeine provoke responses in intolerant people who lack the appropriate enzymes.

The symptoms may resemble those of food allergy when foods containing natural histamine, e.g. chocolate, strawberries, egg white, fish, or tomatoes, are consumed.

Gelling Agents Substances which are capable of forming a jelly. Many of the gelling agents may be used in a stabilising capacity too but not all stabilisers are capable of setting into a jelly.

Glazing Agents Substances which either provide a shiny appearance to the food or provide a protective coat, or both.

GMP Good manufacturing practice.

Humectants These are substances which absorb water vapour from the atmosphere and prevent the food from drying out and becoming hard and unpalatable. Glycerine is added to royal icing in the home as a humectant, to prevent the icing drying out and hardening.

JECFA Joint Expert Committee on Food Additives
Composed of experts appointed by the Directors General of the World

Health Organization (Geneva) and the Food and Agriculture Organization (Rome).

Liquid Freezants Liquids or liquefiable gases which can freeze food by coming into contact with it directly and extracting heat from it.

Mineral Hydrocarbons A wide variety of substances derived from bitumen (paraffin hydrocarbons) whether liquid, semi-liquid or solid. The group includes white oil, liquid paraffin, petroleum jelly, microcrystalline wax and hard paraffin.

M.T.D.I. Maximum Tolerable Daily Intake. This expression is used for chemicals which are essential nutrients as well as unavoidable constituents of food (e.g. phosphorus as phosphates).

Mutation A permanent change in the DNA-coded genetic material of the chromosomes, present in all body cells. When the cells divide, this change is passed on to subsequent generations of cells. This might have cancer-causing implications if it occurs in non-sexual cells, or reproductive implications (birth defects) if it happens in the ovaries or testes which produce the reproductive cells.

NHMRC National Health and Medical Research Council
The objective of the NHMRC is to advise the Australian community on the achievement and maintenance of the highest practicable standards of individual and public health and to foster research in the interests of improving those standards.

The NHMRC prepares recommendations on food additives on the advice of its Australian Food Standards Committee and its Food Science and Technology Subcommittee.

The use of food additives in Australia is regulated by State/ Territory food standards which are based on recommendations made by the NHMRC.

Packaging Gases These are inert gases which are employed to occupy space in packaging which if occupied by atmospheric air would cause oxidation of the contents or encourage the growth of micro-organisms, e.g. nitrogen.

pH Abbreviation of potential hydrogen: a measure of the degree of acidity of a substance. The scale runs from O, extreme acidity, to 14, extreme alkilinity.

Placebo An inactive substance or preparation given to satisfy the patient's symbolic need for drug therapy, and used in controlled studies to determine the efficacy of medicinal substances by giving some patients a placebo and some the medicine. Also, a procedure with no intrinsic therapeutic value performed for such a purpose.

Preservatives Preservatives are substances which inhibit the growth of bacteria, fungi and viruses within foods and thus prevent the spoilage of these foods. Gases such as sulphur dioxide, organic and inorganic acids, are all preservatives.

Propellants Gases or volatile liquids employed in aerosol containers to expel the contents when the button is depressed.

Release Agents Substances added to the machinery or coated on to food to prevent foods from sticking to the surfaces of food-processing equipment such as moulds, conveyors, cooking pans or trays. Release agents such as magnesium stearate are also added to tins in which foods are packaged to allow the contents to slip out easily.

SCF Scientific Committee for Food (UK).
The committee and the working groups meet at the invitation of a representative of the European Economic Commission. The committee may be consulted by the Commission on any problem relating to the protection of the health and safety of persons arising from the consumption of food and in particular on the composition of food processes which are liable to modify food and the use of food additives and other processing aids, as well as the presence of contaminants.

Sequestrants Traces of metals, always present in the environment, can cause deterioration in food by advancing the oxidation process, or cause premature setting in dessert mixes. Sequestrants are substances capable of attaching themselves to the trace metals such as calcium, iron or copper.

Solvents These are liquids which are used to disperse substances either in solution or in suspension. They may also be used for extraction, then can either remain, as can be the case with the alcoholic extraction of a flavour, or be removed, as when oil is dissolved from seed.

Stabilisers Similar in function to emulsifiers and thickeners, stabilisers serve to protect the droplets in an emulsion from collision with one another and consequently their tendency to separate out. Stabilisers reduce coalescence either by adding to the viscosity or thickness of the medium forming a protection to the droplets or by forming protective colloids so the frequency and energy of collisions are minimised. The term 'stabiliser' may embrace thickening and gelling agents.

Starch Chemically starch is a carbohydrate, the basic unit of which is anhydroglucose. Two basic types of polymers are present in most starches — amylose and amylopectin, both of which are made up of anhydroglucose units.

Synergists A synergist is a substance which is capable of increasing or enhancing the effect of another substance. In the context of food additives, synergists are usually used to enhance the effects of antioxidants. These synergists include tartaric and citric acid and their calcium, potassium and sodium salts.

Tenderiser A substance or process used to alter the structure of meat to make it less tough and more palatable. This is achieved by loosening the structure of the muscle fibres. There are three main types of tenderising process:

(1) Mechanical, i.e. beating of meat to disrupt its structure.

(2) Ageing — as in the 'hanging' of game. Natural enzymes and micro-organisms start to decay the meat so loosening the structure.

(3) Artificial — proteins are broken down to their constituent amino acids in the gut by protein digesting (proteolytic) enzymes. Artificial tenderisers are concentrated forms of such enzymes used to disrupt the structure of meat. This is not a new idea. Four hundred years ago Cortez noted that Mexican Indians used to wrap tough meat in leaves from the papya tree. The leaves contain the protein digesting enzyme, papain. Another frequently used tenderiser is bromelain which comes from the pineapple.

Thickeners Food additives which add to the viscosity of a food. Most of the thickeners employed are of plant origin, for example, seaweed or algae derivatives or substances produced from cellulose capable of forming a gel or colloid.

References

100 Nagabushan, M., Amonkar, A. J. and Bhide, S. V., *In Vitro* Antimutagenicity of Curcumin against Environmental mutagens, Food and Chemical Toxicology, Volume 25, No. 7, pp. 545–74, 1987.

102 Murdoch, R. D., Pollock, I., and Naeen, S., 'Tartrazine-induced Histamine Release in Vivo in Normal Subjects', paper presented at British Society for Allergy and Clinical Immunology Spring Meeting, 10 April 1987 (to be published October 1987).
— August, P. J., *Urticaria International Medicine Supplement* No. 6, 1983. Allergy 83: A symposium on recent developments in clinical allergy.
— Truswell, A. Stewart, 'ABC of Nutrition: Food Sensitivity', *British Medical Journal*, 1985, 951–5.
— Supramaniam, G. & Warner, J. O., 'Artificial Food Additive Intolerance in Patients with Angio-oedema and Urticaria', *The Lancet*, 18 October 1986.
— Hesser Lynn (BIBRA), 'Tartrazine on Trial', *Fd. Chem. Toxic.*, Vol. 22, No. 12, 1019–26, 1984. Quoting:
Lockey, S., *An. Allergy*, 1959, 17, 719.
Lockey, S., *An. Allergy*, 1977, 38, 206.
Green, *An. Allergy*, 1974, 33, 274.
Cordas, *J. Amer. Osteop. Assoc.*, 1978, 77, 696.
Lahti, *Acta Derm-vener.*, 60, Suppl 91, Stockholm 1980.
Warin & Smith, *Contact Dermatitis*, 1982, 8, 117.
Trautlein & Mann, Ann, *Allergy*, 1978, 41, 28.
Chafee & Settipane, J., *Allergy*, 1967, 40, 65.
Criep, J., 'Allergy' *Clin. Immunology*, 1971, 48, 7.
Settipane *et al, ibid*, 1976, 57, 541.
Zlotlow & Settipane, *Amer. J. Clin. Nutr.*, 1977, 30, 1023.
Mikkelsen *et al, Archives of Toxicology*, 1978, supplement 1, 141.
Warin & Smith, *Br. J. Derm.*, 1976, 94, 401.
Syvanen & Blackman, *Allergy*, Copenhagen , 1978, 33–342.
— Henschler, D. & Wild, D., 'Mutagenic Activity in Rat Urine after Feeding with Azo Dye, tartrazine'. *Archives of Toxicology*, 57: 214–5, 1985.
— Egger, J., Carter, C. M., Graham, P. J., Gumley, D., Soothill, J. F., 'Controlled Trial of Oligoantigenic Treatment in the Hyperkinetic Syndrome', *The Lancet*, 9 March 1985.

E104 *Food Advisory Committee Final Report on the Review of the Colouring Matter in Food Regulations 1973*, MAFF, HMSO, 1987 quoting:
1) LEMM (1978), 'Metabolism and distribution studies in the rat and the dog of Quinoline Yellow or E104 labelled with 14C', unpublished report dated December 1978, Laboratoire

d'Etudes du Métabolisme et Médicaments, Commissiariat à l'Energie Atomique, France (3 volumes and annexes), SUP 11501–5.
2) IFREB (1981), 'Carcinogenicity study of the OFI mouse with the colouring agent E104-Quinoline yellow', Report No. 110202 dated 2 October 1981, Institut Francais de Recherches et Essais Biologiques, St German-Sur-l'Arbrèsle, France, SUP 11501–11505.
3) Biodynamics Inc. (1973), 'A 3-generation reproduction study of D and C Yellow 10 in rats', unpublished Report No. 71R 740, dated 18 December 1973 submitted to the Cosmetic, Toiletry and Fragrance Association, Inc., by Biodynamics Inc., New Jersey, USA.

110 Jacobson, M. F., Ph.D., *New England Journal of Medicine*, Vol. 313, #7, 15 August 1985, quoting 'Carcinogenic effect seen in preliminary report on FD and C yellow No. 6', *Food Chem. News.*, 1 October 1984, 19.
— Supramaniam, G. & Warner, J. O., 'Artificial Food Additive Intolerance in Patients with Angio-oedema and Urticaria', *The Lancet*, 18 October 1986.

120 'Evaluation of Certain Food Additives', 25th Report of the Joint FAO/WHO Expert Committee on Food Additives, Technical Report Series 669, WHO, 1981, 19.
— Food Advisory Committee, 'Final Review of the Colouring Matter in Food Regulations 1973', FdAC/REP14, 1987.

122 Traghi, E., Marinovich, M. & Galli, C. L., 'The Placental Transfer and Detection of ^{14}C-Carmoisine and Metabolites by HPLC Combined with a Radioactivity Monitor', *Disease Metabolism and Reproduction in the Toxic Response to Drugs and Other Chemicals, Archives of Toxicology*, Supplement 7, 312 (1984).

123 Supramaniam, G. & Warner, J. O., 'Artificial Food Additive Intolerance in Patients with Angio-oedema and Urticaria', *The Lancet*, 18 October 1986.
— Taylor, R. J., *Food Additives*, John Wiley, 1980.

127 Matula, T. I. & Downie, R. H., 'Genetic Toxicity of Erythrosine in yeast', *Mutation Research*, 138 (1984), 153–6.
— Jacobson, M. F., Ph.D., *New England Journal of Medicine*, Vol. 313 No. 7, 15 August 1985, quoting Molotsky, I., 'Heckler puts off action on barring use of six drugs', *New York Times*, 3 February 1985, 24.
— Colombi, M. & Wu, C. Y., 'A food dye, Erythrosine B, increases membrane permeability to calcium and other ions', *Biochem. Biophys. Acta*, 20 October 1981, 648(i) 49–54.
— Wenlock, R. W., Buss, D. H., Moxon, R. E., & Bunton, N. G., 'Trace Nutrients, 4 Iodine in British Food', *British Journal Nutrition* (1982), 47, 381–90.
— Katamine, Shinichiro et al, 'Differences in Bioavailability of Iodine among Iodine-rich Foods and Food Colours', *Nutrition Reports International*, Vol. 35 No. 2, Feb. 87, and quoting Barbano, D. M. & Delaralle, M. E., 'Thermal degradation of FD and C Red No. 3 and release of free iodide', *J. Food Prot.*, 47, 668–9 (1984).

128 WHO 1981 Technical Report, Series 669, 20.
— Combes, R. D. and Haveland-Smith, R. B., 'A Review of the Genotoxicity of Food, Drug and Cosmetic Colours and other Azo Triphenylmethane and Xanthene Dyes', *Mutation Research*, 93 (1982), 101–248.

129 Combes, R. D. & Haveland-Smith, R. B., 'A Review of the Genotoxicity of Food, Drug and Cosmetic Colours and other Azo, Triphenylmethane and Xanthene Dyes', *Mutation Research*, 98 (1982), 112.
— 'Proposed an Additional Colour in the Commission Proposal for an 8th Amendment to the Colours Directive COM (85), 474 Final'.
— 'Annex 3 Report of the Scientific Committee for Food on Colouring Matters Authorized For Use in Foodstuffs Intended for Human Consumption'.
— MAFF 'Food Advisory Committee Final Review of the Colouring Matter in Food Regulations 1973', HMSO, 1987.

132 Supramaniam, G. & Warner, J. O., 'Artificial Food Additive Intolerance in Patients with Angio-oedema and Urticaria', *The Lancet*, 18 October 1986.
— Jacobson, Michael F., *New England Journal of Medicine*, Vol. 313 No. 7, 15 August 1985.
— 'Food Advisory Committee Final Report of the Colouring Matter in Food Regulations 1973', HMSO, 1987.

150 Wood, F., 'Caramel Colours under Review', *Nutrition Bulletin*, January 82, Vol. 7 No. 1.
— Spector, Reynold & Huntoon, Sheryl, 'Effects of Caramel Color (Ammonia Process) on Mammalian Vitamin B_6 Metabolism, *Toxicology and Applied Pharmacology*, 62, 172–8 (1982).
— Noltes, A. W. & Chappel, C. A., 'Toxicology of Caramel Colours: Current Status', *Food Toxicology — Real or Imaginary Problems*, ed. G. G. Gibson and R. Walker. Proceedings of an International Symposium at the University of Surrey, Guildford on 11–15 July 1983, Taylor and Francis, 1985.

154 Haveland-Smith, R. B. & Combes, R. D., Screening of food dyes for genotoxic activity, *Food and Cosmetic Toxicology*, 18, 1980, 215.
— Haveland-Smith, R. B. & Combes, R. D., 'Studies on the Genotoxicity of the Food Colour Brown FK and its Component Dyes using Bacterial Assays', *Mutation Research*, 105, 1982, 51.
— Venitt, S., and Bushell, C. T., 'Mutagenicity of the Food Colour Brown FK and Constituents in *Salmonella typhimurium*', *Mutation Research*, 40, 309.
— Combes, R. D., 'Brown FK and the colouring of smoked fish — a risk-benefit analysis, *Food Additives and Contaminants*, Vol. 1 No. 3, 1987.

160(a) 'Carrots — do they combat cancer?' Citation of work under Prof. Nicholas Wald at St Bartholemew's Hospital in *Chemistry and Industry*, NO. 7, 205, 1 April 85.

160(b) 'Evaluation of Certain Food Additives', Report of the Joint FAO/WHO Expert Committee on Food Additives Technical Report 683, Geneva 1982, 21.

E160(c) Personal communication with D. M. Taylor, T. C. Feeds Ltd, Gt Harwood, Blackburn, Lancs.

E160(g) Food Advisory Committee, 'Final Review of the Colouring Matter in Food Regulations 1973', FdAC/REP/4, HMSO 1987, 58–9.

E161(b&g) Personal communication with D. M. Taylor, T. C. Feeds Ltd, Gt Harwood, Blackburn, Lancs.

163 'Evaluation of certain food additives', Report of the Joint FAO/WHO Expert Committee on Food Additives Technical Report, 683, Geneva 1982, 21.

172 'Evaluation of Certain Food Additives', Technical Report Series 684 and 696, 23rd, 27th Report of the Joint FAO/WHO Expert Committee on Food Additives, WHO Geneva, 1980 and 1983.

E173 Bland, Jeffrey, *Your Personal Health Programme*, Thorsons, 1983, quoting D. P. Perl & C. J. Gibbs, 'Intraneuronal Aluminium Accumulation in Amyotrophic Lateral Sclerosis and Parkinsonism of Guam', *Science*, 217, 1053 (1982).
— Lerick, S. E., 'Dementia from Aluminium Pots', letter to *New England Journal of Medicine*, July 17 1980, 164.
— 'Aluminium dementia link', *Journal of Alternative Medicine*, June 85, quoting 'Acid rain may cause senile dementia', *New Scientist*, April 25 1985, & Lockie, A. 'Comparison of alumina — the drug picture', and 'Alzheimer's disease — the disease picture', *Brit. Hom. J.*, Vol. 73, 2, 92–4 (1984), reviewed in *J.A.M.*'s March 1985 'Update'.

200 Daniel, J. W., *Preservatives in Food Toxicology — Real or Imaginary Problems?* Proceedings of an International Symposium held at the University of Surrey, Guildford, on 11–15 July 1983, ed. G. G. Gibson and R. Walker, Taylor and Francis, 1985.

210 August, P. J., 'Urticaria', *International Medicine Supplement*, 6 November 1983.
— Egger, J., Carter, C. M., Graham, P. J., Gumley, D., Soothill, J. F., 'Controlled Trial of Oligoantigenic Treatment in the Hyperkinetic Syndrome', *The Lancet*, 9 March 1985.

211 Supramaniam, G. & Warner, J. O., 'Artificial Food Additive Intolerance in Patients with Angio-oedema and Urticaria', *The Lancet*, 18 October 1986.

213 27th Report of the Joint FAO/WHO Expert Committee on Food Additives', Technical Report Series 696, Geneva, 1983.

E214 & 216 Daniel, J. W., 'Preservatives' in *Food Toxicology — Real or Imaginary Problems?* Proceedings of an International Symposium held at the University of Surrey, Guildford, on 11–15 July 1983, ed. G. G. Gibson and R. Walker, Taylor and Francis, 1985.

E217 & 218 Tilmen, W. J. & Kuramoto, R., Martindale, 'The Extract Pharmacopoeia', quoting *Journal of the American Pharmaceutical Association, Scientific*, Vol. 46 1957, 211.

220 Weszicha, B., 'Sulphur dioxide in foods', *Nutrition Bulletin*, 42, Vol. 9 (3), 155, 1984.
— Personal communication with Dr S. W. Brewer, University of Lancaster, Dept. of Chemistry.
— Yang, William H. & Purchase, Emerson C. R., 'Adverse Reactions to Sulfites', *Canadian Medical Association Journal*, Vol. 133, 1 November 1985, p. 865.
— Roger, L. J., Kehrl, H. R., Hazucha, M. & Horstman, 'Broncho Constriction in Asthmatics Exposed to Sulphur Dioxide during Repeated Exercise', *Journal of Applied Physiology* 59 (3): 784–791, 1985.
— Truswell, A. Stewart, 'ABC of Nutrition: Food Sensitivity', *British Medical Journal*, Vol. 291, 5 October 1985, 951–5.

221 Roger, L. J., Kehrl, H. R., Hazucha, M. & Horstman, 'Broncho Constriction in Asthmatics Exposed to Sulphur Dioxide during Repeated Exercise', *Journal of Applied Physiology* 59 (3): 784–791, 1985.
—Yang, William H. & Puchase, Emerson C. R., 'Adverse Reactions to Sulfites', *Canadian Medical Association Journal*, Vol. 133, 1 November 1985, 865.
— Personal communication with Dr S. W. Brewer, University of Lancaster, Dept. of Chemistry.
— Huang, A. *et al*, letter to *New England Journal of Medicine*, 23 August 1984, 542.
— *Medical World News*, 12 September 1983, 123.
— Levine, A. S., Labuza, T. P., Morley, J. E., letter in *New England Journal of Medicine*, 15 August 1985, 454.

222 Roger, L. J., Kehrl, H. R., Hazucha, M. & Horstman, 'Broncho Constriction in Asthmatics Exposed to Sulphur Dioxide during Repeated Exercise', *Journal of Applied Physiology* 59 (3): 784–791, 1985.
— Personal communication with Dr S. W. Brewer, University of Lancaster, Dept. of Chemistry.
— Huang. A. *et al*, letter to *New England Journal of Medicine* 23 August 1984, 542.
— *Medical World News*, 12 September 1983, 123.
— Levine, A. S., Labuza, T. P., Morley, J. E., letter in *New England Journal of Medicine* 15 August 1985, 454.
— Yang, William H. & Purchase, Emerson C. R., 'Adverse reactions to Sulfites', *Canadian Medical Association Journal*, Vol. 133, 1 November 1985, 865.

223 Supramaniam, G. & Warner, J. O., 'Artificial Food Additive Intolerance in Patients with Angio-oedema and Urticaria', *The Lancet*, 18 October 1986.
— Roger, L. J., Kehrl, H. R., Hazucha, M. & Horstman, 'Broncho Constriction in Asthmatics exposed to Sulphur Dioxide during Repeated Exercise', *Journal of Applied Physiology* 59 (3): 784–791, 1985.

— Yang, William H. & Purchase, Emerson C. R. 'Adverse reactions to Sulfites', *Canadian Medical Association Journal*, Vol. 133, 1 November 1985, 865.
— Levine, A. S., Labuza, T. P., Morley, J. E., letter in *New England Journal of Medicine*, 15 August 1985, 454.
— *Medical World News*, 12 September 1983, 123.
— Huang, A. *et al*, letter to *New England Journal of Medicine*, 23 August 1984, 542.
— Personal communication with Dr S. W. Brewer, University of Lancaster, Dept. of Chemistry.
— Truswell, A. Stewart, 'ABC of Nutrition: Food Sensitivity', *British Medical Journal*, Vol. 291, 5 October 1985, 951–5.

224 Roger, L. J., Kehrl, H. R., Hazucha, M. & Horstman, 'Broncho Constriction in Asthmatics Exposed to Sulphur Dioxide during Repeated Exercise', *Journal of Applied Physiology* 59 (3): 784–791, 1985.
— Jacobson, Michael F., *New England Journal of Medicine*, Vol. 313 No. 7, 17 August 85.

224–E227 Personal communication with Dr S. W. Brewer, University of Lancaster, Dept. of Chemistry.
— Huang A. *et al*, letter to *New England Journal of Medicine*, 23 August 1984, 542.
— *Medical World News*, 12 September 1983, 123.
— Yang, William H. & Purchase, Emerson C. R., 'Adverse reactions to sulfites', *Canadian Medical Association Journal*, Vol. 133, 1 November 1985, 865.
— Levine, A. S., Labuza, T. P., Morley, J. E., letter in *New England Journal of Medicine*, 15 August 1985, 454.

249–251 Weisburger, J. H., 'Role of Fat, Fiber, Nitrate and Food Additives in Carcinogens: a Critical Evaluation and Recommendation', *Nutrition and Cancer*, Vol. 8, No. 1, 1986.

250 Tanaka, N., Meske, L., Doyle, M. & Traisman, E. A., '*Clostridium botulinum* challenge study on bacon made by the Wisconsin process — a three plant study', United States Department of Agriculture, 1984, quoted by Jacobson, M. F., in *The New England Journal of Medicine*, 15 August 1985.

300–321 Haigh, R., 'Safety and Necessity of Antioxidants: EEC Approach', *Food and Chemical Toxicology*, Vol. 24 No. 10/11, 1986, 1031–4.

300 *New Scientist*, 16 January 1986.

301 Kroes, R. & Wester, P. W., 'Forestomach Carcinogens: Possible Mechanisms of Action', *Food and Chemical Toxicology*, Vol. 24, No. 10/11, 1986 1085, quoting:
Mirrish, S. S., Pelfrene, A. F., Garcia, H. & Shubik, P., 'Effect of Sodium Ascorbate on Tumour Induction in Rats Treated With Morpholine and Sodium Nitrite and with Nitrosomorpholine', *Cancer Letters* (2), 101, 1976, and Fukishima, S. & Ito, N. (1985), 'Squamous Cell Carcinoma Forestomach Rat', in *Monographs on Pathology of Laboratory Animals' Digestive System*, ed. T. C. Jones, U. Mohr and R. D. Hunt, 292, Springer-Verlag, Berlin.
— Ito, N., Fukushima, S., Tsuda, H., Shirai, T., Hagiwara, A. & Imaida, K., 'Antioxidants: Carcinogenicity and Modifying Activity in Carcinogenesis', in *Toxicology — Real or Imaginary Problems?* Proceedings of an International Symposium held at the University of Guildford, Surrey, on 11–15 July 1983, ed. G. G. Gibson and R. Walker, Taylor and Francis, 1985; quoting: Fukushima, S., Imaida, K., Sakata, T., Okamura, T., Shibata, M. & Ito, N., 1983, 'Promoting Effects of Sodium L-ascorbate on Two-stage Urinary Bladder Carcinogenesis in Rats', *Cancer Research*, 43, 454–7.

302 'Evaluation of Certain Food Additives', 25th Report of Joint FAO/WHO Expert Committee on Food Additives, TRS 669, 1981, WHO Geneva.

304 Kahl, R. & Heildebrandt, A. G., 'Methodology for Studying Antioxidant Activity and

Mechanisms of Action of Antioxidants', *Food and Chemical Toxicology*, Vol. 24 No. 10/11, 1007–14, 1986.

306–308 Lindsey, Jennifer A., Zhang, Hanfang, Kaasiki, Hisayuki, Morisaki, Nobuhiro, Sato, Takasi and Cornwell, 'Fatty Acid Metabolism and Cell Proliferation'; 'VII Antioxidant Effects of Tocopherols and Their Quinones', *Lipids*, Vol. 20 No. 3 (1985).
— Thomassi, G. and Silano, V., 'Assessment of the Safety of Tocopherols as Food Additives', *Food and Chemical Toxicology*, Vol. 24, No. 10/11, 1051–61, 1986.

310 Kahl, R. and Heildebrandt, A. G., 'Methodology for Studying Antioxidant Activity and Mechanisms of Action of Antioxidants', *Food and Chemical Toxicology*, Vol. 24 No. 10/11, 1007–14, 1986.

310–312 Furia, *Handbook of Food Additives*, CRC, 1980.

320 Furia, *Handbook of Food Additives*, CRC, 1980.
— Altmann, H. J., Wester, P. W., Matthiaschk, G., Grunow, W. & Van der Heijden, C. A., 'Induction of Early Lesions in the Forestomach of Rats by 3-tert-Butyl-4-hydroxyanisole (BHA). *Food and Chemical Toxicology*, Vol. 23, No. 8, 723–31, 1985.
— Altmann, H. J., Grunow, W., Mohr, U., Richter-Reichelm, H. B. & Wester, P. W., 'Effects of BHA and Related Phenols on the Forestomach of Rats', *Food and Chemical Toxicology*, Vol. 24, No. 10/11, 1183–8, 1986.
— Branen, A. L., Richardson, T., Goel, M. C., and Allen, J. R., 'Lipid and Enzyme Changes in the Blood and Liver of Monkeys Given Butylated Hydroxylene and Butylated Hydroxyanisole', *Food and Cosmetic Toxicology*, Vol. 11, 797–806, 1973.
— Cohen, L. A., Tanaka, T., Choi, K. & Weisburger, J. H., 'Paradoxical Behaviour of Dietary Butylated Hydroxianisole (BHA): Inhibition of Dimethylbenz(A)anthracene(DMBA)-induced Rat Mammary Tumors and Adrenal Nodules; Enhancement of Forestomach Lesions', photocopy of abstract.
— Conacher, A. S. B., Iverson, F., Lau, P.Y. & Page, B. D., 'Levels of BHA and BHT in Human and Animal Adipose Tissue: Interspecies Extrapolation', *Food and Chemical Toxicology*, Vol. 24, No. 10/11, 1159–62, 1986.
— Fisherman, E. W., Rossett, D., and Cohen, G. 'Serum Triglyceride and Cholesterol Levels and Lipid Electrophoretic Patterns in Intrinsic and Extrinsic Allergic States', *Annals of Allergy*, Vol. 38, January 1977.
— Ito, N., Fukushima, S., Tsuda, H., Shirai, T., Hagiwara, A., & Imaida, K., 'Antioxidants: Carcinogenicity and Modifying Activity in Tumorigenesis', in *Food Toxicology — Real or Imaginary Problems*? Proceedings of an International Symposium held at the University of Surrey, Guildford, on 11–15 July, 1983, ed. G. G. Gibson & R. Walker, Taylor and Francis.
— Ito, N., Fukushima, S., Shirai, T., Hagiwara, A., and Imaida, K., 'Drugs, Food Additives and Natural Products as Promoters in Rat Urinary Bladder Carcinogenesis', IART Scientific Publications 1984, Vol. 56 — *Models, Mechanisms and Etiology of Tumour Promoters*, 399–407.
— Kirkpatrick, D. C. & Lauer, B. H., 'Intake of Phenolic Antioxidants from Foods in Canada', *Food and Chemical Toxicology*, Vol. 24, No. 11/12, 1035–7, 1986.
— Kroes, R. & Wester, P. W., 'Forestomach Carcinogens: possible Mechanisms of Action', *Food and Chemical Toxicology*, Vol. 24, No. 10/11, 1083–9, 1986.
— Moch, R. W., 'Pathology of BHA- and BHT-induced Lesions', *Food and Chemical Toxicology*, Vol. 24, No. 10/11, 1167–9, 1986.
— Monroe, D. H., Holeski, C. J. & Eaton, D. L., 'Effects of Single-dose and Repeated-dose Pretreatment with 2(3)-tert-Butyl-4-hydroxyanisole (BHA) on the Hepatobiliary Disposition and Covalent Binding to DNA of Aflatoxin B_1 in the Rat', *Food and Chemical Toxicology*, Vol. 24, No. 12, 1273–81, 1986.
— Report of the Working Group on the Toxicology and Metabolism of Antioxidants, Dr W. G. Flamm (Chairman).

— Shamberger, R. J., 'Antioxidants and Cancer', in *Carcinogens and Mutagens in the Environment*, ed. Hans F. Stich, CRC Press Inc., Florida, 1982.
— Surak, J. G., Bradley, R. L., Branen, A. L., Maurer, A. J. & Ribelin, W. E., 'Butylated Hydroxyanisole (BHA) and Butylated Hydroxytoluene (BHT) Effects on Serum and Liver Lipid Levels in *Gallus domesticus*', *Poultry Science*, 56, 747–53, 1977.
— Talyor, M. J., Sharma, R. P. & Bourcier, D. R., 'Tissue Distribution and Pharmocokinetics of 3H-Butylated Hydroxyanisole in Female Mice', *Agents and Actions*, Vol. 15, 3/4 (1984).
— Tobe, M., Furuya, T., Kawasaki, Y., Naito, K., Sekita, K., Matsumoto, K., Ochiai, T., Usui, A., Kokubo, T., Kanno, J. and Hayashi, Y., 'Six-month Toxicity Study of Butylated Hydroxyanisole in Beagle Dogs', *Food and Chemical Toxicology*, Vol. 24, No. 10/11, 1223–8, 1986.
— Wattenburg, L. W., 'Protective Effects of 2(3)-tert-Butyl-4-Hydroxyanisole on Chemical Carcinogenesis', *Food and Chemical Toxicology*, Vol. 24, No. 10/11, 1099–102, 1986.
— Wurtzen, G. & Olsen, P., 'BHA study in Pigs', *Food and Chemical Toxicology*, Vol. 24, No. 10/11, 1229–33, 1986.

321 Furia, *Handbook of Food Additives*, CRC, 1980.
— Olsen, P. *et al*, *Pharmacologia et Toxicologia* 53(5), 433, 1983.
— Shamberger, R. J., 'Antioxidants and Cancer', Chapter 5 of *Carcinogens and Mutagens in the Environment*, ed. Hans F. Stich, Vol. II, 'Naturally Occurring Compounds, Endogenous Formation and Modulation', CRC Press Inc., Florida, 1982.
— Babich, H., 'Butylated Hydroxytoluene (BHT): A Review', *Environmental Research*, 29, 1–29 (1982).
— Fukayama, M. Y. & Hsieh, D. P. H., 'Effect of Butylated Hydroxytoluene Pretreatment on the Excretion, Tissue, Distribution and DNA Binding of (^{14}C) Aflatoxin B_1 in the Rat', *Food and Chemical Toxicology*, Vol. 23 No. 6, 567–73.
— Branen, A. L., Richardson, T., Goel, M. C. & Allen, J. R., 'Lipid and Enzyme Changes in the Blood and Liver of Monkeys Given Butylated Hydroxylene and Butylated Hydroxanisole', *Food and Cosmetic Toxicology*, Vol. II, pp. 797–806, 1973.
— Brugh, M., 'Butylated Hydroxytoluene Protects Chickens Exposed to Newcastle Disease Virus', Department of Agriculture, Athens, Georgia, May 1977.
— Cohen, L. A., Choi, K., Numoto, S., Reddy, M., Berke, B. & Weisburger, J. H., 'Inhibition of Chemically Induced Mammary Carcinogenesis in Rats by Long-Term Exposure to Butylated Hydroxytoluene (BHT): Interrelations Among BHT Concentration, Carcinogen Dose and Diet', INCL Vol. 76, No. 4, April 1986.
— Conacher, A. S. B., Iverson, F., Lau, P.Y. & Page, B. D., 'Levels of BHA and BHT in Human and Animal Adipose Tissue: Interspecies Extrapolation', *Food and Chemical Toxicology*, Vol. 24, No. 10/11, 1159–62, 1986.
— Fisher, J. A., 'BHT as a Treatment for Herpes', *AntiAging News*, Vol. 3, No. 11, November 1983.
— Fisherman, E. W., Rossett, D. & Cohen, G., 'Serum Triglyceride and Cholesterol Levels and Lipid Electrophoretic Patterns in Intrinsic and Extrinsic Allergic States', *Annals of Allergy*, Vol. 38, January 1977.
— Haigh, R., 'Safety and Necessity of Antioxidants: EEC Approach', *Food and Chemical Toxicology*, Vol. 24, No. 10/11, 1031-4, 1986.
— Ito, N., Fukushima, S., Tsuda, H., Shirai, T., Hagiwara, A. & Imaida, K., 'Antioxidants: Carcinogenicity and Modifying Activity in Tumorigenesis', in *Food Toxicology — Real or Imaginary Problems?*, Proceedings of an International Symposium held at the University of Surrey, Guildford, on 11–15 July 1983, ed. G. G. Gibson and R. Walker, Taylor and Francis.
— Ito, N., Fukushima, S., Shirai, T., Hagiwara, A. & Imaida, K. 'Drugs, Food Additives and Natural Products as Promoters in Rat Urinary Bladder Carcinogenesis', IART Scientific Publications 1984, Vol. 56 — *Models, Mechanisms and Etiology of Tumour Promoters*, 399–407.
— Kirkpatrick, D. C. & Lauer, B. H., 'Intake of Phenolic Antioxidants from Foods in Canada', *Food and Chemical Toxicology*, Vol. 24, No. 11/12, 1035–7, 1986.

— Kroes, R. & Webster, P. W., 'Forestomach Carcinogens: Possible Mechanisms of Action', *Food and Chemical Toxicology*, Vol. 24, No. 10/11, 1083–89, 1986.

— Moch, R. W., 'Pathology of BHA and BHT-induced Lesions', *Food and Chemical Toxicology*, Vol. 24, No. 10/11, 1167–9, 1986.

— Moneret-Vautrin, D. A., Bene, M. C. & Faure, G., 'She Should Not Have Chewed', letter, *The Lancet*, 15 March 1986.

— Olsen, P., Bille, N. & Meyer, O., 'Hepatocellular Neoplasms in Rat Induced by Butylated Hydroxytoluene (BHT)', *Acta Pharmacol. et Toxicol.*, 1983, 53, 433–4.

— Olsen, P., Meyer, O., Bille, N. & Wurtzen, G., 'Carcinogenicity Study on Butylated Hydroxytoluene (BHT) in Winster Rats Exposed in Utero', *Food and Chemical Toxicology*, Vol. 24, No. 1, 1–12, 1986.

— Powell, C. J., Connelly, J. C., Jones, S. M., Grasso, P. & Bridges, J. W., 'Hepatic Responses to the Administration of High Doses of BHT to the Rat: Their Relevance to Hepatocarcinogenicity', *Food and Chemical Toxicology*, Vol. 24, No. 10/11, 1131–43, 1986.

— Report of the Working Group on the Toxicology and Metabolism of Antioxidants.

— Shamberger, R. J., 'Antioxidants and Cancer' in *Carcinogens and Mutagens in the Environment*, ed. Hans F. Stich, CRC Press Inc., Florida, 1982.

— Shilian, D. M. & Goldstone, J., 'Toxicity of Butylated Hydroxytoluene', letter to *The New England Journal of Medicine*, Vol. 314, No. 10, 6 March 1986, 648.

— Snipes, W., Person, S., Keith, A. & Cupp, J., 'Butylated Hydroxytoluene Inactivates Lipid-containing Viruses', *Science*, Vol. 118, 4 April 1975, 64–5.

—Surak, J. G., Bradley, R. L., Branen, A. L., Maurer, A. J., & Ribelin, W. E., 'Butylated Hydroxyanisole (BHA) and Butylated Hydroxytoluene (BHT): Effects on Serum and Liver Lipid Levels in *Gallus domesticus*'. *Poultry Science*, 56, 747–53, 1977.

— Wursten, G. & Olsen, P. 'Chronic Study on BHT in Rats', *Food and Chemical Toxicology*, Vol. 24, No. 10/11, 1121–5, 1986.

E321(c) 'Process for giving flavour to broilers', *Food Processing Industry*, March 1982, i.

338–341 Personal communications with L. R. J. Krakowicz, Albright & Wilson Ltd., Phosphates Division, PO Box 80, Trinity Street, Old Bury, Warley, West Midlands B69 4LN.

E385 Haigh, R., 'Safety and Necessity of Antioxidants: EEC Approach', *Food and Chemical Toxicology*, 101, 24, No. 10/11, 1031–4, 1986.

407 Abraham, R., Benitz, K.-F., Mankes, R. & Rossenblum, I., 'Chronic and Subchronic Effects of Carrageenan in Rats', *Ecotoxicology and Environmental Safety*, 10, 173–83 (1985).

— Boxenbaum, H. G. & Dairman, W., 'Evaluation of an Animal Model for the Screening of Compounds Potentially Useful in Human Ulcerative Colitis: Effect of Salicylazosulfapyridine and Prednisolone on Carrageenan-induced Ulceration of the Large Intestine of the Guinea Pig', *Drug Development and Industrial Pharmacy*, 3 (2), 121–30 (1977).

— CECA SA (Satia) Food Applications — list of booklets and application data sheets, November 1984.

— Collins, T. F. X., Black, T. N. & Prew, J. H., 'Long-term Effects of Calcium Carrageenan in Rats — II, Effects on Foetal Development', *Food and Cosmetic Toxicology*, Vol. 15, 539–45, 1977.

— Engster, M. & Abraham, R. 'Cecal Response to Different Molecular Weights and Types of Carrageenan in the Guinea Pig', *Toxicology and Applied Pharmacology*, 38, 265–82 (1976).

— 'Evaluation of Certain Food Additives and Contaminants', 28th Report of the Joint FAO/WHO Expert Committee on Food Additives, Technical Report Series 710, WHO 1984.

— International Agency for Research on Cancer, *Monographs on the Evaluation of the Carcinogenic Risk of Chemicals to Man*, Lyons, France, Vol. 31, 1983.

— FMC, Marine Colloids Division, Box 308, Rockland Maine, 04841, 'Carrageenan, Current Regulatory Status for Safe Use in Food', personal communication, 16 August 1985.

— Personal communication with David W. Manning, Group Leader, Protein Section, Marine Colloids Division, FMC Corporation, 29 October 1985.

— Jensen, B. H., Andersen, J. O., Poulsen, S. S., Skrovolsen, S., Norbyrasmussen, Rasmussen S., Hansen, S. H., & Hvidberg, E. F., 'The Prophylactic Effect of 5-Amino-Salysilic Acid and Salazosulphapyridine on Degraded-Carrageenan-Induced Colitis in Guinea Pigs', *Scandinavian Journal of Gastroenterology*, 19 (1984).

— Mallett, A. K., Rowland, I. R., Bearne, Carol, A., & Nicklin, S., 'Influence of Dietary Carrageenans on Microbial Biotransformation Activities in the Cecum of Rodents and on Gastrointestinal Immune Status in the Rat', *Toxicology and Applied Pharmacology*, 78, 377–385 (1985).

— Marcus, R. & Watt, J., 'Seaweeds and Ulcerative Colitis in Laboratory Animals', letter to *The Lancet*, 30 August 1969, 489.

— Personal communication with Dr A. J. Marcus, 28 March 1985.

— Marcus, S. N., Marcus, A. J. & Watt, J., 'Chronic Ulcerative Disease of the Colon of Rabbits Fed Native Carrageenans', paper presented to the Proceedings of the Nutritional Society of Medicine, May 1983.

— Mottet, N. K., 'Carrageenan Ulceration as a Model for Human Ulcerative Colitis', letter to *The Lancet*, 26 December 1970.

— Thomson, A. W., Fowler, E. F., Sljivic, V. S. & Brent, L., 'Carrageenan Toxicity', letter to *The Lancet*, 10 May 1980.

— *Official Journal of the European Communities*, written answer by Lord Cockfield to written answer by Mr James Ford on the food additive carrageenan, 25 November 1985, No. C.304–9.

— Onderdonk, A. B., Franklin, M. L., & Cisneros, R. L., 'Production of Experiment Ulcerative Colitis in Gnotobiotic Guinea Pigs with Simplified Microflora', *Infection and Immunity*, April 1981, 225–31.

— Rustia, M., Shubik, P. & Patil, K., 'Lifespan Carcinogenicity Tests with Native Carrageenan in Rats and Hamsters', *Cancer Letters*, 11 (1980), 1–10.

— Watt, J., & Marcus, R., 'Harmful Effects of Carrageenan Fed to Animals', *Cancer Detection and Prevention*, 4 (1981), 129–34.

— Watt, J., Path, M. C. & Marcus, R., 'Hyperplastic Mucosal Changes in the Rabbit Colon Produced by Degraded Carrageenan', *Gastroenterology*, Vol. 59, No. 5, November 1970, 760–768.

— 'Toxicological Evaluation of Certain Food Additives and Contaminants' Joint FAO/WHO Expert Committee on Food Additives, Rome, 19–28 March 1984. WHO Food Additives series 1984, No.19.

412 Sharma, R.D., 'Hypocholesterolemic Activity of some Indian Gums', *Nutrition Research*, Vol. 4, 381–9, 1984.

— Tako, Masakuni & Nakamura, Sanehisa, 'Synergistic Interaction between Xanthan Gum and Guar Gum', *Carbohydrate Research*, 138 (1985), 207–13.

— Jenkins, D. J. A., Reynolds, D., Slarin, B., Leeds, A. R., Jenkins, A. L. & Jepson, E. M., 'Dietary fiber and blood lipids: treatment of hypercholesterolemia with guar crispbread', *The American Journal of Clinical Nutrition*, 33, March 1980, 575–81.

— McIvor, Michael E., Cummings, Charles C. & Mendeleff, Albert I., 'Long-term Ingestion of Guar Gum is not Toxic in Patients with Noninsulin Dependent Diabetes Mellitus', *The American Journal of Clinical Nutrition*, 41, May 1985, 891–4.

413 Eastwood, M. A., Brydon, W. G. & Anderson, D. M. W., 'The Effects of Dietary Gum Tragacanth in Man', *Toxicology Letters*, 21, (1984), 73–81.

414 Sharma, R. D., 'Hypocholesterolemic Activity of some Indian Gums', *Nutrition Research*, Vol. 4, 381–9, 1984.

— Anderson, D. M. W., 'Evidence for the safety of Guar Arabic (*Acacia senegal* (L) Willd.) as a Food Additive — a brief review', *Food Additives and Contaminants*, 1986, Vol. 3, No. 3, 225–30.

— McLean, A. H., Eastwood, M. A., Anderson, J. R. & Anderson, D. M. W., 'A Study on the Effects of Dietary Gum Arabic in Humans', *American Journal of Clinical Nutrition*, 37, March 1983, 368–75.

415 Tako, Masakuni & Nakamura, Sanehisa, 'Synergistic Interaction between Xanthan Gum and Guar Gum', *Carbohydrate Research*, 138 (1985).
— Eastwood, M. A., Brydon, W. G. & Anderson, D. M. W., 'The Dietary Effects of Xanthan Gum in Man', *Food Additives and Contaminants* 1987, Vol. 4, No. 1, 17–26.

416 Eastwood, M. A., Brydon, W. G. & Anderson, D. M. W., 'The Effects of Dietary Gum Karaya (*Sterculia*) in Man', *Toxicology Letters*, 17 (1983), 159–66.

420 Review of the Soft Drinks Regulations 1964 (as amended), FSC/REP/65, MAFF, London, HMSO 1976.

450 Personal communication with L. R. J. Krakowicz, Albright & Wilson Ltd., Phosphates Division, PO Box 80, Trinity Street, Old Bury, Warley, West Midlands B69 4LN.

460 Mackler, Bradley, P. & Herbert, Victor, 'The Effect of Raw Wheat Bran, Alfalfa Meal and Alpha-cellulose on Iron Ascorbate Chelate and Ferric Chloride in three Binding Solutions', *The American Journal of Clinical Nutrition*, 42, October 1985, 618–28.

461 Martindale, 'The Extract Pharmacopoeia', quoting Tilmen, W. J. & Karamoto, R., *Journal of the American Pharmaceutical Association, Scientific*, Vol. 46, 1957, 211.

466 Anderson, D. M. W., Eastwood, M. A. & Brydon, W. G., 'The dietary effects of sodium carboxymethyl cellulose in man', *Food Hydrocolloids*, Vol. 1, No. 1, 37–44, 1986.

471 Hodge, D. G., 'Fat in Baked Products', *Nutrition Bulletin*, 48, Vol. 11(3), 153, 1986, Flour Milling and Baking Research Association, Chorley Wood, Herts.
— Vincent, A. and Harrison, S., 'Stabilising Dressings and Sauces', *Food Trade Review*, Vol. 57, No. 10, October 1987.

E474 Technical Report Series, 'Evaluation of Certain Food Additives', JECFA, WHO, Geneva, 1980.

476 Radiamuls 2253 'A flow improver for chocoloate', Oleofina S.A., 37, rue de la Science, B-1040, Brussels.

500 Anonymous report, *New Scientist*, 5, 2 May 1985.

503 'Evaluation of certain food additives and contaminants', 26th Report of the Joint FAO/WHO Expert Committee on Food Additives, Technical Report Series 683, WHO 1982, 26.

509 'Food Additives in Focus', National Dairy Council, *Journal of Applied Physiology*, 59 (3), 784–91, 1985.

E524 & 525 The Revised Codex Standard for Table Olives; personal communication with Miss B. Toole, Standards Division, Ministry of Agriculture, Fisheries and Food.

526 'Food Additives in Focus', National Dairy Council, *Journal of Applied Physiology*, 59 (3), 784–91, 1985.

540 & 541 Personal communication with L. R. J. Krakowicz, Albright & Wilson Ltd., Phosphates Division, PO Box 80, Trinity Street, Old Bury, Warley, West Midlands B69 4LN.

541 Lione, A., 'The Prophylactic Reduction of Aluminium Intake', *Food and Chemical Toxicology*, February 1983, 21 (1), 103–9.
— Katz, A. C., Frank, D. W., Sauerhoff, M. W., Zwicker, G. M., 'A Six-month Dietary Toxicity Study of Acidic Sodium Aluminium Phosphate in Beagle Dogs,' *Food and Chemical Toxicology*, January 1984, 22(1), 7–9.
Hicks, J. S., Hacket, D. S. and Sprage, G. L., 'Toxicity and Aluminium Concentration in Bone

following Dietary Administration of Two Sodium Aluminium Phosphate Formulations in Rats', *Food and Chemical Toxicology*, 25, 533–8, 1987.

E544 & E545 Personal communication with L. R. J. Krakowicz, Albright & Wilson Ltd., Phosphates Division, PO Box 80, Trinity Street, Old Bury, Warley, West Midlands B69 4LN.

554 & 556 Lione, A., 'The Prophylactic Reduction of Aluminium Intake', *Food and Chemical Toxicology*, Vol. 21, No. 1, 103–9, 1983.

578 Kundu, P. N. & Das, A. A., 'Note on crossing experiments with *Aspergillus niger* for the production of calcium gluconate', *Journal of Applied Bacteriology*, 59, 1–5, 1985.

621 Truswell, A. Stewart, 'ABC of Nutrition Food Sensitivity', *British Medical Journal*, Vol. 291, 5 October 1985, 951–5.
— Noah, Norman D., 'Food Poisoning', *British Medical Journal*, Vol. 291, 28 September 1985, 879–83.
— Choi, Dennis, 'Glutamate Neurotoxicity in Cortical Cell Culture is Calcium Dependent', *Neuroscience Letters*, 58 (1985), 293–7.
— Olney, John W., Labruyere, Joan and de Gubareff, Taisija, 'Brain Damage in Mice from Voluntary Ingestion of Glutamate and Aspartate', *Neurobehavioural Toxicology*, Vol. 2, 125–9, 1980.
— Yamaguchi, Shizuko & Takahasi, Chikahito, 'Hedonic Functions of Monosodium Glutamate and Four Basic Taste Substances Used at Various Concentration Levels in Single and Complex Systems', *Agriculture and Biological Chemistry*, 48 (4), 1077–81, 1984.
— *Sweet, Sour, Salty, Bitter and Umami*, Umami Information Centre, Hosokawa Tsukiji Building, 1-9-9 Tsukiji, Chuo-ku, Tokyo 104, Japan.
— *What is MSG?*, Umami Information Centre, 5–8 Kyobashi 1-chome, Chuo-Ku, Tokyo 104, Japan.
— 'A Handbook for The World of Umami' (video), Umami Information Centre, 1986.
— *Proceedings of the International Symposium on MSG as Flavor Enhancer* (held on 8 December 1983 in Bangkok, Thailand), Ministry of Science, Technology and Energy, The Kingdom of Thailand.
— Kenny, R. A., 'The Chinese Restaurant Syndrome: An Anecdote Revisited', *Food and Chemical Toxicology*, Vol. 24, No. 4, 351–4, 1986.
— Yamaguchi, Shizuko & Takahasi, Chikahito, 'Interactions of Monosodium Glutamate and Sodium Chloride on Saltiness and Palatability of a Clear Soup', *Journal of Food Science*, Vol. 49, 1984.
— Stegink, L. D., Filer, L. J. Jnr. & Baker, G. L., 'Plasma Glutamate Concentrations in Adult Subjects Ingesting Monosodium L-glutamate in Consommé', *The American Journal of Clinical Nutrition*, 42, August 1985, 220–5.
— Wilkin, J. J., & Richmond, M. D., 'Does Monosodium Glutamate cause Flushing (or merely Glutamania)?', *Journal of the American Academy of Dermatology*, Vol. 15, No. 2, Part 1, August 1986.

621–3 Choi, Dennis, 'Glutamate Neurotoxicity in Cortical Cell Culture is Calcium Dependent', *Neuroscience Letters* 58 (1985), 293–7.

907 IRAC monograph on the 'Evaluation of the Carcinogenic Risk of Chemicals to Man', Lyon, Vol. 3, 1973, 30.
— 'Recognized Carcinogens', IARC, 32; Dalton, A., Oil BSSRS, London, 1975, 47–8.
— Adrianova, M., *Voprosij Pitaniya*, Vol. 29, No. 5, 61, 1970: N10SH (note QJ6560000.

E907 Lawrence, Felicity (ed.), *Additives, Your Complete Survival Guide*, Century, 1986.

920 Personal communication with Martin Dove, Croxton & Garry, Dorking.

924 Personal communication with J. E. Allen, British Bakeries, RHM Centre, PO Box 178, Alma Road, Windsor, Berks SL4 3ST.

925 Taylor, R. J., *Food Additives*, John Wiley, 1980.

967 Culbert, S. J., Wang, Y. M., Fritsche, H. A., Carr, D., Lantin, E. and van Eys, J., 'Oral xylitol in American adults', *Nutrition Research*, Vol. 6, 1986.

— Kandelman, D. and Gagnon, G., 'Clinical results after 12 months from a study of the incidence and progression of dental caries in relation to consumption of chewing gum containing xylitol in school prevention programmes', *Journal of Dental Research*, August 1987.

1410–1450 Author unknown, 'Nutritional and Safety Aspects of Modified Food Starches', *Nutritional Review*, 44, No. 2, 74–9, February 1986.

Bibliography

Bender, A. E., *Dictionary of Nutrition and Food Technology*, Butterworths Scientific Publications, 1960.

British Nutrition Foundation, *Why Additives? The Safety of Foods*, Forbes, 1987.

Brouk, B., *Plants Consumed by Man*, Academic Press, 1975.

Combes, R. D. & Haveland-Smith, R. B., 'A review of the genotoxicity of food, drug and cosmetic colours and other azo, triphenylmethane and xanthene dyes', *Mutation Research*, 98 (1982), 101–248.

Denner. W. H. B., 'Colourings and Preservatives in Food', *Human Nutrition: Applied Nutrition* (1984) 38A, 435–49 (E200, E201, E202, E203, E210, E211, E212, E213, E214, E215, E216, E217, E218, E219, E220, E221, E227, E230, E231, E232, E233, E239, E249, E250, E251, E252, E280, E281, E282, E283, E234).

Dietary Guidelines for Australians, Australian Government Publishing Service, 1982.

Dorlands *Illustrated Medical Dictionary*, 26th Edition, W. B. Saunders.

FAO/WHO Food Additives Data System, FAO Food and Nutrition Papers 30 (1984); 30/Rev. 1 (1985) and 30/Rev. 1/Add. 1 (1985) based on the work of the Joint FAO/WHO Expert Committee on Food Additives, 1956–1985.

Food Additives: The Balanced Approach, 1987. Free from MAFF, Freepost, Food Additives, Alnwick, Northumberland NE66 1BR.

Joint FAO/WHO Food Standards Programme, Codex Alimentarius Commission (1981), *Procedural Manual*, 5th edition. FAO/WHO, Rome.

HMSO, 1984 No 1305, 'The Food Labelling Regulations, 1984'.

HMSO, 'Report of the Review of Additives and Processing Aids used in the Production of Beer' (Food Additives and Contaminants Committee: FAC/REP/26, HMSO 1978).

Jacobson, Michael F., *Esters Digest. The Consumers' Factbook of Food Additives: Are they safe?* Anchor Books, Doubleday & Co. Inc., New York, 1976.

Jukes, D. J. *Food Legislation in the UK — A Concise Guide*, Butterworths, 1984.

Martindale, *The Extra Pharmacopoeia*, 28th Edition, 1982.

Miller, Melanie, 'Danger! Additives at Work', a Report on Food Additives, Their Use and Control, London Food Commission, October 1985.

Millstone, E., 'Food Additives: a technology out of control?' *New Scientist*, 18 October 1984.

Painter, A. A., *Meat Products and Spreadable Fish Products*, Special Report prepared for the Food and Drugs Industry. Bulletin December 84 January 1985 presented at a meeting of the Society of Chemical Industry Food Group.

National Dairy Council, *Food Additives in Focus*.

NHMRC Food Standards Code 1987 and Amendment No. 1 to the NHMRC Food Standards Code (1988), Australian Government Publishing Service.

NHMRC Pamphlets — *Nutrition, Food Labels and You 1987*; *Identifying Food Additives*, 1988.

Pyke, M., *Food Science and Technology*, 4th edition 1981, John Murray.

Taylor, R. J., *Food Additives*, John Wiley, 1980.

Trease, G. E. & Evans, W. C., *Pharmacognosy*, 12th edn, Bailliere Tindall, 1983.

Walford, J., *Developments in Food Colours*, Elsevier, 1984.

Welham, R. D., 'The Early History of the Synthetic Dye Industry', *The Journal of the Society of Dyers and Colourists*, Vol. 79, Nos. 3, 4 & 5, 1963.

Windholz, Martha (editor), *The Merck Index 1976*, Merck and Co. Inc., Rathway, New Jersey.

Winter, R., *A Consumer's Dictionary of Food Additives*, Crown Publishers Inc., New York, 1984.

World Health Organization Evaluation of Certain Food Additives and Contaminants. Reports of the joint FAO/WHO Expert Committee on

Food Additives. Technical Report Series: 648 1980; 653 1980; 669 1981; 683 1982; 696 1983; 733 1986; 751 1987; Published by World Health Organization, Geneva.

World Health Organization Principles for the Safety Assessment of Food Additives and Contaminants in Food. Environmental Health Criteria 70. Published by World Health Organization, Geneva 1987.

Government Decrees

'Directive au conseil rélative au rapprochment des règlementations des Etats Membres concernant les matières colorantes pouvant être employées dans les denrées destinées à l'alimentation humaine', *Journal Officiel des Communautés Européennes*, Communauté Economique Européenne, 26 May 1962.

Council Directive of 25 July 1978 laying down specific criteria of purity for antioxidants which may be used in foodstuffs intended for human consumption, 77 & 78/664/EEC. *Official Journal of the European Communities*, 14 August 1978. Annexes to the above.

'Specific Criteria of Purity for Emulsifiers, Stabilizers, Thickeners and Gelling Agents for use in Food Stuffs', *Official Journal of the European Communities*, No. L 223/8, 14 August 1978.

Decree of the President of the Republic 26th March 1980 no. 327. 'Order implementing the law of 30th April 1962 no. 283 and subsequent amendments, governing hygiene standards in the production and sale of foodstuffs and beverages'. LTS 1561/82/Italian/BJH Circular No. 51.

Presidential Decree no. 322 of 18 May 1982, 'Implementation of EEC Directive No. 79/112 relating to the labelling of foodstuffs intended for sale to the ultimate consumer and the advertising of such foodstuffs, and the implementation of EEC Directive no. 77.94 on foodstuffs for particular nutritional use', LTS 574/82.

'Additives in Wine', *Oenological Practices for Wine*, Annex III to Regulations 337/79 published in *Official Journal of the European Communities* no. L54/34 of 5 March 1979; added by R.1990/80; amended by R.3577/81.

Italy (Food Legislation) 'Guide Prepared by Exporters to Europe', Branch Presidential Decree No. 337 of 26 March 1980 (*Gazzetta Ufficiale 193*, 16 July).

'Proposal for a Council Directive amending for the eighth time the

Directive of 23 October 1962 on the Approximation of the rules of the Member States concerning the colouring matters authorized for use in foodstuffs intended for human consumption', Commission of the European Communities, COM (85) 474 final, Brussels, 19 September 1985.

Resource List of Organisations for Asthma, Allergies and Hyperactivity

Australia

Asthma

NSW **Asthma Foundation of NSW**
Unit 1
'Garden Mews'
St Leonards, NSW 2065

Qld **Asthma Foundation of Queensland**
51 Ballow Street (PO Box 394)
Fortitude Valley, Qld 4006

SA **Asthma Foundation of South Australia**
149 Hutt Street
Adelaide, SA 5000

Tas. **Asthma Foundation of Tasmania**
Hampden House
5/82 Hampden Road
Battery Point, Tas. 7004

Vic. **Asthma Foundation of Victoria**
2 Highfield Grove
Kew, Vic. 3101

WA **Asthma Foundation of Western Australia**
2/61 Heytesbury Road
Subiaco, WA 6008

NT **Asthma Foundation of the Northern Territory**
PO Box 41326
Casuarina, NT 5792

Allergies and Hyperactivity

ACT **Allergies and Intolerant Reactions Association**
PO Box 1780
Canberra, ACT 2601

NSW **The Allergy Clinic**
c/o Out Patients Department
Royal Prince Alfred Hospital
Camperdown, NSW 2050

Australian College of Allergy
18 Garnet Street
Killara NSW 2071

Allergy Association Australia — Sydney Inc.
PO Box 74
Sylvania Southgate, NSW 2224

Hyperactivity Association (NSW)
24/29 Bertram Street
Chatswood, NSW 2067

Department of Thoracic Medicine
Royal North Shore Hospital
St Leonards, NSW 2065

Qld **Queensland Allergy and Hyperactivity Association**
Box 107
Yeronga
Brisbane, Qld 4104

Allergy Association Australia–Brisbane
PO Box 45
Woody Point, Qld 4019

SA **Hyperactivity Association of SA**
Room 21, First Floor
Florence Knight Building
Adelaide Children's Hospital
Nth Adelaide, SA 5006

Tas. **Dr Jocelyn Townrow**
Allergy Recognition & Management Group
Box 2
Sandy Bay, Tas. 7005

Allergy Recognition and Management
PO Box 2
Sandy Bay, Tas. 7005

Vic. **Active Hyperkinetic Children's Association**
PO Box 17
East Doncaster, Vic. 3109

Allergy Clinic
Royal Children's Hospital
Flemington Road
Parkville, Vic. 3053

Allergy Association Australia–Victoria Inc.
PO Box 298
Ringwood, Vic. 3134

WA **Allergy Association Australia–Perth**
3 Shark Court
Sorrento, WA 6020
Many public hospitals that are also teaching hospitals have allergy clinics.

New Zealand

Asthma

Auckland Asthma Society Inc.
PO Box 67066
Auckland

Asthma Society
PO Box 13091
Christchurch

Asthma Society Otago Inc.
PO Box 5494
Dunedin

Asthma Foundation of New Zealand
PO Box 1159
Wellington

PO Box 1459
Waikato

PO Box 4169
Hamilton

PO Box 217
Tauranga

PO Box 186
New Plymouth

Allergies and Hyperactivity

Auckland Hyperactivity Association
PO Box 39–099
Northcote
Auckland 9

Australian and New Zealand Myalgic Encephalomyelitis (ME) Society
PO Box 35–429
Brown's Bay
Auckland

Bay of Plenty ME Support Group
13 Tynan Street
Te Puke

Palmerston North ME Group
22 Kent Street
Palmerston North

Rotorua ME Group
PO Box 1678
Rotorua

Allergy Awareness Association (Inc.)
PO Box 12–701
Penrose
Auckland 6

41 Fox Street
Hamilton

La Leche League NZ
PO Box 2307
Christchurch

Dunedin Allergy Support Group
c/- 2 Heath Street
Andersons Bay
Dunedin

Hamilton Support Group
PO Box 15–011
Dinsdale
Hamilton

Allergy and Food Intolerance Support and Help (AFISH)
c/- 5 La Salle Drive
Westown
New Plymouth

22 Nelson Street
Gore

44 Milburn Street
Corstorphine
Dunedin

Sinclair Road
RD1
Te Anau

PO Box 348
Te Puke

15 Grantlea Drive
Timaru

Big Jim's Hill
RD 42
Waitara

Manawatu Hyperactivity and Allergy Support Group
c/- 19 Columbo Street
Palmerston North

Marlborough Allergy Assistance Group
c/- 2 Surrey Street
Picton

c/- 55 Redwood Street
Blenheim

Wanganui Hyperactivity and Allergy Aware Association (Inc.)
c/- 10 Fromont Street
Wanganui

Wellington Hyperactivity and Allergy Association (Inc.)
c/- 93 Waipapa Road
Hataitai
Wellington 3

Open Forum for Health Information NZ
5 Patrick Street
Petone
Wellington

NZ Parents Centres Federation
54 Murphy Street
Wellington 1

Ashburton Allergy Support Group
PO Box 476
Ashburton

Christchurch Allergy Group
PO Box 28032
Thorrington
Christchurch 2

Darfield Allergy Support Group
18 North Terrace
Darfield

Food Allergy and ME Group (FAME)
107 Wilton Street
Invercargill

Foundation for Healing Arts
PO Box 4529
Christchurch

Masterton Allergy Group
13 Durham Street
Masterton

Napier Hastings Allergy Support Group
11 Roskilda Crescent
Taradale

Nelson Allergy Support Group
'The Bracken'
Marahau Valley
RD2
Motueka

Takaka Allergy Support Group
Marama House
9 Waitapu Road
Takaka

Tokoroa Allergy Support Group
147 Elizabeth Drive
Tokoroa

Wairarapa Allergy Group
Norfolk Road
RD1
Carterton